Autobiographical Identities in Contemporary Arab Culture

Edinburgh Studies in Modern Arabic Literature
Series Editor: Rasheed El-Enany

Writing Beirut: Mappings of the City in the Modern Arabic Novel
Samira Aghacy

Autobiographical Identities in Contemporary Arab Culture
Valerie Anishchenkova

The Iraqi Novel: Key Writers, Key Texts
Fabio Caiani and Catherine Cobham

Figuring the Sacred in the Modern Arabic Novel
Ayman A. El-Desouky

Sufism in the Contemporary Arabic Novel
Ziad Elmarsafy

Gender, Nation, and the Arabic Novel: Egypt 1892–2008
Hoda Elsadda

Post-War Anglophone Lebanese Fiction: Home Matters in the Diaspora
Syrine Hout

War and Occupation in Iraqi Fiction
Ikram Masmoudi

Rifa'a Al-Tahtawi: A 19th-Century Egyptian Educationalist and Reformer
Daniel Newman

The Arab Nahḍah*: The Making of the Intellectual and Humanist Movement*
Abdulrazzak Patel

Occidentalism, Maghrebi Literature and the East–West Encounter
Zahia Salhi

Sun'allah Ibrahim: Rebel with a Pen
Paul Starkey

www.euppublishing.com/series/smal

Autobiographical Identities in Contemporary Arab Culture

Valerie Anishchenkova

EDINBURGH
University Press

To Mom and Dad, and all my grandparents

Edinburgh University Press Ltd
The Tun – Holyrood Road
12 (2f) Jackson's Entry
Edinburgh EH8 8PJ
www.euppublishing.com

Typeset in 11/15 Adobe Garamond by
Servis Filmsetting Ltd, Stockport, Cheshire
and printed and bound in Great Britain by
CPI Group (UK) Ltd, Croydon CR0 4YY

A CIP record for this book is available from the British Library

ISBN 978 0 7486 4340 0 (hardback)
ISBN 978 0 7486 4341 7 (webready PDF)

Contents

Series Editor's Foreword

The Edinburgh Studies in Modern Arabic Literature is a new and unique series which will, it is hoped, fill in a glaring gap in scholarship in the field of modern Arabic literature. Its dedication to Arabic literature in the modern period, that is, from the nineteenth century onwards, is what makes it unique among series undertaken by academic publishers in the English-speaking world. Individual books on modern Arabic literature in general or aspects of it have been and continue to be published sporadically. Series on Islamic studies and Arab/Islamic thought and civilization are not in short supply either in the academic world, but these are far removed from the study of Arabic literature qua literature, that is, imaginative, creative literature as we understand the term when, for instance, we speak of English literature or French literature, etc. Even series labeled "Arabic/Middle Eastern Literature" make no period distinction, extending their purview from the sixth century to the present, and often including non-Arabic literatures of the region. This series aims to redress the situation by focusing on the Arabic literature and criticism of today, stretching its interest to the earliest beginnings of Arab modernity in the nineteenth century.

The need for such a dedicated series, and generally for the redoubling of scholarly endeavor in researching and introducing modern Arabic literature to the Western reader has never been stronger. The significant growth in the last decades of the translation of contemporary Arab authors from all genres, especially fiction, into English; the higher profile of Arabic literature internationally since the award of the Nobel Prize for Literature to Naguib Mahfouz in 1988; the growing number of Arab authors living in the Western diaspora and writing both in English and Arabic; the adoption of such authors and others by mainstream, high-circulation publishers, as opposed to the academic publishers of the past; the establishment of prestigious prizes, such as the International Prize for Arabic Fiction (the Arabic Booker), run by the Man Booker Foundation, which brings huge publicity to the shortlist and winner every year, as well as translation contracts into English and other languages – all this and very recently the events of the Arab Spring have heightened public, let alone academic, interest in all things Arab, and not least Arabic literature. It is therefore part of the ambition of this series that it will increasingly address a wider reading public beyond its natural territory of students and researchers in Arabic and world literature. Nor indeed is the academic readership of the series expected to be confined to specialists in literature in the light of the growing trend for interdisciplinarity, which increasingly sees scholars crossing field boundaries in their research tools and coming up with findings that equally cross discipline borders in their appeal.

Autobiography is an area of modern Arabic literature that calls for further study. The genre predates modern Arabic fiction by a few decades, going back to the middle decades of the nineteenth century, as we see, for example, in elements of the writings of two major figures of that time, viz. Rifa'a Al-Tahtawi (1801–73) and Ahmad Faris Al-Shidyaq (1804–87). But autobiography was truly to establish itself in the first half of the twentieth century at the hands of most major men of letters writing at the time, notably Taha Husyan (1889–1973), Abbas Mahmud Al-Aqqad (1889–1964), Ahmad Amin (1886–1954), Muhammad Husayn Haykal (1888–1956) and Tawfiq Al-Hakim (1898–1987), who produced autobiographical texts of varying lengths, form and structure; some direct and others thinly disguised as fiction. Many of these autobiographies have long since become part of the modern classics of Arabic literature, with some translated into English and other languages, such as Husayn's *The Stream of Days* and Amin's, *My Life*, to name but two. The genre has gathered momentum since the second half of the twentieth century, with the last three decades or so witnessing both a qualitative and quantitative leap in its development, as well as a notable growth in its popularity among both writers and readers, with noticeably more women writers contributing to it in a manner commensurate with the rise of their participation in Arab intellectual and literary life generally. There has also been a refreshing openness in the writing, with authors exercising less and less self-censorship, and sometimes showing a readiness, often controversially, to share with their readers the most intimate details of their personal life, as we see, for instance, in the writing of the Moroccan, Muhammad Shukri (1935–2003).

This growth in the genre has yet to be matched by scholarship, and the current volume travels a good distance in that direction. Perhaps most refreshingly, this book does not stop at exploring some of the most interesting autobiographical texts of modern Arabic, but also ventures into little-trodden ground: that of the autobiographical motion-picture and the virtual autobiographical narratives of the blog.

Acknowledgments

I would like to thank Edinburgh University Press for the wonderful partnership, in particular the series editor Professor Rasheed El-Enany and his endless support, and all the staff, especially Michelle Houston and Jenny Peebles, who answered perhaps a million questions and were always there to help in every way.

I am very grateful to the authors, artists and their representatives who generously allowed me to use examples of their work as illustrations: Oreet Ashery and Larissa Sansour; Mona Hatoum and White Cube Gallery; Ghada Abd al-Al; Misr International Films; and especially author and artist Samia Halaby, since our email correspondence has gradually evolved into a wonderful thought-provoking discussion.

There are many people and places whose presence in my life have influenced this book project in both direct and indirect ways, and I particularly want to thank:

Carol Bardenstein: for being the best advisor and mentor a person can ask for.

Anton Shammas: for the thought-provoking graduate classes and discussions, and for always encouraging the most unorthodox and brave research ideas. The initial idea to explore the autobiographical came to me in his class upon reading Jurji Zaydan's *Mudhakkirat*.

The University of Michigan: for the very best graduate school and for opening my eyes to new and exciting horizons of the world. Go Blue!

Students in my "Writing Lives in Arabic" class taught at the University of Maryland in spring 2010, for excellent debates and bright ideas that reenergized my research and inspired me to expand it.

C (Chelsea): for being my best friend, my closest family away from home, and the strongest shoulder a person could wish for in really bad weather; for always inspiring me to do new things. And because sometimes things just ought to be eerie.

Kari: for being my best friend and for making me believe that a friendship can last a lifetime; for continuing questioning everything together since that first "postcolonial studies" class. And because sometimes you just ought to put your thoughts on a T-shirt.

Pete: for taking on the burden of administrative work in fall 2012, which gave me the precious time to finish this manuscript. And because sometimes a plant can make everything better.

Nick: for being a wonderful friend for life, for always being there despite the distance. And because sometimes you just ought to fly to an island.

Jon and Ahmad: for being great friends during the most difficult of times. And because sometimes you just ought to embrace the darkness.

Miha, for dreaming together and seeing each other make all the impossible dreams come true. And because sometimes the grass is just greener in Tahrir.

My Egyptian family, for accepting me unconditionally and for making me love Egypt in all her magnitude.

Sasha and Anya Knysh: for endless care and support during graduate school and beyond.

The city of St. Petersburg: for teaching me resilience.

And most importantly, my deepest gratitude for everything I have accomplished in life, including this book, goes to my wonderful parents and grandparents. Thank you for always believing in me, for always inspiring me to climb the highest mountain, for always being there, for always giving me the strength to do anything. Your love is what defines my life. This book is for you.

Transliterated Names

Personal names, place names, and the names of political parties appear in the main text without transliteration. Properly transliterated forms of these names appear below.

- ʿAbbās, Iḥsān
- ʿAbd al-ʿĀl, Ghādah
- Abū Zayd, Laylā
- Amīn, Aḥmad
- Bassām, Riḥāb
- Ḥassan, Ihāb
- Ḥusayn, Ṭāhā
- Khuḍayrī, Batūl
- Maḥfūz, Najīb
- Maḥmūd, Ghādah Muḥammad
- Manṣūr, Ilḥām
- Mīnah, Ḥannā
- Mūsa, Salāmah
- Qabbānī, Nizār
- Qaraḥ ʿAlī, Muḥammad
- Ramaḍān, Sumayyah
- Shāhīn, Yūsuf
- Shidyāq, Aḥmad Fāris
- Shukrī, Muḥammad
- Suyūṭī, Jalāl al-Dīn
- Ṭūqān, Fadwā
- Yārid, Nāzik Sābā

Figures

The truth is that I am not all that interested in "myself" – I am only curious to see what kind of person is going to emerge from a certain arrangement of personal stories, which are themselves not facts but earlier arrangements, for certain practical uses.

Andrei Codrescu, *Adding to My Life*

Introduction: Writing Arab Selfhood – From Taha Husayn to Blogging

Identity, self, selfhood, subjectivity. In our globalizing, interdependent, and endlessly mutating world with its sporadically changing geopolitical realities, these terms seem to circulate with increasing frequency, performing as symbolic "anchors" that define and contextualize our existence and assign unique qualities to our lives. How do we define who we are and how do others define us? How often do we choose a single attribute – such as ethnicity, language, gender, sexual orientation, religion, and so on – to articulate our selfhood? What methods do we as individuals use to cope with our hybrid, perplexing, twisted subjectivities? In what ways do our personal identities relate to various cultural, societal, and ideological processes surrounding us in particular moments in time?

In the context of these questions, autobiographical discourse becomes particularly relevant and important: it creates a space where individual self-representation merges with different modes of collective identity circulating in the autobiographer's environment. But if life-writing in Western literatures initiated a vast body of critical research, Arab autobiographical discourse – in particular its recent developments – remains largely unexplored. I argue that an inquiry into the ways and methods by which personal identity is constructed in recent autobiographical production by Arab authors offers a personalized insight into the cardinal changes that have occurred in Arab sociocultural zones in the last one hundred years – because, using the words of Sidonie Smith and Julia Watson, "people tell stories of their lives through the cultural scripts available to them, and they are governed by cultural strictures about self-presentation in public" (Smith and Watson 2001: 42).

Although Arab autobiographical discourse has always been an interesting and culturally rich phenomenon, in recent decades it has gone through crucial transformations in both form and method. While numerous new autobiographical genres and subgenres mushroomed in different parts of the Arab world (including various innovative literary works in both prose and poetry, cinematic autobiographies, personal cyber-writing, and other unorthodox forms), authors also began to articulate their personal selfhood using diverse thematic angles. Many chose to reveal split, ruptured, and hybrid subjectivities; cultural constructs of gendered identities; sexual identities and, in more general terms, the autobiographical subject's physicality; and other identity markers that have very rarely been considered in earlier works of the genre. In other words, contemporary autobiographical authors took on revealing the overall *vulnerability* of the autobiographical subject and exposed the essential intricacy at the core of identity making.

In the last several years, the ground-shaking political events in the Arab world have highlighted the problematics of Arab identity in its various manifestations – as an ideological concept, a national affiliation, a cultural belonging, and a political entity. Among other things, the Arab Spring brought to the surface the ongoing clashes between different nationalist discourses and the rejection of both local and foreign identity models, the former being imposed by local autocratic regimes and the latter streaming from the countless satellite channels promoting the Western way of life. The radical shifts in the ideological map of the Arab world in this very short period of time show that we are, indeed, experiencing a crucial historical moment that promises major reconfigurations of Arab selfhood. Within this context, this book offers a perspective on some of the internal identity-making processes that led to the current crisis in that it conceptualizes the most recent autobiographical discourse and its various modes of self-representation.

1 Subjectivity, Identity, and Modalities of Autobiographical Transmission

The primary goal of this study is to offer an analytical framework to contemporary Arab autobiographical discourse by investigating cultural production that articulates novel conceptions of Arab selfhood and highlights complex sociocultural, ideological, and other non-narrative discourses behind identity construction. The book's inquiry goes beyond conventionally published works to include filmic and cyber forms of self-representation: I treat autobiographical narrative as first and foremost *cultural* text, expanding on the traditional definition of the literary.[1]

While including a number of autobiographical works as case studies, I aim to define what I call *modalities of autobiographical transmission* and to offer a preliminary typology that illustrates autobiographical diversity in Arab culture. Each chapter of the book identifies and discusses one of such modalities: nationalist, corporeal, multicultural, cinematographic, and virtual/cyber. My definition of autobiographical modality does not by any means imply a singular manifestation of one's personal selfhood but, rather, it is a vehicle that translates the highly complex and fluid construct of autobiographical subjectivity into a more tangible form – such as a particular literary form, a cinematic narrative, or a cybertext. In addition to the author's personal preference for a particular mode of artistic self-expression, I argue that their choices of autobiographical modalities are also informed by a particular environment surrounding the production of this autobiographical work and by its geographical locality with its distinct cultural and political history. In other words, these modalities situate the autobiographical within a specific sociocultural context.

In their vision of identity, Hazel Markus, Patricia Mullally, and Shinobu Kitayama pointed out that self is inevitably a cultural and historical construct:

> Particularized senses of the self – self-concepts and individuated identities – are always grounded in the complex of consensual understandings and customary behavioral routines relevant to being a self in a given sociocultural and historical context. Such sociocultural understandings and practices will influence the form and function of the psychological processes that comprise the self – what people notice and think about, what they feel moved to do, what they feel, how they feel, and how they organize, understand, and give meaning to their experiences. (Markus, Mullally and Kitayama 1997: 15)

Therefore, the notions of the "self," "selfhood," and "identity" are always charged with various cultural, social, and ideological connotations, which continue to change over time and take diverse forms in different societies and in different strata of the same society. As theoretical terms, "identity" and "subjectivity" are often defined in markedly different ways depending on the field, the school of thought, and the subject matter. However, in humanities the two terms are frequently used interchangeably as synonyms. In this study, I treat identity and subjectivity as two different constructs, drawing on Chris Weedon's conceptualization in his *Identity and Culture*:

> How can we usefully conceptualize the relation between subjectivity and identity? Identity is perhaps best understood as a limited and temporary fixing for an individual of a particular mode of subjectivity as apparently what one *is*. One of the key ideological roles of identity is to curtail the plural possibilities of subjectivity inherent in the wider discursive field and to give individuals a singular sense of who they are and where they belong. This process involves recruiting subjects to the specific meanings and values constituted within a particular discourse and encouraging identification. A wide range of social practices, for example, education, the media, sport and state rituals, offer subject positions that encourage identification. (Weedon 2004: 19)

Whereas Weedon's theory is primarily concerned with the place of an individual within ideological institutions and practices, I utilize a similar approach to conceptualize the making of identity within autobiographical discourse. For the purpose of this study, I view autobiographical subjectivity as an individual's metatextual accumulative construct of selfhood, a synthesis of one's life experience, a highly complex hybrid of our various selves (gendered, national, linguistic, social, religious, and so on) that are in the state of perpetual transformation through time and space.

Building on Althusser's theory of ideology and subjectivity and Foucauldian discursive practices, Weedon sees identity as subjectivity's singular "fixing" at a particular moment in a particular place, where identity is an ideological construct formulated within various power structures aiming to give individuals a sense of belonging (*ibid.*). While the process of identification can in actuality become a practice of counter-identification (that is, individuals can elect to construct their sense of self against available ideological models), Weedon's theory suggests that identity models have already been fully formulated as fixed and specific "locations" of subjectivity within available ideological discourses. For the purpose of this study, I argue that, on the contrary, identity is a *product* of autobiographical transmission.

Autobiographical identity is a singular manifestation of the autobiographical subjectivity in a particular place and time, but such an identity does not necessarily have a predetermined shape. Rather, autobiographical identities are formulated *in the process* of narrative self-representation channeled through a particular modality. When we examine Muhammad Shukri's outrageous, overly sexual, and explicitly physical subject in *al-Khubz al-Ḥāfī* (*The Bare Bread*) discussed in Chapter 2, the making of identity does not adopt an already available cultural model. Instead, the autobiographical identity is constructed *in the process of writing* – through corporeal modality – creating a "snapshot" of Shukri's metatextual subjectivity.

Certainly, the metatextual autobiographical can have multiple modes of transmission, generating multiple narrative autobiographical identities; for example, in two or more autobiographical works by the same author. Likewise, when I choose a particular modality for my analysis, it does not mean that the constructed autobiographical identity is void of other modalities of transmission: a "nationalist" identity could be approached simultaneously as "gendered" or "multicultural," and so forth. In other words, the choice to create a framework of autobiographical modalities does not reduce the complexity of identity construction, nor does it disregard the essential heterogeneity of human selfhood. But, I argue, it helps to understand the mechanics behind identity politics in a given sociocultural zone at different historical moments. Whereas some of the modalities are thematic (nationalism, physicality, multiculturalism), others have more to do with the medium of expression (cinematography and cyberspace), but each of them serves as a vehicle of autobiographical transmission, as a tool of communication between autobiographical authors and their audiences.

The modalities discussed in this book are only some examples within the increasingly pluralistic Arabic autobiographical discourse. It is important to emphasize that my main objective is to offer a *method* to contemporary Arab autobiographical production, rather than to produce an all-inclusive study of works published within this genre in recent decades. The proposed method of accessing selected cultural texts from the scope that goes beyond the oeuvre of separate authors, or national boundaries, or even language (I include works by Arab authors written in languages other than Arabic) generates the "big picture" framework that offers an insight into current modes of self-representation and self-expression in Arab societies. Such a framework highlights the remarkable internal diversity within the cultural category of "Arab identity" and, at the same time, establishes certain commonalities in identity-making practices among different autobiographical texts and authors. Therefore, I include works produced in different localities of the Arab world – Egypt, Iraq, Morocco, Syria, Lebanon, and Palestine – in order to explore the construction of autobiographical identities across national boundaries. With regard to linguistic diversity, the study offers a range of texts composed in literary Arabic (*fuṣḥā*), dialects, and English.

2 Scope and Goals of Study

The majority of texts I chose to discuss in this book are not explicitly labeled as "autobiographies" by their authors, and there are several important reasons behind my selection. One of many paradoxes of autobiography is a discrepancy between theoretical discussions behind the genre and its perception by the audience. Most contemporary schools of thought view autobiographical identity as a necessarily complex and heterogeneous construct,[2] where the author is set on a quest to produce an account of the self, rather than an accurate depiction of facts from his or her life. However, autobiographical readership continues to demand factual accuracy from a life story, and there is definitely an obsession with the "truth" that readers often seem to mandate from an autobiography. As the Australian novelist Nicholas Jose put it, "We seem to be very complex creatures when it comes to questions of representation, willing to be deceived, yet not completely."[3] Perhaps an extreme, yet very telling, example is the 2006 James Frey–Oprah Winfrey scandal, where Frey's extremely popular memoir *A Million Little Pieces*, after being praised and promoted on the Oprah Winfrey show, was proved to have been fabricated by the author.[4] The story quickly became the national fable in the United States on the *necessity* of truthfulness when presenting your life to an audience. Philippe Lejeune's formulation of autobiographical pact, where the author and the reader enter into an implied contractual relationship of factual truthfulness sealed by "the affirmation in the text of [autobiographical] identity, referring back . . . to the name of the author on the cover" (Lejeune 1989: 14),[5] has been a conservative demarcation of the genre since the 1970s. Shirley Neuman summarized the foundational principle of the autobiographical author–audience dynamic: "The assumption that, from his privileged position vis-à-vis himself, the autobiographer will tell the truth . . . is the most fundamental article of good faith between autobiographer and his readers" (Neuman 1981: 319). In this context, the *A Million Little Pieces* scandal became a TV spectacle of Lejeune's pact, Oprah's couch being the courtroom where the author was put on public trial for violating the autobiographical truth-telling contract with the audience and, as Oprah put it, for "presenting a false person" in his pseudo-memoir.

The James Frey episode is only one of many examples of our society's fascination with the lives of others. Reality television, celebrity following, obsessive reading of Facebook and Twitter posts, and watching YouTube personal videography – numerous autobiographical genres of all formats and modes continue to mushroom in popular culture, and we continue to consume, it seems, every manifestation of confessional life-telling. Despite proclamations of the death of the genre by Derrida and de Man,[6] the constantly mutating autobiography seems to be very much alive, and the autobiographical author remains "a person of interest." Going back to the *A Million Little Pieces* example, the fact that following numerous unsuccessful attempts to sell his book to a publisher as a "novel" Frey succeeded almost immediately after changing it to a "memoir" (thereby entering into an autobiographical pact with the readership), highlights the undying popularity of the genre.

Expanding on the Foucauldian framework of power and Shotter's approach to social articulation of personal selfhood in the field of psychology, Paul Eakin theorizes a system of social accountability within contemporary autobiographical discourse:

> the interpersonal exchange of self-narrations is a rule-governed regime and . . . the rules are enforced. Others police our performance, and it is also true that we do this policing ourselves. We monitor and judge what others tell us . . . The psychologist John Shotter claims that our participation in what I am calling a narrative identity system is governed by "social accountability": "What we talk of *as* our experience of our reality is constituted for us very largely by the *already established* ways in which we *must* talk in our attempts to account for ourselves – and for it – to the others around us . . .

> And only certain ways of talking are deemed legitimate" (141, emphasis in original). The analyses of Chaloupka, Foucault, and Shotter sensitize us to the presence of social constraints in the exercise of self-narration; our sense of autonomy, of total control, is something of an illusion when it comes to talking about ourselves. (Eakin 2008: 24–5)

Therefore, not only does the confessional mode remain at the core of autobiography – at least when it comes to readers' expectations – but it has evolved into a complex, yet rigid, power system. An author who self-identifies as an autobiographer through Lejeune's pact is basically expected to become a truth-telling, fact-checking, self-confessing writing machine where literary text no longer functions within the categories of fiction/non-fiction. Instead, autobiography is now called to operate within the uncompromising binary of truth versus lie.

Related to the reader's demand for autobiographical truthfulness, there is also an expectation that through the act of autobiographical writing the author would reveal his or her true identity: the core of the core *real* self which is seen as concealed behind the many layers of one's societal attributes, familial roles, education, political affiliations, and ideological and religious beliefs. This singular self is anticipated to expose the ultimate truth about the author's selfhood and *explain* his or her life to the reader. In his philosophical and yet very personal work *In the Name of Identity: Violence and the Need to Belong*, Amin Maalouf talks about the oversimplification imposed on the autobiographical subject, resulting from the audience's quest for the ultimate truth:

> ". . . but what do you really feel, deep down inside?" For a long time I found this oft-repeated question amusing, but it no longer makes me smile. It seems to reflect a view of humanity which, though it is widespread, is also in my opinion dangerous. It presupposed that "deep down inside" everyone there is just one affiliation that really matters, a kind of "fundamental truth" about each individual, an "essence" determined once and for all at birth, never to change thereafter. As if the rest, all the rest – a person's whole journey through time as a free agent; the beliefs he acquires in the course of this journey; his own individual tastes, sensibilities, and affinities; in short his life itself – counted for nothing. (Maalouf 2001: 2)

When it comes to methods of self-representation, such demands for truthfulness inflict certain limitations on the autobiographical author. The expectations of the genre with its enforced "contract" between the autobiographer and the reader basically requires authors to avoid any fictionalized elements in their narratives and, therefore, restrains them creatively. I argue that an excessive focus on truth-telling has a negative impact on the making of autobiographical identity because it imposes a dichotomy of Truth versus Lie, and confines the imaginative and abstract aspects of subjectivity. Therefore, I am most interested in literary texts that are *implicitly* autobiographical, that is, texts that are not bound by Lejeune's autobiographical pact, namely, autobiographical novels. In such narratives authors can exercise more freedom of self-expression while avoiding scrutiny from their readers for being untruthful.

One might argue that all writing could be considered autobiographical since authors use their life experience when creating their works, and everything that they produce reflects their worldview in one way or another. "As I look back, I suspect that no matter how I tuned the lyre, I played the same tune. All my writing – and yours – is autobiographical," Donald Murray wrote in an essay-overview of his oeuvre.[7] If this were the case, how could one demarcate an autobiographical novel? I define a novel as autobiographical when the principal function of the text is the *making of autobiographical identity*. This practice is not limited to a mere inclusion of facts and experiences from the author's personal history, since various snippets of one's life may have countless other narrative purposes external to the self-referential discourse. The autobiographical novel is a narrative form that articulates human selfhood in all its complexity, with all the dreams, thoughts, imaginary worlds, and alternative realities that exist in the human psyche. This is a narrative form that is free from the convention to strictly follow the factual storyline of one's life, which makes it more versatile. As Paul Eakin reminds us, "fictions and the fiction-making process are a central constituent of the truth of any life as it is lived and of any life devoted to the presentation of this life" (Eakin 1985: 5).

The autobiographical novel contains a number of autobiographical elements that function as connecting points between the author, the narrator, and the protagonist. These autobiographical elements take various forms, such as similarities between the narrative story and the author's personal history; physical resemblance, especially with presence of unusual physical traits; similarity of the surrounding environment (family house, street, city); resemblance of family members and friends and their life stories, and so on. Whereas fictionalized elements create a discourse that lies outside the "truth-telling" mode of the autobiographical pact and the limitations imposed by it. In Arab cultural contexts, a salient factor behind the author's choice to narrate personal selfhood through a novel is the question of censorship – both institutional and social – in that it is far less acceptable to reveal intimate details of one's life and to talk openly about taboo aspects of autobiographical subjectivity, such as family relationships, sexuality, political activity, unconventional religious beliefs. As Layla Abu Zayd stated in the preface to her autobiography *Return to Childhood*, "a Muslim's private life is considered an *'awra* (an intimate part of the body), and *sitr* (concealing it) is imperative" (Abu Zayd 1998: iii).

For all these reasons, I focus on autobiographical novels as primary case studies in the first three chapters, where I discuss literary autobiographical modalities. The only exceptions are Ihab Hassan's *Out of Egypt* (subtitled *Scenes and Arguments of an Autobiography*) and Muhammad Shukri's *The Bare Bread*[8] (subtitled *Sīrah Dhātīyah Riwā'īyah* (*A Novelistic Autobiography*)), neither of which are conventional autobiographies. Each subsequent chapter of the book discusses a particular modality of autobiographical transmission. Chapter 1 investigates nationalism, which has gradually become one of the most popular vehicles of self-representation. The postcolonial period in the Arab world brought about a large number of literary works concerned with constructing new national identities. Autobiographical production is particularly important in this context because it renegotiates the complex triangular relationship between the individual, his community/nation, and the Western Other. Anticolonial and nationalist aspects of contemporary Arab life-writing highlight new modes of ideological and cultural identity that emerged in the process of nation-building. My case studies in this chapter are Hanna Minah's *Fragments of Memory* (1975) and Layla Abu Zayd's *Year of the Elephant* (1984). These works, produced in two distinct geopolitical locations of the Arab world – Syria and Morocco, respectively – illustrate how different colonial histories, local cultural traditions, and religious discourses inform the construction of diverse nationalist autobiographical identities.

If the human body was virtually absent in early works of the genre, physicality has gradually become an important site for the construction of autobiographical identity. Chapter 2 investigates the corporeal modality of autobiographical transmission by examining Muhammad Shukri's *The Bare Bread* (1973) and Nazik Saba Yarid's *Improvisations on a Missing String* (1992), with a focus on various cultural dimensions of the autobiographical body. In Chapter 3, I explore the multicultural–multilingual modality and discuss a selection of autobiographical writings informed by displacement and exile, where the three selected case studies offer markedly different forms of displacement and cultural hybridity. In Sumayyah Ramadan's *Leaves of Narcissus* (2001), the bilingual autobiographical subject is situated in a permanent limbo between its Arabic- and English-speaking identities. In Batul al-Khudayri's *A Sky So Close* (1999), the narrator attempts to (re)negotiate her two ethnicities – Iraqi and British, whereas Ihab Hassan's autobiographical subject in *Out of Egypt* (1986), written in English, labors to completely erase his Egyptian self in favor of an American(ized) identity.

Cinematographic autobiographical modality is examined in Chapter 4. The importance of this unorthodox mode of self-expression cannot be underestimated, taking into consideration cinema's increasing popularity among Arab audiences. Filmic autobiography renders a visual dimension to the identity construction and, I argue, formulates a more intimate relationship between the filmmaker-autobiographer and his or her audience. With regard to selected case studies, this chapter focuses on Youssef Chahine's trilogy: *Alexandria . . . Why?* (1978), *An Egyptian Story* (1982), and *Alexandria, Again and Forever* (1989). Chapter 5 is dedicated to one of the newest and most versatile autobiographical genres – Internet blogs. With its rising popularity, cyber-writing represents perhaps the most dynamic mode of autobiographical construction. Blogging culture has fundamentally altered the very nature of autobiographical narration by putting authors in direct communication with their readers, often in real time. No longer a retrospective prose, autobiographical cyber-writing devoid of censorship restrictions in most parts of the Arab world has truly become the voice of Arab youth. Therefore, such autobiographical blogs offer a fascinating insight into discourses of cultural identity among younger generations. This chapter will focus on the genre of autobiography, looking at Ghada Abd al-Al's weblog "wanna b a bride" and its book version *I Want to Get Married!* as the primary case studies.

3 Modes of Arab Cultural Identity

Given that each and every cultural area renders different understandings of selfhood and different ways of constructing collective identities, it is important to recognize that Western formulations of individual identity might not be always applicable to Arab contexts. When discussing sociocultural identity in the Arab world, one should take into consideration that it is not by any means a monolithic construct, since it contains distinctly diverse cultural areas. However, it is also possible to trace some overarching tendencies in configurations of cultural identity throughout the area. A number of interesting studies offering various conceptualizations of Arab identity have been published in recent decades, among them Stephen Sheehi's *Foundations of Modern Arab Identity* (2004), Rashid Khalidi's *Palestinian Identity: The Construction of Modern National Consciousness* (1997), Halim Barakat's *The Arab World: Society, Culture, and State* (1993), and Yasir Suleiman's *The Arabic Language and National Identity: A Study in Ideology* (2003) and *Arabic, Self and Identity: A Study in Conflict and Displacement* (2011) particularly stand out. While approaching different aspects of Arab identity – be it ethnic, religious, national, linguistic, or cultural – from different fields and analytical angles, all these studies highlight the essential complexity of Arab selfhood and its intricate relationship with Western configurations of subjectivity. Stephen Sheehi even suggests that the very confrontation with the West inspired the formation of modern Arab selfhood: "Arab identity came unto itself through the negative image of the West as Other . . . the Arab intellectual of the nineteenth century began to conceptualize his selfhood in terms of his own otherness to Europe" (Sheehi 2004: 34–5).

During the nineteenth and twentieth centuries Arab conceptions of the self have been significantly influenced by Western paradigms as a result of ongoing cultural and economic exchanges, as well as colonial encounters, but the relationship between traditional Arab cultural norms and necessary ideological borrowings from the West was always a complicated one: "much writing from the Arab Renaissance exhibits a tension between the need to maintain Arab cultural authenticity and the need to assimilate Western positivist knowledge and social principles in the pursuit of national 'progress' (*taqaddum*)" (Sheehi 1999). Not only were the indigenous forms of selfhood preserved, but they evolved into highly complex sociocultural constructions, hybrids of traditional and modern. One of the important aspects of Arab selfhood is that of collective identification and valorization of the communal. If in Western modes of selfhood individualism takes the central place, the perception of the self in many Arab cultural and philosophical traditions is largely based on the sense of *belonging* – to a family, tribe, religious community, social group, and so forth. This important marker of Arab selfhood is deeply rooted in various cultural and religious traditions of the area. For example, the Islamic theological concept of the *ʾummah* (community of the believers) serves to reinforce Muslim unity based on religious affiliation. Another important influence on the collective notion, which became particularly critical during the colonial period, was the ideological necessity to unify Arabs in order to confront the Western Other. In addition to that, traditional family structures in Arab societies often reinforce and promote close ties between family members. Halim Barakat argues that family remains at the core of traditional Arab selfhood:

> The fact that the family constitutes the basic unit of social organization in traditional contemporary Arab society . . . may explain why it continues to exert so much influence on identity formation. At the center of social and economic activities, it remains a very cohesive social institution, exerting the earliest and most lasting impact on a person's affiliations. (Barakat 1993: 38–9)

The notion of collectiveness is certainly not the only aspect of Arab conceptions of identity. Moreover, these broad categories of the collective – religious, ethnic, familial, and so on – are neither monolithic nor neatly structured, and are often unstable due to continuous internal shifts. As Barakat points out, "the Arab sense of belonging has to be assessed in the light of overlapping and conflicting affiliations" (*ibid.*: 35). Nonetheless, the collective aspect of identity must be taken into account when comparing Western and Arab constructions of selfhood.

The constantly, and often violently, developing political and ideological landscape in the Arab world guarantees the continuous emergence of new modes of identity. The chain of revolutions that have shaken the Arab world very recently, where in all likelihood, the process of rapid political transformations is far from being over, have had a profound effect on all aspects of cultural life and have stimulated the process of fundamental self-(re)evaluation, in particular with regard to national identity. Naturally, the historic changes in national consciousness and ideological configuration of Arab society will also have a major impact on individual identity in the near future. In a recent interview, the Moroccan author Tahar Ben Jelloun made an interesting suggestion about possible developments of Arab sense of selfhood in the post-revolutionary period:

> Until now the individual was not recognized in the region. Tribes or ethnic groups were recognized but not the individual. In Libya, Moammar Gadhafi exploited the conflict between ethnic groups and played one tribe off against another. But now Arab revolts have been driven by individuals' urgency for change. The concept of the "individual" has been born during these revolts. At the same time, tribal structures and ethnic traditions will not simply disappear. Tribal culture will have to enter into a modern framework and that is very complicated but individualism is here to stay. (Ben Jelloun 2011)

Therefore, Arab cultural identity should be approached as a highly complex construct, a hybrid of different cultural modes and traditional affiliations. It offers great regional variety, where local histories and cultural traditions have profound influence on how collective forms of selfhood are formulated. In addition to that, one should take into account the diversity within the Arab societal infrastructure, where the three types of community – urban, rural, and tribal – continue to shape different worldviews.

All these factors ought to be considered when discussing conceptions of identity in Arab cultural zones and comparing them with Western modes of selfhood. One should be equally mindful of these differences when applying Western theory to Arab autobiographical texts, since Western theories of the self are based on Western cultural heritage and Western conceptualizations of human subjectivity. Autobiographical writing, being in its essence "literature of the self," is very sensitive – perhaps to a larger degree than other literary genres – to ideological shifts in a given society. This means that autobiographical production from different cultures and different historical periods reflects the changing conceptions of subjectivity peculiar to these localities at specific points in time.

4 Arab Premodern Autobiographical Writing

Modern Arab autobiography dating back to the early twentieth century has undergone a phenomenally rapid development during the past one hundred years. Not only has it been recognized as an essential component of contemporary narrative discourse, but it now offers a well-established and rich tradition, which is particularly remarkable considering all the important changes that this genre experienced during a relatively short period. Although in early studies of the genre it was a common opinion that the arrival of autobiography on the Arabic literary scene was a direct influence of Western literatures, recent criticism has shown that this process was a much more complex phenomenon, brought about by both external influences and internal forces within Arab narrative discourse.

Eurocentric views that autobiography as a genre is an exclusive prerogative of Western culture were challenged by many scholars, who asserted that various forms of life-writing and autobiographical storytelling have long been present in cultural traditions outside Europe. One well-known example of orientalist attitudes toward non-Western literatures and cultures could be found in George Gusdorf's article "Conditions and Limits of Autobiography," where he famously claimed:

> It would seem that autobiography is not to be found outside of our cultural area; one would say that it expresses a concern peculiar to Western man, a concern that has been of good use in his systematic conquest of the universe and that he has communicated to men of other cultures. (Gusdorf 1980: 29)

Gusdorf further suggests that even if some autobiographical works are found in non-Western cultures, these appeared directly under European influence. Certainly, such extreme views emphasizing European cultural hegemony has long been proven wrong by scholars in postcolonial studies, feminism and queer studies, and other relevant fields within humanities and social sciences. As Bart Moore-Gilbert argues: "Western autobiography studies' failure to properly recognize alternative traditions derives not simply from ignorance but from narrow, if not plainly ethnocentric, conceptions of what autobiographical self consists of and how it should be written" (Moore-Gilbert 2011: 106). Indeed, when approaching Arab literary heritage, one should not overlook a rich tradition of cognate autobiographical forms in classical literature. The examination of this early autobiographical material is particularly important considering a substantial number of Arab autobiographies of the twentieth century that borrowed some narrative models from premodern life-writing.

Recently, a number of scholars have argued that several genres in medieval Arabic narrative discourse were indeed premodern autobiographies.[9] A crucial study in this area was Dwight Reynolds' monograph *Interpreting the Self: Autobiography in the Arabic Literary Tradition* (2001), in which he examined a large number of classical Arab literary productions ranging from the ninth to the nineteenth centuries, and offered a compelling argument for a rich tradition of premodern Arab autobiography and indigenous conceptualizations of narrative identity present in these works. In an earlier study, *In My Childhood: A Study in Arabic Autobiography* (1997), Tetz Rooke, although not considering Arab premodern works of life-writing as autobiographies in the modern sense of the word, offered a useful classification of classical literary production containing autobiographical elements. Here the three main categories are: biography (*sīrah* or *tarjamah*), which was a dominant form in Arabic historical literature during the Middle Ages; travelogues and geographical texts (*ʾadab al-riḥlah*); and medieval religious tracts[10] (Rooke 1997: 75–83). Notably, numerous elements from all three premodern autobiographical categories are clearly present in many modern works of the genre. The *sīrah*/*tarjamah* was usually written as a *curriculum vitae* of scholars and other prominent figures, and I believe it introduced the idea that it was practically a *required* endeavor for a renowned Arab intellectual to write an autobiography as an important part of his oeuvre (hence, a large number of autobiographies by famous writers, politicians, religious and ideological leaders that appeared in Arabic literature in the first half of the twentieth century). As for travelogues, not only were they rejuvenated during the Arab

Renaissance – *al-Nahḍah al-ʿArabiyah*[11] – but *ʾadab al-riḥlah* initiated the emergence of modern Arab autobiography, and travel memoir continues to be an important element of contemporary life-writing. Finally, the medieval genre of autobiographical religious tracts had a profound impact on conceptualization and the narrative style of Arab autobiography in the early twentieth century, as I will illustrate further.

In his analysis of Jalal al-Din al-Suyuti's autobiography *Al-Taḥadduth bi-Niʿmat Allāh* (*Speaking of God's Bounty*) dated as early as 1485, Dwight Reynolds points out the remarkable contrast between early forms of European autobiographies, most of which were composed as confessions, and premodern Arabic autobiographical writing, which emphasized the author's virtuous life:

> One tradition seems to be framed to make the statement, "These are the ways in which I have enjoyed a moral and productive life – imitate me in them," while the other seems to imply, "These are the ways in which I have been deficient or in error – beware of similar pitfalls!" Each frame produced its own moral tensions and anxieties of representation, as well as literary strategies for resolving those issues (Reynolds 2001: 3)

Interestingly, the tradition of presenting an exemplary life continued through centuries and influenced modern forms of autobiographical writing, in particular the category of what I call *conventional* autobiographies that flourished in the first half of the twentieth century. Al-Suyuti indicated that his predecessors' and his own motivation for writing an autobiography was "praiseworthy intentions, among which is speaking of 'God's bounty' in thanks, and also to make known their circumstances in life so that others might emulate them in these" (quoted from Reynolds 2001: 1). These objectives of autobiographical writing are certainly traceable in the works of Ahmad Amin, Salama Musa, Muhammad Qarah Ali, and others who defined the early developments of the genre in Arabic literature. Indeed, various forms and modes of contemporary Arab autobiographical discourse, I argue, offer a remarkable mélange of traditional and modern, Western and local cultural influences and conceptualizations of human selfhood.

5 The Beginnings of Modern Arab Autobiography: Conventional Autobiographies

The formation of the new reading public and the new worldview during the Arab *Nahdah* in the nineteenth and early twentieth centuries created the conditions for the emergence of modern forms of autobiography in Arabic literature,[12] where the rejuvenation of the *riḥlah* literature became a crucial step in this process. Writers who chose to express their experiences in other countries in *ʾadab al-riḥlah* (travelogue literature) "were able to gain new insights and exercise an influence on their countrymen," and regardless of the quality of the material, these *riḥlah* works "are important as expressions . . . of values, and as indication of individual attitudes toward novel situations" (Chejne 1962: 214). This new form of travel literature was evidently more personal than its classical predecessor, which led some critics to consider Faris al-Shidyaq's satire *al-Sāq ala al-Sāq fima Huwa al-Fāryāq* (*The Cross-Legged*), perhaps the most interesting example of the revived *ʾadab al-riḥlah* written in 1855, a pioneering autobiographical work of the modern period. Sabry Hafiz, one of proponents of this idea, argues that not only was *al-Sāq* the first modern Arabic autobiography, but it significantly influenced subsequent autobiographical works by offering three core narrative components which gradually became principal structural elements of the genre: coming-of-age, journey, and language (Hafiz 2002: 18, 23). C. Nijland, too, suggested that although this work "is not an autobiography in the strictest sense . . . [it] contains enough elements to consider it the first Arabic autobiography in modern times" (Nijland 1975: 67).[13] Others, in contrast, consider *al-Sāq* a work of pure fiction. For example, Mattityahu Peled argued that "even if some episodes related in *al-Sāq* can be traced to events in the life of the author, the sum total of all the events told in *al-Sāq* is meant to construct a fictitious history" (Peled 1985: 42). There is also a third approach to Shidyaq's work offered by Pierre Cachia and Paul Starkey who combined the other two opinions, suggesting that *al-Sāq ala al-Sāq* is a "fictionalized autobiography employed as a frame story for a satirical work of social and literary criticism, with philological and poetic digressions" (Starkey 1998: 37).

If anything, such extensive discussions of *al-Sāq* only highlight the intricate relationship between fictional and autobiographical discourses in Arabic literature from the very beginning of the modern period. An important aspect of modern Arab self-referential literature is that its two main subgenres – autobiographical novel and conventional autobiography – developed side by side, where Taha Husayn's *Al-ʾAyyām* (*The Days*), written in 1926/7 and published in 1929, was the literary catalyst that defined the development of autobiographical writing in the twentieth century.[14] Indeed, many Arab authors of later generations looked back at Husayn's work as a model for their own autobiographical production. For instance, Fedwa Malti-Douglas argues that even the Egyptian über feminist Nawal al-Saadawi followed in Taha Husayn's footsteps by "re-writing" *al-ʾAyyām* into a gender context in her *Mudhakkarat Ṭabībah* (*Memoirs of a Woman Doctor*) (Malti-Douglas 1991). Sayyid Qutb, another prominent Arab writer and intellectual, dedicated his own autobiography *Ṭifl Min al-Qaryah* (*A Child from the Village*), written in 1946, to Taha Husayn:

> To the author of *al-Ayyām*, Doctor Taha Hussayn Bey:
> These, dear sir, are "days" like your "days," lived by a village child, some are similar to your days and some are different. The difference reflects the difference between one generation and another, one village and another, one life and another, indeed the difference between one nature and another, between one attitude and another. But they are, when all is said and done, also "days." (Qutb 2004)

Because of its narrative structure, *al-ʾAyyām* is an autobiographical novel, rather than an autobiography. It is composed from the third-person point of view, the text is not labeled as autobiography, the name of the author is never mentioned in the text,[15] and the reader's perception of Husayn's narrative as autobiographical is based merely on external factors. In other words, *The Days* avoids the "commitments" of *le pacte autobiographique*.

Although following the publication of *al-ʾAyyām* some writers did choose novelistic discourse as a mode of autobiographical expression, the majority of autobiographical production in the first half of the last century took the form of *conventional autobiography*, and this subgenre continued even in more recent developments of Arabic literature. Among the most prominent examples of conventional autobiography are Ibrahim al-Mazini's *Qiṣṣat Ḥayātī* (*The Story of My Life*, 1943), Salama Musa's *Tarbiyat Salāmah Mūsā* (*The

Education of Salama Musa, 1947), Ahmad Amin's *Ḥayātī* (*My Life*, 1952), Abd al-Majid Bin Jallun's *Fī al-Ṭufūlah* (*In Childhood*, 1957), Mikhail Nu'ayma's *Sab'ūn* (*Seventy*, 1959/60), Fadwa Tuqan's *Riḥlah Jabalīyyah, Riḥlah Ṣa'bah: Sīrah Dhātīyyah* (*A Mountainous Journey, a Difficult Journey: An Autobiography*, 1985), and Muhammad Qarah Ali's *Suṭūr Min Ḥayātī* (*Lines From My Life*, 1988).

Arabic conventional autobiography became a literary canon by the mid-twentieth century and it shares numerous structural elements with American autobiography of the eighteenth century, such as that by John Adams, John Woolman, Thomas Jefferson, and Benjamin Franklin. This style of autobiographical writing presents an "image of self which synthesizes private and public histories" (Banes 1982: 226). As I stated earlier, in Arab cultural contexts the articulation of one's life as exemplary can be traced back to premodern autobiographical production. The twentieth-century Arab autobiographer was expected to present himself to his audience as a distinguished individual, and to portray a righteous persona preoccupied with documenting the story of his education, the development of his political consciousness, the details of his spiritual/ideological/scholarly journey and his encounters with other famous contemporaries. The reading public anticipated the writers' active involvement in the political and social life of their respective countries, and, indeed, many of them were prominent figures of their time. Therefore, it is not surprising that many early autobiographies were structured as *historical* narratives where the construction of the autobiographical self was often overshadowed by reports on various important historical and political events that took place during the course of their lives. Susanne Enderwitz suggests that the autohistory style of writing is rooted in some unique features of Arabic literary discourse:

> the first generations of autobiographers, oscillating between history and fiction, sought to stay as far as possible within the boundaries of history as the more respectable genre. Moreover, the heroic gesture also added to the identification of [Arab] autobiography with history. (Enderwitz 1998: 81)

The historiographic aspect of many Arab conventional autobiographies situates them within memoir literature: "a mode of life narrative that historically situates the subject in a social environment, as either observer or participant;

the memoir directs attention more toward the lives and actions of others than to the narrator" (Smith and Watson 2001: 198). Evidently, this mode of self-referential writing generates a particular configuration of narrative identity:

> Whereas autobiography promotes an "I" that shares with confessional discourse an assumed territory and an ethical mandate to examine that interiority, memoirs promote an "I" that is explicitly constituted in the reports of the utterances and proceedings of others. The "I" or subjectivity produced in memoirs is externalized and . . . dialogical. (Quinby 1992: 299)

That is to say, an autobiographical identity of a memoir is likely to manifest a more explicit notion of the *collective* than in a traditional autobiography, in that the former is more keen to embrace the identities of others – of a generation, a political or ideological movement, a religious denomination, particular social and academic circles – in the autobiographical act. It is not surprising, then, that some critics classified many conventional Arab autobiographies as memoirs, since substantial parts in these works were dedicated to detailed depictions of the authors' milieu and famous contemporaries. For instance, Thomas Philipp argues that Salama Musa'a work (especially the chapter "Some Men of Letters I Knew") is a memoir, rather than what he calls a "clear-cut" autobiography (Philipp 1993: 579).

One of the principal features of conventional autobiographies is a clearly conveyed Lejeune's autobiographical pact – either in the title (*The Education of Salama Musa*; *My Life*) or the subtitle (*ḥikāyat ʿumr* ("a life story") in Mikhail Nuaymah's *Seventy*). The story is related from the first-person point of view and contains ample evidence that the author, the narrator, and the protagonist are identical. Usually, the sameness of names is confirmed by the author's first and/or last name mention in the text, and furthermore, the autobiographical pact is often reinforced in the *muqaddimah* (introduction or preface). The author of a conventional autobiography is usually a man (with some exceptions, such as Fadwa Tuqan's *A Mountainous Journey*), and he is a figure of high stature and impeccable moral character, hence, the educational aspect of his life story. The narrative chronology is very linear with hardly any interruptions, and the language is consistently transparent, all of which gives an impression of a "life reportage."

Most importantly, Arab conventional autobiography introduced and disseminated a particular mode of narrative identity: a clearly delineated conception of self, in many ways comparable to the Western notion of the universal subject. In these early autobiographies, the *I* of the narrator was formulated as a self-defined, self-knowing, and static construct. Among the important attributes of the identity-making process in these works is a particular focus on human intellect and spirituality. Conventional autobiographers believed that the intellectual, rational, and cognitive self, completely detached from any notion of the bodily, is the primary signifier of one's subjectivity. Because of the conceptual similarities between Arabic conventional identity and Western humanist ideas on selfhood, it is very likely that European autobiographical discourses influenced early Arab works of the genre. Such influences were very much anticipated, bearing in mind the large number of fundamental European works translated into Arabic during *Nahdah*. Sabry Hafiz wrote about the cultural importance of Western translations:

> translations answered a real need for fresh literature . . . the appearance of many translated novels and short stories reflected the readers' thirst and fondness for the new narrative discourse. Translation not only familiarized them with the conventions of narrative and answered their need for new reading material, but also served as a training ground for would-be writers. (Hafiz 1993: 89–90)

Some autobiographers openly admitted that they modeled their monographs on well-known Western counterparts. For instance, Salama Musa, whose *The Education of Salama Musa* bears an obvious resemblance to *The Education of Henry Adams*, pointed out in the introduction to his book that: "I borrow its title from Henry Adams, finding in it a deep significance from which the reader may well benefit" (Musa 1961: 6).

The concept of the Cartesian subject was very much in tune with many traditional Arab cultural paradigms. For example, depictions of the human body, female as well as male, were very limited in the mainstream Arabic literature of the time. The writer was judged on his moral character, intellectual achievements, spirituality, and other exemplary traits almost as much he was judged on his literary work. Naturally, autobiography was expected to convey an educational message and to satisfy the public's expectations. Thus, the adoption of literary models from Western autobiographical tradition should not be looked at as a blind borrowing of all things European, but as a careful selection of certain concepts and narrative devices that fit into the local cultural framework. Certainly, Western literary, cultural, and ideological influences did participate in the reshaping of the Arab literary system throughout the twentieth century, including the emergence of new literary genres and forms, but these were only some of the many factors that took part in the development of modern Arab narrative discourse.

In addition to the "exemplary life" mode rooted in premodern autobiographies, another feature illustrating authentic Arab conceptions of self and narrative devices expected from self-referential literature was a distinct apologetic tone that outlined the majority of conventional autobiographies. Layla Abu Zayd wrote in the English preface to her *Return to Childhood* about the incompatibility of autobiography's focus on the individual self and traditional Arab cultural norms:

> autobiography has the pejorative connotation in Arabic of *madihu nafsihi wa muzakkiha* (he or she who praises him- or herself). This phrase denotes all sorts of defects in a person or a writer: selfishness versus altruism, individualism versus the spirit of the group, arrogance versus modesty. That is why Arabs usually refer to themselves in formal speech in the third person plural, to avoid the use of the embarrassing "I." In autobiography, of course, one uses "I" frequently. (Abu Zayd 1998: iii)

Early Arab autobiographers insisted on linking their personal stories to broader social, generational, national, and other histories so enthusiastically that it almost seemed like they were renouncing their individualism. Frequent and detailed depictions of social and political conditions in these works, as well as the dedication of substantial portions of the text to other prominent intellectuals, indicated the need to produce a justification of their autobiographical endeavors and to downplay the individual aspect of their life stories. The apologetic tone in many autobiographical *muqqadimāt* (introductions), which became an important narrative element of the genre, often outlined the autobiographer's attempt to avoid accusations of self-indulgence and hedonism.[16] For instance, Ahmad Amin boldly asks in the preface to his autobiography: "Why am I publishing *My Life*?," which he rationalizes by situating his story as *illustrative* of his generation:

> perhaps it may portray one aspect of our generation and describe one type of our life, perhaps it may benefit a reader today and help a historian tomorrow, for I have been concerned to describe my surroundings as they affected myself, and myself as I was affected by my surroundings. (Amin 1978: 4–5)

Salama Musa takes a very similar approach in his own introduction to *Education of Salama Musa*: "This is the history of the age in which I lived, and the history of the generation of which I was a member" (Musa 1961: 4). I do not believe that these writers' inclination to assign universal meanings to their autobiographical accounts means that they intended to compose memoirs. Rather, this phenomenon illustrates a distinctive feature of early Arab autobiographies to formulate an identity where the individual and the collective are intricately entangled.

However, as the genre continued to develop, conventional autobiographies of a later period gradually departed from the collective mode, and some even showed an entirely opposite attitude by focusing on the *I* of the narrator and by emphasizing the individual and private nature of the autobiographical story. In the first, introductory chapter of her *A Mountainous Journey* (1985) Fadwa Tuqan asserts the singularity and individuality of her autobiographical subject by using numerous first-person verbs and pronouns in virtually every sentence. Here the autobiographical *I* is front and center, which, especially in the Arabic original, stands in sharp contrast with the aforementioned Layla Abu Zayd's quote:

> I yearned continually to escape from my time and place . . . Fate threw me on to a rough path and on it I began my journey up the mountain. I carried the rock and endured the fatigue of the endless ascents and descents . . . I realized that action is the obverse of the coin, the reverse being dream and will-power. I determined to do business with this two-sided coin: will and action. (Tuqan 1990: 12)

Another indication of a collective aspect of Arab conventional autobiography is the author's efforts to bond with the audience by comparing his or her personal life with their reader's. For instance, Mikhail Nu'aymah, addressing his audience in an introductory chapter, typical for those forms of autobiographical writings, refers to the reader in the second person which creates a sense of intimacy between the author and the reader: "Seventy years! . . . My dear reader, all this and a thousand other things are the atoms and particles constituting my life and yours" (Nuaymah 1962: 7–8).[17]

To illustrate the self-referential discourse formulated in conventional autobiographies with a specific example, let us look at Ahmad Amin's *Ḥayātī* (*My Life*) – one of the typical works of the genre. Amin's autobiography, written in 1950, is a clear-cut case of Lejeune's pact. Not only does the title of the book clearly indicate that the narrative is the author's life story, but there is also an explicitly indicated identicalness of the name in the text itself: "In 1948 the College of Arts Council and the Fuad I University Council decided to award me an honorary doctorate, and so I was called Dr. Ahmad Amin" (Amin 1978: 221). Furthermore, the text contains an excerpt from Amin's diploma, which mentions his full name, "Dr. Ahmad Amin Ibrahim Bey," leaving no uncertainty about the narrator-protagonist's identity.

Like other conventional autobiographers, Amin is preoccupied with presenting an exemplary life story to his reader. *My Life* is first and foremost a story of class struggle, education, and intellectual growth. Even the opening chapters of the book, where we hear about Amin's childhood, are written as a social criticism piece rather than his childhood reminiscences. The environment and events from his early years are analyzed from the perspective of a grown-up intellectual who wants to *explain* his character and personality to his reader:

> All the characteristics of the home which I mentioned were reflected in my nature and formed the most important distinctive qualities of my personality. If you discern in me an excessive bent towards seriousness and a disgraceful negligence of merriment, or if you see in me patience for work and endurance for hardships . . . then know that all this has been the echo of my home's teachings and principles. (Amin 1978: 20–1)

The narrator's early memories are intertwined with – even overshadowed by – the detailed discussion of the political situation, social conditions, and cultural values that were representative of Egyptian society at the time. Such *reflective* narrative mode was characteristic of Arab conventional autobiography. It is not little Ahmad, a child growing up in Cairo, who tells the story, but it is Dr. Ahmad Amin, a prominent Egyptian intellectual and reformer who critiques his society in retrospect: "Our neighborhood offered an example of family life in the Middle Ages before it was invaded by the materialism and the concepts of civilization" (*ibid*: 26).

The autobiographical subject here is a monolithic and predetermined construct. It is a subject who seemingly *knows* his essence, his personality, and his selfhood *prior* to the act of autobiographical writing. In this regard, Amin's autobiography references George Gusdorf's definition of the genre as "the mirror in which the individual reflects his own image" (Gusdorf 1980: 33). Amin asserts that in his book he is "the displayer and the displayed, the describer and the described. The eye cannot see itself except in a mirror" (Amin 1978: 3). From the narrator's perspective, there is never any doubt in the autobiographical self's uniformity, and the making of identity is seen as a very straightforward and unambiguous process of self-depiction. Finally, *My Life* presents an idea of the autobiographical self that is in many ways similar to the Cartesian subject whose quintessence is defined by mind and soul, but never the body: "this 'I,' that is to say, the mind, by which I am what I am, is entirely distinct from the body" (Descartes 1968: 54). In Amin's narrative, the self is, too, a highly abstract, bodiless category; he views it as a thought and a feeling:

> the self has depths like those of the seas and an obscurity like that of the night. The conscious and the unconscious mind, the simple and the complex feeling, the superficial and the deep motive, the near and the distant purpose. (Amin 1978: 3)

These and other works representing Arab conventional discourse offered a particular kind of autobiographical modality: a modality that promoted the notion of a uniform, homogeneous, self-knowing, intellectual, and bodiless autobiographical subject. This type of narrative identity was articulated in direct reference to the metatextual persona of the author, whereas the text's main objective was to offer a retrospective literary account of his or her life describing – often in an educational manner – the intellectual path of the autobiographer.

6 Recent Developments of Arab Autobiographical Genre

The production of new conventional autobiographies has certainly declined in recent decades, which led some literary critics to announce the death of the autobiographical genre in Arabic. In 1993, Thomas Philipp wrote that "the mid-twentieth century constitutes a certain zenith of autobiographical writing in Arabic . . . [and] with perhaps the noteworthy exception of women authors, this genre of writing and self-expression seems to have stagnated since then" (Philipp 1993: 601). This might be true of conventional autobiographies, but a careful examination of new modes of life-writing in Arabic evidences that not only does this form of self-expression continue to develop, but, I argue, that autobiographical production is now more popular than ever – both among authors and their audiences. Novel experimentations with the genre offer new sites and new possibilities for autobiographical identity construction by incorporating and mixing elements of traditional Arab and popular Western sociocultural discourses, presenting a broad variety of narrative techniques, and introducing new mediums for self-representation, such as audiovisual and cyber texts.

On the literary scene, if conventional autobiography became a popular means of literary expression for prominent intellectuals, autobiographical novel stemming from the groundbreaking *Al-ʾAyyām* was often chosen by writers who either belonged to a minority of sorts (for instance, women authors often elected this mode of writing) or by those who were willing to take risks – either in content or form. Hanna Minah's depictions of extreme poverty, Muhammad Shukri's blunt displays of sexuality, and Batul al-Khudayri's struggle between the two polar opposite identities, Iraqi and English – autobiographical novel gave freedom to these and other risk-taking, bold, and candid life stories that conventional autobiography was much less likely to offer.

But why did the number of autobiographical novels grow exponentially in the second half of the last century? On the one hand, looking for purely literary reasons, one might suggest that because the novel continued to rapidly develop as a genre, for their autobiographical expression the new generation of Arab writers were eager to pick a literary form that was more popular with the reading public and easier to publish. On the other hand, one should take

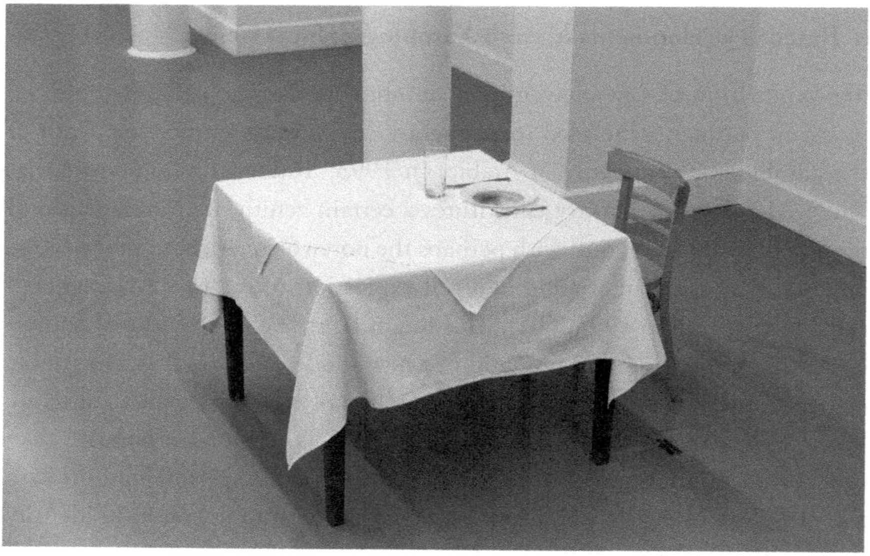

into consideration a number of major historic events that created conditions for fundamental reconfigurations of identity discourses in Arab societies, urging a new means of autobiographical narration. The process of decolonization generated the need to conceive and formulate national identity and, at the same time, highlighted the complexity of this process, given the intricate dynamics between pan-Arab and local forms of nationalism. The Arab defeat of 1967 shook the whole Arab world and triggered major transformations of all aspects of Arab society and culture, including the quest to conceptualize modern authentic Arab identity.[18] A number of other important ideological, political, and social processes had, and still have, an ongoing effect on Arab selfhood. Among these are the effects of Western cultural and economic influences and globalization; an unprecedented growth of radicalized Islamic movements and their influence on political and sociocultural life; the emergence of both secular and Islamic feminist movements. In other words, the twentieth century witnessed some fundamental changes in Arab society, which had a profound impact on both individual and collective notions of identity. Naturally, under these circumstances Arab autobiographical production continued to develop and search for novel modalities.

Figure 1 *Deep Throat* (1996), Mona Hatoum

Table, chair, tablecloths, plate, fork, knife, water glass, monitor and DVD player
35 1/16 × 33 7/16 × 51 3/16 in. (89 × 85 × 130 cm)
Photo: Hadiye Cangokçe

Courtesy: *Arter, Istanbul and White Cube*

The Beirut-born Palestinian Mona Hatoum is the multidimensional artist whose artwork features an unconventional range of media, including installations, sculpture, video, photography, works on paper, as well as performance art. Much of her early work focuses on the body and body politics.

The art installation *Deep Throat* features a restaurant setting with the endoscopic video of the artist's digestive system is shown on a white plate. Part of Hatoum's "endoscopic journey" (also presented in another work entitled *Corps étranger*), the artwork explores the complex relationship of selfhood and corporeality and the representational discourse of the autobiographical body.

With the extraordinary growth of visual culture, autobiography is in a state of perpetual metamorphosis. Autobiographical paintings, photography, and filmmaking continue to expand our understanding of human agency by offering new media of expression. In this book, I explore the cinematic modality of autobiographical transmission in the example of Youssef Chahine's (Yusuf Shahin) Alexandrian Trilogy. Among other things, film expanded the notion of the autobiographical author and autobiographical reader, and highlighted the non-verbal aspects of one's selfhood. I imagine that the audiovisual mode of autobiographical narration will only continue to grow, taking into consideration the expansion of the TV culture, Internet streaming videos (such as YouTube), independent filmmaking, and the general accessibility of currently available video-capturing technology.

Cyber-writing offers yet another space for autobiographical expression. The arrival and growth of the Internet completely transformed the relationship between the author and the audience by putting them in direct communication, often in real time. The Internet, especially web blogging, has assigned writing a new attribute – that of *immediacy*, where texts are created, released, and circulated, and then receive the reader's response so quickly that this process has completely reconfigured discursive practices. Virtual texts are also very fluid, with their easily changeable forms, lack of tangible

format, inclusion of non-linguistic – visual and auditory – formats (photographs, pictures, videos, music, and so on), and potential anonymity of both the author and the reader. Given its heterogeneous and unstable nature, cyber-writing becomes a fascinating site of autobiographical production. In the context of this study, I am particularly interested in blogging, where

Figure 2 *I Found Myself Growing Inside an Old Olive Tree* (2005), Samia Halaby

(Archive No. D1896) Acrylic on tyvek, approximately 36 × 24 in. (91.5 × 61 cm). A soft bas-relief sculpture with parts of the tree's foliage made of folded attachments.

Photographic representation and excerpts from the accompanying essay courtesy of the artist.

Samia A. Halaby is a Palestinian artist, scholar, and a life-long advocate of the Palestinian cause, who lives and works in New York. She is recognized as one of the Arab world's leading contemporary painters.

This self-portrait challenges the boundaries of self-representational discourse and illustrates the complex, multilayered relationship between the individual selfhood and the Palestinian collective identity. The following are the excerpts from the artist's essay accompanying the painting:

> I had just spent 7 precious days inside the green line in occupied Palestine (the Israeli entity) staying at a hostel and using a rented car to drive to one of the oldest stands of olive trees in the Galilee in the northern parts of historic Palestine and spending 8 to 10 hours painting. On the very day of my return to New York, I found an invitation from the Art Car Museum in Houston, Texas, to participate in an exhibition titled "Faces." The deadline to mail the artwork was on the following day. I decided to participate and thus at dawn of the following day, jet-lagged, existing between time zones, still full of the impressions of the old trees, full of the ruminations regarding Zionist oppression, I made this self-portrait and wrote on it: "I Found Myself Growing Inside an Olive Tree in Palestine. We are ancient trees now. We lost many friends cut by Israeli butchery" . . .
>
> The experience of painting the olive trees all day for seven consecutive days while living the quiet life of a monastic hostel allowed them to permeate my being. My mental sight was full of olive trees. I saw them clearly when I closed my eyes and they overlay all I saw with my eyes open. I began to be one of them rather than just looking at them. When I made the self-portrait I was mentally not yet in New York and existing in the isolation of my own studio. I did it aware of my most recent artwork and wanting the challenge of doing it in that same formal manner. I was really hesitant and full of doubt about it and was not sure if I should tear it up or send it. Eventually, out of the fatigue of everything, I decided to just do some final bold gestures and just send it no matter how doubtful I felt. I am now glad that I did it. It seems to tell people just what I experienced there with the ancient olive trees about which I began to feel very sisterly, as though they were accepting me into an ancient collective of those who have seen tragedy and joy. I am rarely mystical but sometimes the romance of it assuages the pain imposed on Palestine. (Samia Halaby, 2007)

the formation of plural immediate fixations of autobiographical subjectivity (blog entries), combined with the reader's direct involvement in the autobiographical act, creates a unique and previously impossible modality of identity making. From the Arab sociocultural perspective, cyber-writing is an even more appealing medium because, on the one hand, it avoids the hurdles of institutional censorship imposed on printed literature and the difficulties

GUUH..
COULD I HAVE A WORD WITH YOU OUTSIDE THE FRAME FOR A SECOND, LARISSA.
I'M SORRY, NONEL, BUT THAT NAME REFERS TO MY ARTISTIC EX-PERSONA ONLY.
STOP CLINGING TO THE PAST, WOMAN.
YEAH, I KNOW. BUT IT'S, LIKE, A META TYPE THING. PLEASE.
WHAT'S UP, OREET?
I DON'T KNOW, LARISSA. AS MUCH AS I ENJOY SEEING OUR CHARACTERS BAILED OUT MARTIAL ARTS STYLE, ISN'T A NINJA A LITTLE TOO ELIA SULEIMAN?

Figure 3 *Nonel and Vovel* (2009), Oreet Ashery and Larissa Sansour

Graphic novel, Charta: Milan and New York, 183 pp.

Reproduction of a page from the novel courtesy of the artists. Information about the artists taken from the website dedicated to their work at: http://nonelandvovel.net/book.

Oreet Ashery is from Israel and lives in London. Larissa Sansour is from Palestine and lives in Copenhagen. The collaborative work of these two artists produced a very special graphic novel, featuring Ashery's and Sansour's alter egos. The graphic novel raises questions on artistic agency, collaborative processes, the nature of authority, and art and politics, and offers an eye-opening take on Palestine. *Nonel and Vovel* represents the pioneering voices of Middle Eastern graphic novel artists, whose self-referential works challenge the boundaries between word and image, and the relationship between an individual and political discourses.

behind finding publishing opportunities for unknown authors. On the other hand, the anonymity that cyber-writing offers is a particularly important feature as far as Arab authors are concerned because it gives more freedom to be open without fear of being judged by society and family.

Recent developments of Arab autobiographical discourse are certainly not limited to the types of cultural texts that I discuss in this book. There are also autobiographical poems, oral narratives, music, paintings, photography, graphic novels, autobiographical documentaries (a genre very different from autobiographical feature films), webcam videos, Facebook and Twitter posts, and other continuously evolving and expanding modes of autobiographical expression (Figures 1–3 offer some recent examples of unorthodox autobiographical works by Arab authors: painting, art installation, and graphic novel). Here is a hope that future scholars will continue exploring this rich tradition. My aim is to offer a method by which to approach the incredibly diverse contemporary Arab autobiographical production and identity-making practices, some of whose modalities I will proceed to explore and conceptualize in subsequent chapters.

Notes

1. Sidonie Smith and Julia Watson mention a group of European theorists of autobiography, among them Jorg Dunne and Christian Moser, who have recently published research about new mediums of autobiographical production and developed a term of *automediality*, expanding "the definition of how subjectivity is constructed in writing, image, or new media" (Smith and Watson 2010: 168).

2. The essential heterogeneity of identity as a concept has been outlined by scholars from different fields: from literary criticism to political science. Rogers Brubaker and Frederick Cooper wrote about the term "identity" and its unavoidable embracing of numerous – at times conflicting – meanings: "Clearly, the term 'identity' is made to do a great deal of work. It is used to highlight non-instrumental modes of action; to focus on self-understanding rather than self-interest; to designate sameness across persons or sameness over time; to capture core, foundational aspects of selfhood; to deny that such core, foundational aspects exist; to highlight the processual, interactive development of solidarity and collective self-understanding; and to stress the fragmented quality of the contemporary existence of 'self,' a self unstably patched together through shards of discourse and contingently 'activated' in differing contexts. These usages are not simply heterogeneous; they point in sharply differing directions" (Brubaker and Cooper 2000: 8).
3. The quote is taken from the online essay "Any Resemblance is Unintended" by Jose, available at: http://www.nla.gov.au/events/history/papers/Nicholas_Jose.html.
4. *The Oprah Winfrey Show* is a highly popular American syndicated talk show that aired nationally from 1986 to 2011. In 2006, James Frey's memoir, *A Million Little Pieces*, was chosen as an Oprah's Book Club selection. Shortly after, TheSmokingGun.com published a piece accusing Frey of fabricating and embellishing parts of the book. A media firestorm ensued, and Frey returned to *The Oprah Winfrey Show* for a controversial interview that made headlines around the world. This incident proved to be the biggest controversy in the history of Oprah Winfrey's show (facts taken from www.oprah.com, accessed August 1, 2013).
5. For more on Lejeune's autobiographical pact, see his *L'autobiographie en France* (1971) and *Le pacte autobiographique* (1975).
6. Derrida's theoretical works, in particular *The Ear of the Other* (1985) and "Living On/Border Lines" (1979), and de Man's "Autobiography as De-facement" (1979) played a fundamental role in the postmodern reconceptualization of the autobiographical subject. Not only did the new analytical framework call for the author's disappearance from the text, but it also announced the death of subjectivity. For de Man, the biographical self is displaced by a trope in the act of autobiographical composition: it becomes disfigured and dies in the process of literary self-representation. Thus, autobiographical discourse becomes the writer's symbolic suicide: "The dominant figure of the epitaphic or autobiographical

discourse is . . . the *prosopopeia*, the fiction of the voice-from-beyond-the-grave" (de Man 1984: 77).

However, one might approach these claims of autobiographical author's and subject's "death" as highlighting the deconstruction of the uniform subjectivity and the authoritarian role of the author. Theorists of poststructuralism saw autobiography as "an exemplary instance of the impossibility of self-presence, the radical split between the self that writes and the self that is written, and the crucial role of language in the constitution of the subject" (Marcus 1994: 183).

7. The quote is taken from "All Writing is Autobiography" (Murray 1991: 66).
8. There is a circulating Paul Bowles English version of Shukri's autobiographical narrative *al-Khubz al-Ḥāfi* titled *For Bread Alone*, however, I chose not to use Bowles translation as it presents a number of substantial divergences with the Arabic text which I find problematic.
9. One should point out, however, that as early as 1951 Carl Brockelmann argued that Arabic medieval literature produced various autobiographies, in which list he included Al-Ghazali, Usamah Ibn Munqidh, and Umarah of Yaman (Brockelmann 1951).
10. Some prominent examples of medieval *sīrah/tarjamah* are those by Ibn Buluqqin (d. 1094), Abu Shama (d. 1266), Ibn Khaldun (d. 1405), al-Jazri (d. 1429), Ibn Hajar al-Asqalani (d. 1449), Ibn Abi Usaybia's (1203–1270) dictionary of physicians *Kitab Uyun al-Anba' fi Tabaqat al-Attiba'*, and Yaqut al-Hamawi (1179–1229) *Mu'jam al-Udaba'*. Ibn Jubayr (1145–1217), who recorded his pilgrimage to holy Muslim sites in Arabia, and later Ibn Battuta (1304–1368/9) with his famous *Rihlah* (*The Journey*) are considered the most celebrated writers of medieval travelogue literature. The stand-out examples of the autobiographical religious tracts genre are Imam al-Ghazali's (1058–1111) *al-Munqidh min al-Dalal* (*The Deliverer from the Error*) and Jalal al-Din al-Suyuti's (1445–1505) *al-Tahadduth bi-Ni'mat Allah* (*Speaking of God's Bounty*).
11. *Al-Nahḍah* (also spelled as *Al-Nahḍa*), or *Al-Nahḍah al-ʿArabiyah*, refers to the period of cultural and intellectual renaissance, including the revival of Arabic literature, translations of European masterpieces into Arabic, the emergence of the press, crucial changes in the reading public, and other similar cultural phenomena in the Levant and Egypt from the mid-nineteenth century to the First World War. Authors sought to revive classical forms of Arabic, develop language in ways appropriate to modern times, make compatriots aware of new ideas coming from Europe, and develop a common patriotism to transcend sectarian differences. This eventually developed into pan-Arab sentiment (facts

taken from Oxford Islamic Studies Online, available at: http://www.oxfordislamicstudies.com/article/opr/t125/e1692?_hi=0&_pos=20, accessed August 11 2012.

12. For more on the subject of new cultural discourses that emerged during *Al-Nahdah*, see Sabry Hafiz's *The Genesis of Arabic Narrative Discourse* (1993). Among other things, he highlights the favorable conditions that promoted self-awareness and self-representation: "the growing sense of individualism and the development of a clear sense of national identity had altered the very nature of the experience of life, and, more significantly, the individual's perception of it and made it more conductive to narrative" (Hafiz 1993: 104)
13. Among Arab literary critics subscribing to this view are Ihsan Abbas (Abbas 1967) and Mahir Hasan Fahmi (Fahmi 1970).
14. Numerous scholars of Arabic literature pointed out the literary significance of *Al-ʾAyyām*. Tetz Rooke states that "most historians of literature consider this work to be the first Arabic autobiography of literary consequence" (Rooke 1997: 85). Other scholars, among them Rashidah Mahran, emphasized the remarkable place that *al-ʾAyyām* occupies in Arabic literature with regard to its unique narrative aspects that in many ways determined the further development of the genre (Mahran 1979: 371–4).
15. Here I specifically refer to the first part of *al-ʾAyyām*.
16. Some Arab and Western critics accounted a remarkably common use of introductions or introductory passages in early Arabic autobiographies to the newness of the genre and the authors' need to make their audiences accustomed to it. Stefan Wild, for instance, noted that the phenomenon of numerous *muqaddimāt* could be a sign that the author is not sure of the reaction of the reader toward the genre of autobiography. The *muqaddimah* in this case serves the function of a *captatio benevolentiae*, a gesture made to a reader who is not sufficiently used to the genre (Wild 1998: 83). Among Arab critics who hold to this view are Zakariya Ibrahim (Ibrahim 1967) and Ali Adham (Adham 1978).
17. My translation.
18. Among others, Anouar Abdel-Malek wrote about this crucial shift in self-realization triggered by the 1967 defeat: "Since then, the Arab masses and the Arab intelligentsia have critically scrutinized the structure of national life in its entirety, from the economic to the ideological, and not excluding the apparatus of state . . . This scrutiny was like a blade turned in the wound, and orientated the Arab people towards a revolution lying beyond the national liberation" (Abdel-Malek 1983: 21).

1

Autobiography and Nation-Building: Constructing Personal Identity in the Postcolonial World

1 Nationalizing the Autobiographical Subject

In 1993 – almost a decade before the events of September 11, 2001 triggered a global crisis of Arab identity, and two decades before the Arab Spring – Martin Kramer wrote in his article "Arab Nationalism: Mistaken Identity":

> Three lines of poetry plot the trajectory of Arab national consciousness. "Awake, O Arabs, and arise!" begins the famous ode of Ibrahim al-Yaziji, penned in 1868 in Lebanon . . . "Write down, I am an Arab!" begins the poem of resistance by the Palestinian poet Mahmoud Darwish, written in 1963 . . . In the century that separated these two lines millions of people gradually awakened and arose, insisting before the world and one another that they should be written down as Arabs. (Kramer 1993: 171)

Indeed, the question of Arab national identification remains at the core of Arab cultural life. Tracing the formation of modern Arab subjectivity back to the early days of the Arab Renaissance or *al-Nahḍah al-ʿArabīyah* (Sheehi 2004: 3) and looking into the development of Arab national narratives during the last 150 years, one cannot underestimate the complexity of modern Arab nationalism, both as an ideological construct and as a social movement. In 1993, Halim Barakat identified three main "nationalist orientations" circulating in the Arab world:

> one is pan-Arabism, which dismisses existing sovereign states as artificial creations and calls for Arab unity. Another is the local nationalist

> orientation, which insists on preserving the independence and sovereignty of existing states. In between these two is a regional nationalist orientation that seeks to establish some regional unity, such as a greater Syria or a greater Maghrib, either permanently or as a step toward a larger Arab unity. (Barakat 1993: 38)

However, the recent politico-ideological crises throughout the Middle East and North Africa (particularly in Egypt) have brought to the fore a new confrontational dynamic between pan-Arabism, pan-Islamism, and local nationalisms, where the latter strives to become a ruling entity in a given nation-state, rather than endeavoring to initiate an Arab and/or an Islamic unity.

In addition to the already complex character of Arab nationalism, its cultural representations are further problematized by a multiplicity of colonial discourses (Ottoman, British, French, Spanish, Italian), as well as ethnic and religious diversity in the area. Therefore, an inquiry into the nationalist modality with autobiographical discourse will illustrate how these ideological and cultural processes participate in the construction of personal selfhood. How do autobiographical authors situate their subjectivities between several conflicting forms of Arab nationalism? What roles do ethnic and religious affiliations play in this process? How did Arab configurations of national identity manifest in the postcolonial period? These are my central questions in this chapter.

The corpus of postcolonial autobiographical literature represents one of the most interesting developments in modern Arabic narrative discourse. In the context of my study, I define postcolonial autobiographical writing as works where the autobiographical construction is informed by continuous negotiations between colonial, anticolonial, and postcolonial discourses on both thematic and linguistic levels. Within this category, I am particularly interested in works of postcolonial life-writing that emphasize the construction of national consciousness. The two case studies in this chapter are Hanna Minah's *Baqāyā Ṣuwar* (1975), translated by Olive and Lorne Kenny as *Fragments of Memory: A Story of a Syrian Family*,[1] and Layla Abu Zayd's *ʿĀm al-Fīl* (*Year of the Elephant*, 1980). These works, which I approach as autobiographical novels, illustrate how different colonial histories and nationalist movements inform discourses on identity in two distinctly different locations of the Arab world: Syria and Morocco, respectively. The nationalist autobiographical modality discussed in this chapter highlights the relational[2] and collective aspects of human subjectivity. In Minah's text, for instance, the construction of autobiographical identity relies on intricate relationships with the three members of the narrator's family who embody different forms of Syrian nationalism. In Layla Abu Zayd's *Year of the Elephant*, the autobiographer, who did not personally participate in the Moroccan movement for independence, projects her personal self onto the context of Moroccan national struggle by constructing an *imagined* autobiographical subject of a common Moroccan woman.

In my discussion of nationalist modality of autobiographical production, on the one hand, I look at the selected texts as a melting pot of colonial, postcolonial, and anticolonial discourses that inform the formation of the national narrative. On the other hand, it is also important to investigate the relationship of the newly formulated national identities with the local hegemonic discourses on both linguistic (colloquial languages versus *fuṣḥā*) and ideological (such as local nationalism versus pan-Arabism) levels. An insight into how these complex cultural and ideological processes inform autobiographical identity-making in texts under study will illustrate how discursive practices of nationalism influence the construction of personal selfhood.

Although much of the recent research in postcolonial and feminist studies addresses the diversity of postcolonial writing, there is still a tendency to generalize about these literatures. For example, this literary production is often placed into strictly defined categories – by language (such as "Francophone writings" or "literature in Arabic"), by colonizer (such as "literatures of British colonies"), and so on.[3] Instead, my approach is to examine postcolonial autobiographical writing across geographical localities and languages, allowing us to observe a full range of metatextual discourses which participate in the autobiographical process. Indeed, not only do different areas of the Arab world have distinct colonial histories,[4] but they also show substantial variations in their cultural and religious contexts, ideologies, social conditions, narrative traditions, and so forth. The linguistic situation is no less complicated. In addition to Arabic diglossia[5] and the constant negotiations between local (dialects) and dominant (*fuṣḥā*) linguistic discourses, Arabic's relationship with colonial languages is evidently complex as well. For example, while North African literatures contain a significant body of Francophone writings, in Egypt colonial languages – French and English – were never institutionalized.

With regard to my methodology in this chapter, I incorporate the two main schools of postcolonial studies: the "textual" approach and the "materialist" one. Early critical works on postcolonialism promoted a theoretical position "freed from the categories of political theory, state formation, and socio-economic relationships" (Parry 2004: 4), where the most influential analytical contribution was Homi Bhabha's anti-Marxist theories. Bhabha's groundbreaking work, especially the notion of hybridity, highlighted the internal complexity of postcolonial writing, and offered a theoretical basis for the rapidly developing global studies and other disciplines focusing on multiplicity of culture. However, other scholars criticized the textual approach to postcoloniality. Among others, Simon During warned that such a narrowly defined method is in danger of becoming exclusively elitist and indifferent to the main purpose of postcolonial autobiographical texts which is, in During's view, the anti-colonial struggle: "by deploying categories such as hybridity, mimicry, ambivalence . . . all of which laced colonized into colonizing cultures, postcolonialism effectively became a reconciliatory rather than a critical, anti-colonialist category" (During 1998: 31). More recent research in postcolonial studies, such as works by Laura Chrisman, Simon During, Benita Parry, Kwame Appiah and others, reasserted Marxist-materialist positions in the field, focusing on ideology as the main analytical tool.

Although my methodology favors the second, "materialist," approach due to my focus on cultural identity and relationships between autobiographical narratives and metatextual ideologies, one certainly cannot dismiss postcolonial textuality, particularly in relation to Arabic cultural contexts where language plays a crucial role. Therefore, the subsequent discussion of nationalist autobiographical modality in Hanna Minah and Layla Abu Zayd focuses on both the narrative texture of the text, and the ideological, cultural, and historical processes surrounding the text's production.

2 National Consciousness and the Syrian Subaltern in Hanna Minah's *Baqāyā Ṣuwar* (*Fragments of Memory*)

Hanna Minah's autobiographical novel *Baqāyā Ṣuwar* was published in Arabic in 1975 and translated into English in 1993 under the title *Fragments of Memory: A Story of a Syrian Family*. Resembling the Western literary form of *Bildungsroman*, the narrative centers on the narrator's childhood memories in northwest Syria during the late 1920s to the early 1930s. A great deal of attention is placed on the hardships suffered by the narrator's impoverished family, who were forced to constant migration as a result of worsening economic conditions in Syria while the country was going through a drastic change from one colonial rule (Ottoman) to another (French). Minah's novel situates the autobiographical identity in the middle of complex negotiations between the two colonial discourses, Ottoman and French, and the rapidly forming Syrian national narrative. Interestingly, the conceptualization of nationalism in *Baqāyā Ṣuwar* is foregrounded in the Christian religion – a particularly remarkable aspect of the narrative, since religious contexts here do not appear to be in confrontation with the religion of the Western colonizer, unlike Islamic discourses.

Although the text is labeled as a novel (*riwāyah*) with no explicit indication of Lejeune's autobiographical pact in the title or subtitle, most literary critics agree that *Baqāyā Ṣuwar* contains at least some autobiographical elements.[6] Choosing novel as a site of autobiographical production was a common practice among postcolonial writers. Sidonie Smith and Julia Watson point out that a novelistic autobiographical narrative was a natural choice that emphasized the complex, unstable, and heterogeneous character of a decolonized subject:

> Many writers take the liberties of the novelistic mode in order to mine their own struggle with the past and with the complexities of identities forged in the present. This fluid boundary has particularly characterized narratives by writers exploring the decolonization of subjectivity forged in the aftermath of colonial oppression. (Smith and Watson 2001: 9–10)

Numerous facts from the family history indicate that the protagonist resembles the author, who grew up in a poor Christian Syrian family in the same time period covered in the book. Moreover, Hanna Minah himself later confirmed that *Baqāyā Ṣuwar* is, in fact, an autobiographical work. In his *Hawājīs fī al-Tajribah al-Riwā'īyah* (*Thoughts on Experiences with the Novel*), he stated: "I wrote *Baqāyāh Ṣuwar* which narrates the biography of my life" (Minah 1988: 9).[7] In one of his interviews elsewhere he classified this work as *tarjamah dhātiya wa ghayr dhātiyah fī ān*, which could be translated either as "a combination of autobiographical facts and fiction," or as "a combination of personal and social history" (Rooke 1997: 47).

Baqāyā Ṣuwar offers a notable duality of autobiographical representation where the narrator and the protagonist have two distinct voices (or lack thereof). Minah's protagonist spends his early years in extreme poverty at the bottom of Syrian society which is in the midst of an agonizing transition from Ottoman to French colonial rule. Following Gayatri Spivak's argument that the true subaltern is characterized by permanent and complete silence, the protagonist's *voicelessness* is so apparent that it constantly reinforces his position as an oppressed colonial subject: he cannot speak, but can only be spoken for. In contrast, Minah's narrator has a strong voice of an educated adult telling a story of his troubled childhood, a silenced history that he strings together from scattered memories. In other words, the narrator is a decolonized subject who speaks of and for his colonial subaltern past.

From the very first pages of *Baqāyā Ṣuwar*, the subordinate position of the autobiographical protagonist is emphasized through the ambiguity behind the place and the time of his birth, and the absence of name. The first chapter pays a great deal of attention to the uncertainty as to when and where the protagonist was born: not only were all records lost, but even the house in which his mother gave birth has been torn down. What is important though is that this *lack of origin* becomes a defining characteristic of the autobiographical subject. Minah-the-narrator tells the reader that the mistake is forever imprinted on his *huwiyah*, which in Arabic means both an identification document and identity as a concept:

the date of birth was not the only mistake: the family's origin was in the village of al-Suwaydiya, near Antioch . . . the *mukhtār* had put down al-Suwaydiyya as the birthplace of every member of the family, including me. This mistake[8] is still on my identity card . . . and will remain there. (Minah 1993: 2)[9]

The lack of the protagonist's name is, too, an important aspect of the autobiographical representation. On the one hand, in most traditional approaches to identity studies name functions as a primary tool of self-representation and as a means to situate the subject in time and space. In Victoria Cook's words, "names are capable of providing verification; they have the power to distinguish, substantiate and confirm, and above all they confer identity and establish identification. To be named, therefore, is to belong, to be located" (Cook 2005: 8). In this case, namelessness indicates an impossible identity, an identity under erasure whose very existence is called to question. On the other hand, namelessness can be looked at as an actual identity-making practice that is freed from the constraints imposed by one's inherited name. In his essay "No Name is My Name," Robert Kroetsch suggests that in order to truly express one's selfhood, we should "hold those names in suspension, to let the identity speak itself out of a willed namelessness. To avoid a name does not . . . deprive one of an identity; indeed, it may offer a plurality of identities" (Kroetsch 1989: 51). Such a fluid and limitless site for identity construction is particularly relevant for a colonized subject who "is not only nameless but who finds himself unnameable" (*ibid.*: 49). It is noteworthy that most other characters in the novel also do not bear names. The protagonist's father, siblings, neighbors, and other characters remain nameless and voiceless, their identities blurred and impossible to clearly situate in time and space. The most blatant representation of the Syrian subaltern takes place with the birth of the protagonist's blind sister, symbolizing the most extreme version of the oppressed colonized subject – a helpless, impoverished, nameless female who cannot speak or see.

In contrast, Minah's narrator – a decolonized subject – has a strong presence in text, in particular in the narrative language. As the narrator speaks for, and gives a voice to, the subaltern protagonist – little Minah – this takes place through a very formal language of *fuṣḥā*, which is used not only for the narration, but also in all dialogs and instances of direct speech. This technique creates a sharp contrast between the protagonist's state of affairs (him being a homeless, starving child) and an educated elite's rhetoric. Even if the subaltern were to speak, his only language of communication would be Syrian colloquial. It is true that the Arab writer's choice between *fuṣḥā* and vernacular language(s) continues to be a source of heated debates,[10] but from the perspective of a postcolonial reading of the text, this phenomenon raises a number of important issues. As many scholars of postcolonial studies have argued (among those Francoise Lionnet, Trinh T. Minh-ha, and Abdelkebir Khatibi), the presence of colloquial and its synthesis with the colonizer's language, or the local official language, categorize the text as postcolonial. The institutionalized language of *fuṣḥā*, which is not commonly used in daily communication and can be acquired only through education, can be viewed as a pillar of the authoritative discourse and a linguistic manifestation of power structures, if not colonial then those of the local elites. In Trinh Minh-ha's words, the transparency of a written official language is an instrument of reinforcing order and hierarchical power: "clarity is a means of subjection, a quality both of official, taught language and of correct writing, two old mates of power: together they flower, vertically, to impose an order" (Minh-ha 1989: 16–17).

In this context, one may suspect that Hanna Minah's autobiographical novel, being written in a language accessible exclusively to educated intelligentsia, not only lacks the postcolonial quality, but also further marginalizes the Syrian subaltern by voicing him in a hegemonic language. However, I suggest a completely different interpretation of the role of language in *Baqāyā Ṣuwar*. First, it is important to acknowledge that many Arab authors preferred to write their works in *fuṣḥā* because it was a literary convention and often a necessary condition for these works to be published. Second, if a traditionally established hierarchal relationship between Arabic formal and vernacular languages implies that *fuṣḥā* represents authority, then a postcolonial, marginal text composed in the highly proper language of the official discourse could be a means to *destabilize* this very discourse. Therefore, the discursive contradiction of voicing Minah's subaltern protagonist in a hegemonic language subverts traditional power structures. The subversive aspect of the narrative language is particularly evident because, in fact, Syrian colloquial occasionally paves its way into the text. For example, although the illiterate mother's speech is usually produced in a conventional proper *fuṣḥā*, she sings Syrian folk songs to her children in colloquial Arabic.[11] These sporadic explosions of vernacular language only emphasize the tension between authoritarian and marginalized discourses in the narrative.

In addition to that, the use of *fuṣḥā* in a postcolonial narrative should be viewed in a larger context of Arab nationalism. Language being one of the unifying principles of pan-Arabism, many Arab intellectuals chose *fuṣḥā* for their writing for ideological reasons. In his examination of Arab nationalist ideologies, particularly Sati' al-Husri's, Yasir Suleiman gives an excellent summary of linguistic conceptualization of Arab nationalism:

> what the Arabs need is a unified language which can in turn unify them, an instrument of fusion rather than fission . . . the Arabs need a "unified and unifying language" ("lughah muwahhada wa-muwahhidah" . . .), rather than a series of dialect languages which will lead to further fragmentation in the Arab body politic. (Suleiman 2003: 142–3)

From this perspective, the nationalist and anticolonial aspect of Minah's autobiographical narrative is emphasized through the uniform language of *al-'ummah al-ʿarabīyyah* (the Arab Nation). A telling example from the text that illustrates the role of language in establishing the sense of *belonging* is a humorous scene describing the protagonist's Greek neighbor. The neighbor, named Kiryakou, is a local fool and a target of mockery for his lack of mastery in Arabic. His Syrian wife uses his inability to effectively communicate in Arabic to curse and humiliate him in front of others:

> [his wife] took advantage of her husband's weakness in Arabic to lash out at him. She would yell at one of the children in his presence: "Damn your father!" Kiryakou would reply, "Why don't you curse my mother?" (He meant his son's mother). "Damn your mother, too!" the wife would retort. She would keep up her curses until she made him lose his self-control. (Minah 1993: 10–11)

As amusing as this episode may appear, it emphasizes an important binary of "us" versus "them" based on a purely linguistic factor and reinforces the unifying quality of the Arabic language in a Syrian community composed of Christians and Muslims. This leads us to the discussion of anticolonial discourses in *Baqāyā Ṣuwar* and their role in the newly emerging Syrian national narrative.

As I have pointed out earlier, the identity-making process in the text occurs between two colonial discourses – Ottoman and French – whereas Minah's autobiographical subject creates radically different relationships with each of the two oppressive power structures. The story takes place during the time when the French seized control of Syrian territories from the Ottoman Empire in the 1920s. The change from one colonial system to another created the need to construct a clear sense of national identity in order to resist and confront the colonizing Other. Although anti-Turkish sentiments are present in the text (such as in the scene describing the protagonist's uncle's vehement refusal to eat any Turkish food), in general the attitude toward the Ottomans is considerably less hostile than it is toward the French.

In *Baqāyā Ṣuwar*, the two colonizers are allegorically represented as insects: silk worms and locusts. Portraying the cultural and ideological Other as insects is not unusual in Western literary traditions: "the insect society has always suggested Otherness", Christopher Hollingsworth points out in his study *Poetics of the Hive* (Hollingsworth 2001: 152). During the colonial conquests of the nineteenth century, European writers often used insect metaphors to illustrate the hostile strangeness of the colonies: "the Hive was . . . put to work in the colonies describing 'them' . . . serving as the template for the West's first truly alien threat" (*ibid.*: 154–5). On the contrary, in Minah the insect society symbolizes the colonizing intruder, whose antagonistic otherness is described from the perspective of the Syrian colonized subject. Different natural qualities of the two insect groups vividly illustrate the principal elements of the two colonial regimes. The greedy and voracious Ottoman silk worms constantly need to be fed, but they are generally harmless and often described as "blessed worms" that provide villagers with a source of income. Even the protagonist's father – a useless but harmless member of the family – is compared with a silk worm:

> He was in such a turmoil that Mother's fears of his leaving us increased. Not because he had no work or that he showed any inclination of leaving, like the silk worms who had shown signs of fasting before they spun their cocoons, but because he was desperate. (Minah 1993: 76–7)

Silk worms, the Ottomans, the father – they all represent the old world order, which despite its unjust and oppressive practices is still a better alternative to the violently tyrannical French rule, represented by swarming locusts – a much more negative and appalling image symbolizing a complete devastation of the land. The use of insect metaphors in *Baqāyā Ṣuwar* emphasizes the dehumanizing and economically destructive effects of colonialism.

As for French rule, at first it was seen as a positive change: "we were free of the Turks . . . The French are better; they are civilized, white people, blue-eyed" (Minah 1993: 84). I should point out that whiteness, representing the French and the West, is depicted as both the object of desire and the source of oppression. On the one hand, there is a hope that the white Europeans will bring a better life, the protagonist's recurring dreams about white bread, and the father's sexual desire toward fair women. On the other hand, white skin is synonymous with parasitic lifestyle and tyranny: "he [the landlord] definitely was fair-complexioned since he was one of the overlords" (*ibid.*: 124). The rapidly worsening economic conditions forced the protagonist's family to move to the city, signifying the urbanization and industrialization of Syrian society with the arrival of the French, as opposed to agricultural production and rural households under the Ottomans. The family members are hired as servants for the new master, Christou – an embodiment of European swanky lifestyle (suit pants, hat, and a whip) and French colonization. New circumstances made their life even more unbearable and brought about nostalgia for the old good days under the Turks:

> [our] conditions at the new landlord's rapidly deteriorated. I heard mother saying, "We have jumped from the frying pan into the fire . . . Life was better there in al-Suwaydiya. At least we were free; we weren't hired servants and we had a house to ourselves." (*ibid.*: 97)

Minah's autobiographical narrator is compelled to formulate an authentic national identity in order to challenge the two clashing colonial discourses. Interestingly, the nationalist narrative in *Baqāyā Ṣuwar* is for the most part figurative and subdued, and it lacks a clearly delineated political or ideological message. I argue that this important aspect of the identity-making process in the text illustrates the character of Syrian nationalist struggle which, although it included several big revolts (such as the 1925 Great Revolt), was in general less bloody and violent than, for example, the Algerian or Moroccan wars for liberation. In Minah, criticism of the dire economic situation is at the core of the anticolonial narrative, as opposed to an ideological agenda. As for the autobiographical subject's nationalism, it is constructed through multilayered symbolism, such as anticolonial metaphors[12] and secondary characters representing different aspects of Syrian nationalism. The Ottoman–French dual colonial discourse complicates the construction of national identity where the autobiographical subject has certain cultural attachments to both: he shares many cultural traditions with the Ottomans who were present in the area for a long time, and, as a Christian, he also shares religious affiliation with the French.

In addition to a complex set of relationships with the two colonizers, the process of self-representation in *Baqāyā Ṣuwar* also incorporates various communal affiliations, such as the Syrian Christian community, impoverished social classes, rural population, and so on. Instead of focusing on the autobiographical subject's personality and individualism, which would be the audience's natural expectation from the genre, the narrative valorizes the *collective*. I argued earlier that the absence of the autobiographical protagonist's name and the ambiguity behind the time and place of his birth represent the voiceless Syrian subaltern. Another important aspect here is the notion of communal identity, where a lack of clarity behind the autobiographical protagonist's origins is a means to construct a *collective image* of the colonized Syrian population. Such a move from private to collective is not unusual in Arab autobiographical works focusing on nationalism and anticolonialism. In addition to Layla Abu Zayd's *Year of the Elephant*, which is discussed later in this chapter, Assia Djebar's *L'Amour, La Fantasia*, Ahlam Mosteghanemi's *Memory in the Flesh*, Latifah Al-Zayyat's *The Open Door*, and the literary works of Sahar Khalifeh also belong to this category where collective identities and shared communal experience are at the core of autobiographical selfhood.

In *Fragments of Memory*, the collective aspect of personal selfhood is manifested in two ways: by emphasizing the autobiographical subject's generational memory; and through his self-identification with three characters embodying different elements of Syrian nationalism: Ibrahim, Rizqallah, and Zanuba. Minah's narrator stresses the importance of family stories, particularly his mother's, for his own identity: they evoked his self-awareness and helped him to situate his selfhood as an integral link on a generational chain of his family. Memories of others are intertwined with his own in a way that makes them indistinguishable from one another: "The past has always found a lively reception in me. It matures in my being, is clarified and becomes translucent as drops of clear water, regardless of all the profundity I live among in the present" (Minah 1993: 3–4). The collective is continuously reinforced in the text. Not only does the narrator share his memories and his identity with others, but his father and other members of his family are portrayed as typical representatives of impoverished Syrian society: "He [the father] isn't alone in his misfortune since this is a fate shared by all who, like him, stumble about in the mire of a disintegrating life" (*ibid.*: 105), and further: "We're not alone. Whatever has happened to us has happened to other people" (*ibid.*: 69). Even the title of the novel – *Baqāyā Ṣuwar* ("remnants of pictures") – stems from the Arabic root *bā-qaf-yā*, which has connotations of continuity, survival, permanence, and immortality, implying the importance of collective memory to one's individual subjectivity. The linguistic meaning of the root offers an interesting binary: on the one hand, it emphasizes the fragmented and plural nature of identity, but on the other hand, it also gives a hope of immortality through generational continuity.

The communal aspect of the identity-making process in the text is not limited to the autobiographical subject's identification with his community, but it also generates a subtle but elaborate discourse on Syrian nationalism. The collective here is a means to transform the silenced subaltern into a decolonized nationalist subject. Although Minah's protagonist is seemingly passive and lacking any sense of national consciousness, the narrative valorizes the explicitly nationalist characters. Uncles Rizqallah and Ibrahim, and the rebellious Zanuba – incidentally, these are among the few named characters – are the center of the nationalist discourse in the text. They are agents of the autobiographical subject's decolonization, each of them symbolizing a distinct aspect of Syrian nationalism. Uncle Rizqallah embodies an anti-Ottoman discourse, whereas Uncle Ibrahim represents the oppressed population's struggle against local authorities. As for Zanuba, on the one hand, she is a symbol of Syrian resistance against the French colonizers, and, on the other hand, she is a manifestation of the glorious Syrian past, since her character alludes to the legendary Queen Zenobia.[13] I argue that these three agents of nationalism actively participate in the self-representational discourse, and as a result, the autobiographical *I* in *Baqāyā Ṣuwar* is a hybrid of several identities: the silenced colonized protagonist of the little Hanna; the decolonized narrator of Minah's prominent intellectual; and the characters of Rizqallah, Ibrahim, and Zenobia, representing the nationalist element.

Rizqallah is the narrator's late uncle whom he never met in person, and who appears early in the narrative through the mother's reminiscences. Rizqallah's figure is idealized and romanticized to the point of becoming not only a prominent family member, but a national hero who led his people against Ottoman Turks:

> Your uncle, son, was a man amongst men: as lively, generous, and brave as any hero in a story. Everyone loved him, even death. Death loved him and took him . . . Your father was one of your uncle's followers. They were crazy about him, and stuck to him until he left us for our father Abraham's bosom. (*ibid.*: 5–6)

Rizqallah's very being is completely defined and dominated by the anti-Ottoman struggle. His expression of nationalist sentiments is bold and literal, including his oath not to eat any form of Turkish food under any circumstances:

> Your uncle, son, took an oath not to eat the Turkish *qarwana*, stuck to his oath and didn't eat it . . . One day when he was in the city he was arrested and conscripted. The men said, "This time he'll definitely eat the *qarwana*." But he didn't eat it. (*ibid.*: 6–7)

The importance of the anti-Ottoman discourse for the autobiographical identity is highlighted in the text, especially in the following episode where the protagonist completely identifies with Rizqallah. One of the relatives calls little Hanna the "little Rizqallah" (*ibid.*: 92), and by linking the autobiographical protagonist directly to the epic figure of anti-Ottoman struggle he is inevitably assigned a nationalist quality.

Uncle Ibrahim's character is yet another symbol of Syrian nationalism, representing a different layer of Minah's anticolonial autobiographical identity. He is the mother's relative who serves as the family's guardian. His nationalism is as ideologically articulated as Rizqallah's, but his eagerness to fight injustice with his gun, which appears to be the main attribute of his identity, indicates a calling for armed resistance: "[I hoped] that he and his gun would spend the night with us; that he would even stay until we departed so the *mukhtār*[14] would no longer have any power on us" (*ibid.*: 92). Unlike Rizqallah, Uncle Ibrahim does not rebel directly against colonial rule; instead, he fights those representing local oppressive power structures that exploit and abuse the poor. The narrator's family members are not the only ones he defends, but he is the protector of all people who come to him for help:

> Thereafter, I found a new profession: an escort of travelers! . . . I didn't ask for a piaster or millieme from the women and children . . . People would come to me complaining: "Uncle Ibrahim, we were robbed on the road . . ." The women and children would cry . . . some of them would fling themselves into my arms. My heart isn't made of stone . . . (*ibid.*: 25)

Ibrahim's heroic stature is highlighted by comparison with the legendary Rizqallah: "[this] uncle's part in rescuing [our] sister magnified the uncle so in our eyes that he became as great as the other uncle who was dead" (*ibid.*: 94). Both uncles are equally important for the autobiographical subject's decolonization, it is through them that he acquires a voice and constructs his nationalist identity. An interesting note is that their names, Rizqallah and Ibrahim, carry ambiguity with regard to their religious community affiliation, since these two names are equally used by Christians and Muslims,[15] which, in turn, suggests unity between the two communities for anticolonial and nationalist purposes. I must point out that religious discourses play a crucial role in the articulation of nationalism in *Fragments of Memory*, and this narrative aspect will be illustrated further in this chapter.

The central, and perhaps the most explicitly nationalist, figure in the text is Zanuba, a local drunk and prostitute who has an affair with the father. At first, Zanuba is portrayed as an immoral woman who drinks like men and does not respect any communal or social norms of behavior. The narrator juxtaposes her "satanic" power over men with his mother's traditional feminine attributes of "gentleness, weakness, compassion, and serenity" (*ibid.*: 127). However, as Zanuba's character develops, it becomes apparent that she symbolizes the famous ancient Syrian Queen Zenobia (Arabic "Zaynab"[16]) – a ruler of Palmyra, at that time a Roman colony, who not only rebelled against

Rome, but even conquered a number of Roman eastern provinces. Zanuba becomes the guardian of the family and substitutes for the father – a weak and irresponsible man – in protecting little Hanna, his mother, and his sisters. In a way, she replaces Uncle Ibrahim in his role as the family's guardian angel. Much like the warrior Queen Zenobia, who fought side by side with men, Zanuba is courageous and protective, and she becomes the leader of villagers. In her fearlessness and her strong, outrageous character, she constantly provokes men and strips them of their masculinity: "By way of provoking the men and disparaging them indiscriminately, she took to denouncing their masculinity, saying that they were already dead; they were no longer good for anything" (*ibid.*: 174).

By the end of the novel, Zanuba metamorphoses from a local prostitute into the organizer of the revolt against the detachment of soldiers and their merciless sergeant who arrived to supervise the peasants' battle with locusts. This episode is particularly significant since it illustrates the double oppression of the Syrian subaltern: locusts are the symbol of the ruthless French colonial rule, while the detachment of soldiers represents local tyrannical authorities. I argue that this riot scene references the great Syrian revolt of 1925 against French rule, which began in villages and indicated the emergence of grassroots nationalism in the Arab world. As Michael Provence stated:

> The Great Revolt was a mass movement . . . Its leaders were not members of the great landowning notable families who sought to become national leaders in an incremental process of negotiation with the French. The revolt was one of the signal events in the emergence of mass politics in the Arab world. (Provence 2005: xi)

Zanuba's spontaneous leadership of the peasants, on the one hand, symbolizes the emergence of national consciousness under the French rule, and, on the other hand, it illustrates the distinct nature of the Syrian nationalist movement that came from the rural areas. Certainly, far from being an exemplary and moral figure, Zanuba is the new kind of national hero: she is an impoverished and marginalized colonized female whose flaws and shameless behavior highlight the lengths one is forced to go to in order to survive in a country devastated by the colonizers. But despite all her imperfections, this new Queen Zenobia finds the strength not only to claim her own voice, but also to unite others to resist oppression. When the sergeant who was leading the soldiers tried to rape her, Zanuba – famous for her frivolous acts with the villagers – fought him fiercely and made him retreat with shame. Symbolizing a country that is repeatedly violated by both the new vicious colonizers and the local powers whose tyranny makes the life of the oppressed population even more unbearable, Zanuba is able to challenge authority against all odds. Portrayed as the Syrian Joan of Arc, her personal strength reveals the strength of her people and her land: "[she] was urging the men on, begging them to burn the boss and not let him escape. She was standing on the edge of the roof, her clothes torn, her hair disheveled, laughing boisterously like a legendary demon" (*ibid.*: 179). Even though the police eventually kill Zanuba and violently stop the riot, the narrative ends with a hope for the future independence of the Syrian people.

Zanuba's character, especially in her active resistance to the French colonial rule, contributes to the autobiographical subject's nationalism. Her association with Queen Zenobia indicates the urge to return to the country's glorious past and to reintroduce the legendary national heroes into the struggling present. The form of nationalism represented by Zanuba constitutes perhaps the strongest element of the autobiographical subject's national identity, since it offers a framework for the future decolonization of the autobiographical self. Her powerful voice, her bravery, and her eagerness to resist oppression show Minah's subaltern a path by which to gain his own voice.

The three characters discussed above – Rizqalla, Ibrahim, and Zanuba – are important elements of the nationalist autobiographical discourse in *Baqāyā Ṣuwar*, since they illustrate how various national narratives participate in the construction of personal selfhood. Uncle Rizqallah symbolizes resistance against the Ottomans and the old world order. Uncle Ibrahim represents the struggle against local power structures that support and reinforce colonial oppression. Finally, Zanuba is the embodiment of national heroism originating from marginal and underprivileged rural classes where references to the great historical past offer a hope and a means for decolonization. These three figures are important catalysts for the construction of autobiographical identity and, in their diversity, they showcase the complexity of Syrian national discourses. It is through these three nationalist narratives that Minah's autobiographical subaltern acquires the means for self-representation:

the intricate process of self-awareness mirrors the difficult process of nation-building.

Religion is another crucial participant in *Baqāyā Ṣuwar*'s autobiographical discourse. Since Minah's narrator comes from the Syrian Christian community, one might assume that there should not be any significant confrontations with the colonial French culture, as they both seemingly belong to the same religious domain (unlike, for instance, the Muslim population). However, a close reading of the text proves that Biblical mythology is utilized to *subvert* Western Christian religious discourses and to establish the autobiographical subject's authority over them by reclaiming Christianity as an authentically Syrian discourse. The narrator's use of Biblical images and symbols presents Christianity as a local indigenous religion originating from this area, rather than an import from the West imposed by French colonizers. Numerous episodes throughout the narrative serve to establish the autobiographical subject's authority over Christian discourses: among those are the connection between little Hanna's birthday and Easter, tracing his family's origins to Antioch, and family members' identification with prominent Biblical figures. Subtly, but firmly, religion in Minah's text serves as a powerful tool of decolonization.

One such image is Antioch, which became a default birthplace for everyone in the narrator's family: "the family's origin was in the village of al-Suwaydiya near Antioch . . . the *mukhtār* had put down al-Suwaydiya as the birthplace of every member of the family, including me" (*ibid.*: 2). Antioch – Great Antioch or Syrian Antioch – is considered one of the most important centers of the Eastern Church, a place where Peter and Paul preached in the early days of Christianity, and where the followers of Jesus were first called Christians: "And when he had found him, he brought him to Antioch. So it was that for a whole year they assembled with the church and taught a great many people. And the disciples were first called Christians in Antioch" (Acts 11:26).[17] Therefore, this image represents a return to the roots of the religion and to its pre-Western times. The narrator establishes a symbolic ownership over Christianity, and treats it as a native religion that had been present in the area long before it spread in Europe. On the one hand, Antioch represents nostalgia for the old glory of Eastern civilization and the impossibility of returning to its long-gone greatness: "Antioch was far away, heaven was far away and there was no one to give ear to their pleas" (Minah 1993: 89). But on the other hand, the legendary Antioch – a city that survived despite numerous foreign invasions and destructions by devastating earthquakes – is a site of continuous self-resurrection and it symbolizes the deep-rooted resilience of the narrator's family and the whole local Christian community under colonial rule and a hope for survival. The narrator's association of his own existence with Easter further highlights the theme of resurrection:

> My consciousness of existence in this village begins with this picture: a slaughtered cow hanging from the branch of a gnarled tree, a small olive grove, a fire, some men, and Father. That was on Holy Saturday. Fifty days of fasting and the next day would be Easter. At dawn Christ would rise from the dead and then we would eat the cakes and eggs. (*ibid.*: 19)

From the perspective of identity construction in *Baqāyā Ṣuwar*, these religious symbols of resurrection signify the future transformation – a metaphorical rebirth – of a voiceless colonized autobiographical subaltern into a decolonized autobiographical narrator. In other words, Christian discourses are utilized to empower the silenced and oppressed autobiographical subject.

Another interesting example of Biblical imagery utilized in the narrative is a fig tree that became the family's home when the desperate state of affairs in the countryside forced them to move to the city. According to the New Testament, the fig tree was cursed by Jesus and it is mentioned in the Gospels of Luke, Mark, and Matthew: "And seeing a fig tree by the road, He came to it and found nothing on it but leaves, and said to it, 'Let no fruit grow on you ever again.' Immediately the fig tree withered away" (Matthew 21:19). In Minah, the tree is the source of despair and disease, symbolizing the god-forsaken Syria with the arrival of French colonialism: "But our condition worsened after that due to the fact that sleeping under a fig tree brought on disease, and we sickened. The fellahin said that the air under the fig tree was so foul" (Minah 1993: 106).

A powerful tool of reclaiming authority over Christian discourses in the text is the family members' association with prominent Biblical figures. Some of them can be even recognized in the names of central characters: for example, the mother's name "Miriam" is the Arabic version of "Mary," and Uncle Ibrahim stands for "Abraham." Interestingly, all Biblical characters in *Baqāyā Ṣuwar* are highly humanized – a narrative technique that offers a remarkable contrast to the ways in which other Arab Christian writers approached Biblical figures by presenting them as highly abstract and idealized constructs. For instance, Sasson Somekh pointed out that "thanks to Jubran Khalil Jubran and several other *mahjar* writers, Jesus was transformed into a purely spiritual, indeed universal idea, detached from the practices and theology of a specific religion" (Somekh 1995: 195). On the contrary, in Minah these characters are not only humanized, but also portrayed as "common people," with an emphasis on their ancestral relation to the Syrian countryside folk. For example, when the narrator's mother tells him about the Biblical Abraham, he thinks of him as his own grandfather:

> "Your father was one of your uncle's followers. They were crazy about him, and stuck to him until he left us for our father Abraham's bosom." I recall lifting my head from her knee to ask, "Who is Abraham? My grandfather?" (Minah 1993: 6)

Virtually all characters surrounding little Hanna reference canonical Christian figures. Uncle Ibrahim/Abraham, the legendary protector of not only the narrator's family, but of everyone who sought his help, identifies himself with poor folk, which, in turn, challenges the view of Christianity as a religion of power and colonial authority. The story of the narrator's older sisters, forced to work as servants at the rich people's houses in order to provide for the family, evokes the betrayal of Jesus and the story of Joseph: "The night she [the mother] gave up our sister she was as wretched as if she were damned. Mother didn't wash Sister's feet like Christ did his disciples . . . my mother didn't sell my sister for thirty pieces of silver" (*ibid.*: 51–2); and further:

> Joseph was in the well. They were the ones who threw him in the well. We didn't throw our sister in the well. We didn't take her blood-stained shirt to father. But in our encounter with her, we were just like Joseph's brothers were with Joseph. (*ibid.*: 83)

Little Hanna's parents are juxtaposed as embodying Judas and Jesus. The resentment toward the father – a reckless character who abandoned his family on numerous occasions, and treated his wife and children very poorly – portrays him as a Judas-like figure who goes as far as selling his own daughters to service the *mukhtār*: "It was Father who concluded this contract and handed over our sister to be crucified on the cross of service. He returned to us in our bare forsaken field bearing brass, not silver" (*ibid.*: 87). On the other hand, the narrator's admiration of his mother depicts her as an embodiment of virtue, patience, forgiveness, and love for her children – all the characteristics of Christ. The scene where the mother finds out that her newborn child is blind references Jesus' conversation with God before the crucifixion: "A month later mother discovered that our baby sister was blind . . . Mother cried and lamented, reproving God in her usual way: 'Lord! What have I done to deserve this?'" (*ibid.*: 154). Even Zanuba's character, who I argued symbolizes the ancient Queen Zenobia, also brings to mind Mary Magdalene: she is a local prostitute who after spending time with the mother becomes a better person and later protects the family. The scene where Zanuba humbly sits on the doorstep when meeting the family calls to mind Mary Magdalene's standing at Jesus' feet, as the mother shows her love and forgiveness, despite the fact that Zanuba was her husband's mistress: "You are good, a good neighbor, we aren't blaming you for anything. Zanuba was jubilant. She struggled to her feet" (*ibid.*: 135). Therefore, religious contexts are a crucial element in the making of the nationalist autobiographical identity in *Baqāyā Ṣuwar*. The identification of important Biblical figures with the Syrian subaltern is a rhetorical means of revolt against colonization by stripping colonial religious discourses of their authority. Thus, Minah's silenced autobiographical subject is given a powerful discursive device to construct a decolonized nationalist identity, which is *legitimized* through canonical Christian discourses, configured as local, indigenous, and, consequently, anticolonial.

Another important factor that highlights nationalist sentiments and further separates local Christian discourses from their Western counterparts is a close relationship between local Christian and Muslim communities. This relationship is shown as lacking any form of antagonism or hostility, and the two communities share their daily routines and customs. For instance, after the protagonist's birth, his mother brings him to the mosque in observation of a ritual meant to keep the baby healthy: "Some months after your birth

I was advised to take you to the mosque on Friday, stand under the minaret at the time of the call to prayer and slap you on the mouth with your father's slipper" (*ibid.*: 16–17). Other scenes, such as little Hanna's receiving protective amulets from a sheikh (*ibid.*: 101) or being offered meat during Muslim charity distribution (*ibid.*: 116–17), only highlight the Christian community's close connections to Islamic cultural life and traditions. For the narrator, there is one community of colonized Syrians who are unified in their oppression and whose religious affiliation does not affect their living conditions or interactions with each other. This perspective reinforces the *collective* aspect of the autobiographical in Minah's narrative. Not only does the autobiographical embrace the diversity within the Syrian nationalist discourse, represented in the characters of Rizqallah, Ibrahim, and Zanuba, but it also emphasizes the unity of Christians and Muslims in their common struggle. Despite his belonging to a particular Christian community, Minah's decolonized autobiographical narrator gives a voice to a *common* Syrian subaltern and renders a *shared* Syrian national identity.

On the one hand, the autobiographical process in *Baqāyā Ṣuwar* focuses on formulating a solid national(ist) identity, and this process is performed on three different but interconnected levels. One of these is the use of the formal *fuṣḥā* language, which in a larger context denotes a unified and unifying Arab identity. Second, national affiliation is strengthened through valorization of the three characters in the novel, who symbolize various forms of local Syrian nationalism. Finally, the religious aspect of identity "nationalizes" Christian discourses by emphasizing their local origins and by reinscribing them into local mass culture. On the other hand, the identity-making in Minah's text is preoccupied with decolonization of the subaltern autobiographical subject. Little Hanna, representing silenced, oppressed, and impoverished social classes, acquires a voice and transforms into Hanna Minah's educated autobiographical narrator who is able to speak – in an eloquent *fuṣḥā*, no less – for his community and his nation. Perhaps the most remarkable aspect of the autobiographical identity in this text is that in its journey from the colonial to the decolonized it appears to be an unavoidably *collective* construct. In order to conceptualize a personal identity that labors to formulate its national affiliation, other communal identities ought to be incorporated in this process.

3 The "Common" Moroccan Womanhood in Layla Abu Zayd's *ʿĀm al-Fīl* (*Year of the Elephant*)

Layla Abu Zayd's novella *ʿĀm al-Fīl*, translated by Barbara Parmenter as *Year of the Elephant*, first appeared in a serialized form in the Moroccan newspaper *Al-Mithaq* in 1983, and was published in book form the following year. *ʿĀm al-Fīl* gained instant popularity with the Arabic-speaking public (the first edition sold out immediately), which Roger Allen explains by the author's bold approach to rewriting national history from a woman's perspective: "a female narrator gives the reader her perspective on the events in the final phase of Morocco's struggle for independence" (Allen 1991: 676). Author Layla Abu Zayd was born in a small Moroccan village where her father worked as an interpreter for the French and actively participated in the nationalist resistance movement. She received her education in Rabat and London, and later worked as a journalist in Morocco, in addition to serving as a press agent for the Moroccan government.[18] Besides *Year of the Elephant*, she wrote numerous short stories, articles, poetry, translations, and published two more books: *Rujūʿ ʾila al-Ṭufūlah* (translated as *Return to Childhood: The Memoir of a Modern Moroccan Woman*) in 1993, and *Al-Faṣl al-Akhīr* (*The Last Chapter*) in 2000.

Year of the Elephant is an important milestone in the development of national Moroccan literature for two reasons. First of all, it is written in literary Arabic (as opposed to Francophone texts) which, as the author stated on multiple occasions, became an ideological message on its own. Second, it was the first novel by a Moroccan woman to be translated from Arabic to English. As in the case of Hanna Minah's *Baqāyā Ṣuwar*, Abu Zayd's novella is not explicitly autobiographical: it neither has a subtitle that would clearly situate it within the corpus of autobiographical literature, nor does it contain an autobiographical pact, since the protagonist's name (Zahra) is different from the author's. A common view among literary critics is that *Year of the Elephant* is much less autobiographical than her other two novels – *Return to Childhood* and *The Last Chapter*. However, I argue that *ʿĀm al-Fīl* is precisely the narrative where the author's subjectivity, freed from the biographical constraints of traditional autobiographical discourse, manifests itself through the prism of a marginalized Moroccan female subaltern.

In one of her interviews, the author stated that the protagonist of *Year of the Elephant* was modeled on her mother: "I wrote . . . of a woman I knew – my mother. I wanted to tell her story" (Munro 2003: 4). At the same time, she pointed out that this book was also her way of articulating her own selfhood: "I wrote to express myself, to talk about my experience of the people I knew" (*ibid.*: 4). Elsewhere, Abu Zayd emphasized that all her characters are drawn from reality, and even suggested that these stories have not been fictionalized, since she is simply a "transmitter" of real-life events:

> The main events and characters throughout the whole collection are real. They have surprised or moved me in real life, and I wanted by their reconstitution in this book to provide the same feelings for the reader . . . I have not created these stories. I have simply told them as they are. (Abu Zayd 1989: ix–x)

Similarly to *Baqāyā Ṣuwar* discussed earlier, Abu Zayd's narrative displays a symbolic move from private to communal in an effort to negotiate the nationalist qualities of her autobiographical "I." Subverting the traditional Western view of autobiography as a story of individual selfhood, here we encounter a *hybrid* autobiographical subject in the character of Zahra – a subject that combines the articulation of the author's personal self with the collective identity of marginalized social groups. Therefore, *Year of the Elephant* offers an interesting case of merging autobiographical and nationalist discourses where the "elite outsider" (the author – an educated, multilingual, liberated feminist) reimagines herself as an "oppressed insider" (a subjugated female of the colonized Morocco), in order to express and highlight the nationalist aspect of her subjectivity. By empowering a traditional Moroccan woman who participated in the country's struggle for liberation, but was unable to tell her own story, Abu Zayd – a representative of the intellectual elite – rewrites her own identity as a common Moroccan freedom fighter. In other words, Zahra is Abu Zayd's subaltern alter ego. *Year of the Elephant* offers an interesting case of postcolonial identity-making where the autobiographer reimagines herself as a colonized subject, bridging her decolonized subjectivity with the marginalized and oppressed fellow Moroccan female who Abu Zayd *could have been* had she been born into different circumstances.

Unlike Minah's careful and often allegorical formulation of nationalist identity, the *Year of the Elephant* takes a much more politically explicit stance: from the opening dedication of the book – "to all those women and men who put their lives in danger for the sake of Morocco" – to bold ideological statements against both the French colonizers and the local government. Parts of the text are so ideologically charged that they sound like excerpts from a political pamphlet. One such example is when the protagonist talks to the reader about her disappointment with the country's conditions in the post-Resistance period and makes a daring statement about international struggle with colonialism:

> In the beginning of the Resistance, we believed the struggle would wash away all spite and malice, just as we thought that independence would relieve our cares and heal our sores like miracle cures sold in the market. In fact, we loaded Independence down with a burden it could not bear, and now we are besieged day and night by new struggles in the world – Palestine, Vietnam, Kashmir, Biafra. How many others are to come? (Abu Zayd 1989: 67)[19]

Even the very language of the narrative delivers a political message. Although Layla Abu Zayd claimed in one of her interviews that writing in Arabic was not exactly a deliberate choice,[20] the fact remains that her preference of Arabic over French – her language of education – does carry ideological weight, especially since the content of the book is dedicated to the Moroccan anticolonial struggle. Abu Zayd is also famous for her passionate disapproval of Francophone authors in that they implicitly support French cultural colonization: "when a Moroccan writes in French, he writes for France and must comply with what it understands and what pleases it. He must maintain its preconceived images about Moroccans" (Hall 1995: 70).[21] Her writing, she argues in the same interview, stands in sharp contrast to Francophone works because she writes of, and for, her fellow countrymen:

> When I write I talk to my people. I use their idioms, the specific expressions that are linked to their inner self and deep feelings. I write for my people and have to do it in their language. And because I do so, my writing comes from within my culture, my messages are direct, sincere and hence human and universal. (Hall 1995: 71)

Another issue that is at the core of the text's ideological framework is gender – referencing both its author Layla Abu Zayd and its protagonist Zahra. As Sidonie Smith pointed out in her study *A Poetics of Women's Autobiography*, the relationship between a female autobiographer, her life narrative, and her audience has always shown a great deal of tension and complexity:

> Since autobiography is a public expression, she speaks before and to "man." Attuned to the ways women have been dressed up for public exposure, attuned also to the price women pay for public self-disclosure, the autobiographer reveals in the speaking posture and narrative structure her understanding of the possible readings she will receive from a public . . . They [female autobiographers] understand that a statement or a story will receive a different ideological interpretation . . . attributed to a man or to a woman. (Smith 1987: 49)

This statement is particularly true of *Year of the Elephant*, which both critics and readers often perceive as a distinctly female text. Ahmad Abd al-Salam al-Baqali wrote in the introduction to the 1987 Arabic edition of the novella: "Layla does not let you forget for a single moment that you are reading [a text] that belongs to a *woman*" (Abu Zayd 1987: 5).[22] My position is, on the contrary, that *Year of the Elephant*, despite being authored by a female writer, leans toward the masculine discourse within the Arabic literary tradition. First, its strong and ideologically informed narrative voice resembles Arabic "literature of commitment" (*'adab al-'iltizām*), pioneered and dominated by male writers. At the same time, its structural and ideological composition is very similar to the Western narrative model of social realism that is representative of European discourses of social change and revolutionary movements – once again, a prerogative of a politically engaged male. Targeted borrowing of certain colonial cultural modes is not, however, uncommon among postcolonial writers. These adopted modes, symbols, and cultural codes are manipulated to reverse the power relationships between a dominant Western narrative form and a local marginal one. As Ashcroft, Griffiths, and Tiffin argued, "radical dismantling of European codes and a post-colonial subversion and appropriation of the dominant European discourses" often characterize postcolonial literature (Ashcroft *et al.* 1989: 195). In other words, the colonizer is battled with his own weapon.

Another important factor that puts *Year of the Elephant* outside so-called "female literature" is the construction of its protagonist Zahra's identity. While some critics suggested that this narrative illustrates "identity politics" that "reduce women to mere sexual objects who must be protected against male gaze and sexual advances" (Moukhlis 2003: 71), I argue that Abu Zayd erases Zahra's femininity and sexuality in order to construct a *gender-less* autobiographical subject. Although the novella consistently addresses gender relationships in both colonial and postcolonial Moroccan society and sharply criticizes them, Zahra is anything but a sexual object. Her very character displays no evident signs of female corporeality: her body, veiled by *djellābah*,[23] is invisible and we learn nothing about her physical appearance or her age: "Forty years have left me haunted by bitterness. I say forty although it might be more. It seems like a hundred" (Abu Zayd 1989: 1). The account of her married life lacks any physical aspect: she offers a detailed description of the wedding ceremony and the first year of marriage, but she completely avoids any references to her wedding night or any other sexual experiences. Zahra's femininity is further relegated when she becomes more involved with the liberation movement. She rejects the traditional feminine attributes as she enters the masculine discourse of political struggle: "I happily sold my olive trees, my jewels . . . Resistance took the place of emeralds and rubies in my life, and today I feel only contempt for such trinkets" (*ibid.*: 20).

A very telling episode is when Zahra juxtaposes her newly formed genderless identity of the guerrilla fighter with the women who continue playing conventional female roles: "In the courtyard I found a group of women peeling vegetables. 'I am one of the guerrilla fighters,' I told them" (*ibid.*: 37).[24] The Arabic original makes the interplay between the genders more visible: *qultu lahunna:ʾana min al-fidāʾiyīn* (Abu Zayd 1987: 48). Interestingly, the plural "guerrilla fighters" (*al-fidāʾiyīn*) is in a masculine form, which creates a vivid linguistic contrast with the feminine plural of "them the women" (*hunna*). This narrative nuance illustrates Zahra's consistent distancing of herself from the feminine and her assuming the masculinized nationalist identity. The configuration of the autobiographical subject as lacking traditional feminine qualities is highlighted by other female characters who appear to be as strong – if not stronger – than men. For instance, Zahra describes a fellow fighter, Roukia, as more masculine than her husband: "What a woman!

Much more capable than her husband, and by far more steady" (*ibid.*: 38).

In addition to that, *Year of the Elephant*'s male characters are being incorporated into female discourse. Here the Muslim veil – a symbolic attribute of Islamic femininity – is utilized not as a representation of patriarchal oppression, but rather as a *unifying* factor in the construction of a solid national identity. Numerous scenes talk about male freedom fighters disguising themselves in women's clothing as a successful strategy in fighting the colonizer. Veiling helps men to kill the enemy and to escape the authorities, and it often saves their lives:

> He [Zahra's imprisoned husband] asked me to bring a *djellabah* and veil on my next visit . . . He bent over and picked it up. "We're worried about one of our detainees," he whispered. "They might kill him." "You're going to smuggle him out of here?" (*ibid.*: 46)

On the one hand, the integration of such a distinct feminine signifier into a masculine nationalist discourse indicates a symbolic alliance of both genders in their fight against the colonizer. On the other hand, the veil serves as a separating line between the freedom fighters and the colonizers, and as a tool to hide their identity from the outsider. A number of scholars pointed to the performative function of Islamic veiling. In contrast to the common Western perception of the veil as a symbol of oppression, it is seen as a practice of concealing national identity from the colonial powers. In Valentine Moghadam's words, "purdah provides the opportunity for preserving one's own identity and a certain stability in the face of external pressures" (quoted in Hirschmann 1998: 352). Therefore, the traditional binary of male versus female identity is replaced by the ideological binary of colonized versus colonizer, where internal diversity is downplayed in order to represent the nation *as a whole*.

Religious discourses in *ʿĀm al-Fīl* play as significant a role as they do in Minah's *Baqāyā Ṣuwar*: in both narratives religion is a key strategy to formulate the autobiographical subject's nationalism. But if Minah uses Biblical imagery in an apolitical and figurative manner, Abu Zayd presents Islam as a powerful force of resistance. Perhaps the most important function of Islamic discourses in the national identity-making process is that they offered an ideological alternative when the liberation movement had failed. As Zahra becomes increasingly disillusioned with the results of the anticolonial struggle, Islam is her answer. *ʿĀm al-Fīl* suggests that the main reason that the Moroccan liberation movement has failed is that it was modeled after Western social movements and represented, using John Halstead's definition, "colonial nationalism . . . characterized in part by xenophobia, by the desire to modernize, and by a rising elite's drive for power" (Halstead 1969: 86). This kind of secular nationalism ultimately received its greatest support from the local authoritarian institutions looking to take over power following the colonizer's departure: "It is consciously employed by the Westernized elite as an agent for achieving national unity, a vehicle to carry all the people along to a new world" (*ibid.*: 87). In the novella this social group is represented in Zahra's husband, a French teacher fascinated by everything European, who divorced and kicked her out immediately after the end of colonization.

This brings us to the discussions, presented among others by Trinh Minh-ha, Homi Bhabha, and Christopher Miller, on the corruptive nature of nationalist movements, that replicate metropolitan discourse in that they eventually reinstate colonial violence and oppression within local power structures. As early as 1961, Franz Fanon argued in his *The Wretched of the Earth* that local elites are not at all interested in "transforming the nation"; on the contrary, their mission "consists, prosaically, of being a transmission line between the nation and a capitalism, rampant though camouflaged, which today puts on a mask of neocolonialism" (Fanon 1968: 152). Numerous episodes support the presence of such epistemology, in particular those describing the sultan's role in the liberation movement where his importance is magnified to the degree of a sanctified status:

> For the Independence appearance, the Sultan came out on the balcony between his two sons, and the crowd in the Mechouar Court raised an incredible roar. People cheered and ululated, laughed and cried. Fantastic what effect he had on our hearts! His exile had wrapped him in a sacred cloak, and for his sake the people had joined the resistance, as if he became an ideal or a principle. (Abu Zayd 1989: 50)

This excerpt shows that for many the primary reason for liberation struggle was essentially to reinstate local authoritarian powers. The movement's fiasco and Zahra's disappointment with its ideas are rooted in its ideological substance, which was not to eliminate oppression, but to shift authority from the colonial to the local elites. The seeds of neocolonization that would follow the nationalist movement were already embedded in its ideological bond with the Western metropolis. As J. M. Blaut warned, "if nationalism is merely a European idea, we could absolve colonialism of all historical blame and maintain that national liberation movements arose because colonialism brought civilization, not oppression" (Blaut 1986: 6).

Zahra bitterly describes the return of colonial powers into the country's economic and cultural life immediately after liberation:

> How quickly we forgot! She [France] rained blow after blow upon our heads, filling between her and us a sea of blood I thought would never be bridged. Never did I imagine diplomatic relations and trade treaties, and . . . communities of Moroccans laboring in French cities. Who could have believed such a thing? (Abu Zayd 1989: 42)

Another meaningful episode symbolizing the rise of neocolonialism comes at the very end of the novel when, having experienced social injustice following her divorce, Zahra is forced to work for the French:

> A woman tells me that the French Cultural Center is looking for a cleaning woman. I don't like the idea and decline, saying I'm waiting for an answer from the factories . . . But no answer comes and finally I realize there will be no reply, and then I come face to face with the basic fact that we can't do without the French after all. (*ibid.*: 67)

The ideological substance of this scene cannot be any more obvious. The French may have lost their military presence in Morocco, but their "cultural centers" – symbolizing their ongoing influence on sociocultural sphere – remain an integral part of the country's infrastructure. Zahra, who despite her participation in the liberation struggle was completely dismissed by her husband and her society after it was over, represents the marginalized and silenced social groups who always end up "cleaning" after whoever comes to power.

However, Abu Zayd's narrative does offer an alternative to this form of nationalism, which did not succeed because of its mimicking the West and, therefore, its inadequacy for Moroccan cultural contexts ideology. The alternative path is the autobiographical protagonist's turn to Islam, where religion is seen as able to achieve what secular nationalism failed to do – to unify the nation. The need to formulate an authentic Moroccan national identity – an identity that would reflect the unique aspects of local culture – engages Muslim discourses as being capable of erasing the signs of Europeanness.[25] The narrative offers plentiful examples of Islam's ideological importance for the process of nation-building where reformulated ideas of nationalism are sought in Islamic beliefs and traditions. The wise sheikh, symbolizing Muslim faith, urges Zahra to be true to her local identity: "Your accent is a local one," the sheikh observes. "Don't try to hide it" (Abu Zayd 1989: 8). Zahra's divorce from her Francophone husband, which was immediately followed by her getting close to the sheikh, could serve as an allegorical departure from nationalist ideas that were corrupted by European influences, as personified in her husband, and which eventually brought about neocolonialism. Closeness to the sheikh symbolizes Zahra's acceptance of a new view of her religion and her understanding of its wisdom, and she begins to see Islam as an ultimate means to resurrect nationalism.

While reminiscing about her life as a guerrilla fighter, Zahra looks for analogies of the current liberation movement in the Muslim tradition. She stresses that struggle has always been an essential constituent of Islamic history and women have always played a crucial role in it:

> I fastened my belt, slipped the pistols . . . inside my blouse and recalled my grandfather speaking of Asma, who took food to the Prophet Mohammed and to her own father Abu Bakr, when they were hiding from their enemies in a cave during their flight from Mecca to Medina. "She tore her belt in two, fastened one part around herself, tied the other around her provisions, then slipped out of Mecca." . . . The comparison shook me and made me realize that the struggle has been the same down through the centuries, in that women, too, have always taken their part in it. (*ibid.*: 39)

When Faqih, one of the resistance leaders, returns to his people, they welcome him as the Hajj – a person who has completed the holy pilgrimage to Mecca: "women pressed around him to kiss his hand as though he had just returned from pilgrimage" (*ibid.*: 47). Later, Zahra emphasizes that the nation gained its independence due to godly powers: "everyone saying how great was the Almighty's power to bring change. The general awe of divine power heightened when we saw the gate opening and the prisoners coming out one by one" (*ibid.*: 49). Finally, the very title of the book – *ʿĀm al-Fīl* (*Year of the Elephant*) – alludes to an important event in Islamic history. Around 570 ad, the Christian king of Saba, Abraha al-Ashram, set out on a mission to Mecca with a large Ethiopian army, planning to destroy the sanctuary of Kaaba. Upon arriving at the Meccan territory, the war elephant leading the troops knelt and refused to advance any further. After that flocks of birds came and threw small stones on the soldiers, and this is how the army was defeated.[26] This event is also referenced in the Quran at Sura 105 (*al-Fīl/The Elephant*), and according to the Islamic tradition the Prophet Muhammad was born in the Year of the Elephant.

Therefore, despite the failure of the nationalist movement, Abu Zayd's narrative does anticipate a better future – a future that will be possible if people have faith and unite under the banner of their religion. Just as the Ethiopian army was destroyed by divine intervention, the seemingly impossible-to-defeat French were expelled out from Morocco. The reference to the Prophet's birth suggests the beginning of a new era for Moroccans. *ʿĀm al-Fīl* concludes on a hopeful note that the Islamic faith will prevail in uniting the people and connecting the dispersed pieces of nationalism into one uniform Moroccan identity that will persist in the face of continuing encounters with the West: "The important thing is that I remember God and concentrate on this idea of mine that we are passing through this life to build a road to the next one" (*ibid.*: 68)

Thus, by consistent merging of nationalist and Islamic discourses the narrative presents an emerging anticolonial and anti-Western, authentic Moroccan nationalist subject. Through her autobiographical reincarnation into Zahra, Abu Zayd demonstrates the need to decolonize the Moroccan female subaltern and empower her with ideological tools that will enable her to acquire a voice of her own. *Year of the Elephant* proves that such tools of decolonization cannot be imposed from external discourses (French, Western, and so on), but they should be located within authentic Moroccan cultural and social contexts. Zahra's decolonization and emerging national consciousness are found in Islamic religiosity, which serves as a powerful discursive device for national unity. Even the name "Zahra" is significant: in Arabic it means a "blossoming flower", and it also references the legendary Islamic figure Fatima al-Zahra – the youngest daughter of the Prophet Muhammad, and the only one of his children who gave him descendants. She symbolizes a promise for new beginnings when a powerless and doubly oppressed female subaltern would "blossom" into a decolonized and ideologically informed nationalist subject.

4 Conclusion: Voicing my Self – Voicing my Nation

The two autobiographical novels analyzed in this chapter illustrate a number of interesting tendencies in the construction of the postcolonial modality of the autobiographical in contemporary Arabic narrative discourse. Indeed, *Baqāyā Ṣuwar* and *ʿĀm al-Fīl* were produced in socioculturally and historically different locations of the Arab world, which evidently affected the autobiographical processes in these texts. For example, if Minah's autobiographical identity is formulated through complex negotiations with the two colonial discourses, Ottoman and French, in a highly metaphorical language, Abu Zayd constructs her "imagined" autobiographical subject in a much more ideologically assertive manner. Among other things, such distinct narrative practices could be explained by the fact that the Syrian anticolonial movement was considerably different from the Moroccan one, the latter being more militarily involved and more politically organized.

However, the two narratives also show some important discursive similarities that shed more light on how Arab constructions of individual selfhood communicate with the highly complex framework of Arab nationalism – or, rather, nationalism*s*.

First of all, the identity-making processes in both texts are preoccupied with the voicing of the subaltern – a colonial Arab subject, oppressed and silenced – and providing this subject with effective ideological tools of decolonization. And both texts view religion as the primary catalyst for both decolonization and nationalization. *Baqāyā Ṣuwar*'s autobiographical subject reclaims authority over religious discourses through intricate manipulation of Biblical imagery and presents Christianity as an indigenous local religion, as opposed to being a Western cultural import imposed by the French colonizers on the Syrian population. In *ʿĀm al-Fīl*, Islam functions as a powerful ideological tool with the means to unite and mobilize the oppressed social classes in their anticolonial struggle. Following the failure of secular nationalism, modeled after European movements, Islam is seen as a core element in reconfiguring Moroccan nationhood and in constructing an authentic Moroccan identity. Thus, in both works religious discourses perform a key function in the construction of autobiographical identity that is defined through nationalist semiotics.

Second, autobiographical identities formed in *Baqāyā Ṣuwar* and *ʿĀm al-Fīl* exhibit a strong notion of the collective which, I argue, is a crucial aspect of Arab nationalist selfhood. In Minah's text, in addition to acquiring authority over Christian discourses, the autobiographical subject's decolonization involves symbolic identification with the three overly nationalist characters. Rizqallah, Ibrahim, and Zanuba, each of whom embody an aspect of Syrian nationalist ideology (anti-Ottoman and anti-French nationalism, the resistance to local autocratic structures, and the valorization of the glorious Syrian past), constitute essential elements of *Baqāyā Ṣuwar*'s autobiographical identity. As for *Year of the Elephant*, it shows an even stronger collective aspect, where the subjectivity of a postcolonial author is rewritten into a colonial context. Abu Zayd's Zahra is a collective autobiographical subject – a hybrid of autobiographical elements and the image of a "common" Moroccan woman, oppressed by both colonial powers and local authorities. In this case, the autobiographical act aims to decolonize the Moroccan female subaltern by empowering her with the strong nationalist and feminist voice of Abu Zayd.

Notes

1. A close translation of *Baqāyā Ṣuwar* is "remnants of pictures."
2. Here I refer to the concept of relationality developed by Paul Eakin, who claimed that "all selfhood is relational" (Eakin 1999: 50) in that personal identity is never singular and self-contained, and its construction is unavoidably influenced by other identities that it comes in contact with, such as parents, friends, social class, nation, and so on. Therefore, *all* representations of personal selfhood contain at least some aspects of the collective.
3. A number of scholars have warned about such generalizing practices, among them Chidi Okonkwo, who stressed the negative consequences of such approach: "'Postcolonial literature' has . . . been defined as a catch-all category for the lit-

eratures of the world's peoples (including the United States of America) outside the male-authored texts of the dominant European imperial powers . . . The ragbag approach favored by homogenizing postcolonial theories compelling eliding major distinctive features of decolonization literatures for the purpose of assimilating the literatures within the universal broth, or infiltrating the literatures with issues derived from European cultural history and social conflicts" (Okonkwo 1999: ix–x). Sidonie Smith and Julia Watson have offered similar criticism of Western intellectual practices with regard to postcolonial writing: "we need to resist the tendency of Western theorizing to install another colonial regime, albeit now a discursive regime that works to contain 'colorfulness' inside a Western theoretical category" (Smith and Watson 1992: xv)

4. While most of the Arab world long constituted part of the Ottoman Empire, in modern times Syria came under French mandate, Libya was an Italian colony, North African countries were under French rule, and Egypt was briefly colonized by the French (1798–1801) and finally by the British (1882–1952).
5. Diglossia of the Arabic language refers to a complex relationship between *fuṣḥā* (formal or literary language) and *ʿāmmiyah* (colloquial or vernacular). Each Arab country has its own dialect, as well as numerous regional and social variations of the colloquial/patois, while *fuṣḥā* remains a canonized form in literary production. Although in recent decades Arabic dialects have received a wider acceptance in media, literature, and other forms of official discourse, narratives in colloquial, both oral and written, are still often marginalized and considered to be low-brow, "improper" literature.
6. Among critics who hold to this view are Tetz Rooke, Yumna al-ʿId, John Maier, as well as Khaldoun Shamaa, who wrote an introduction to the English translation of the text. The latter compared Minah's novel with Maxim Gorky's autobiographical works *My Childhood*, *In the World*, and *My Universities* (Minah 1993: xi)
7. Quoted in Ostle *et al.* (1998: 315, n. 19).
8. As a matter of fact, the protagonist, as well as Hanna Minah himself, was born in the Syrian city of Latakiya (my note).
9. The original text only has the word *huwiyah* (identity), as opposed to *biṭāqat huwiyah* (identity card): "wa lā yazāl hādhā al-khaṭaʾ fī huwiyatī, wa sa-yabqā" (Minah 1978: 55). This allows for a broader interpretation of the sentence: "this mistake is still a part of my identity and will remain so."
10. The linguistic diglossia phenomenon is one of the most controversial issues in Arabic narrative discourse. Sasson Somekh points out that this problem is most

clearly manifested in fiction and drama (Somekh 1991: 5). The rapid development of new literary genres and the demands of new reading public in the late nineteenth to the early twentieth centuries called for major reconfigurations of the old literary system in order to produce more realistic forms of representation. This resulted in the creation of the so-called "mixed" language which contains both linguistic registers – formal and colloquial. Most commonly, the narrative would be composed in *fuṣḥā*, and dialogues, in order to imitate oral speech, would be written in vernacular. A number of Arab writers resorted to composing some of their works exclusively in a dialect, such as Luwis Awad's *Mudhakkirāt Ṭālib Ba'thah* (1940), but these attempts continue to be "treated by Arab critics as aberrations" (Somekh 1991: 71).

11. The following excerpts illustrate an interesting linguistic dichotomy between formal and colloquial languages in the text. The first is the mother's direct speech written in a proper and stylized *fuṣḥā*; the second is an *ʿāmmiyah* song that she sings to her children:

    (1) "*Qālat: Wa lakinnana ghurabāʾ, wa nanwī ʾan narḥal, wabnatunā marhūna ʿinda al-mukhtār . . . wa la ʾastaṭīʾ ʾan ʾatrukahā khādimah wa rahīnah ʿindahu*" (Mina 1978: 163)

    (2) "*Kānat tughannī:*

Yā rayḥīn ʿala Ḥalab	Ḥubbī maʿākum rāḥ
Yā mḥammlīn il-ʿinab	W foʾ il-ʿinab tufāḥ
Kill mīn liwlīfu lafa	W ʾana wlīfī rāḥ
Yā rabbī nismit hawā	Tridd el-wlīf ilayā" (Mina 1978: 119).

12. In addition to the insect metaphors discussed earlier, there is a peculiar recurring image of an old Ford car. A Ford car symbolizing Western colonial power is an interesting metaphor, taking into consideration the notion of Fordism that defined the post-war Western capitalism: "The stabilization of capitalism in the core societies of Western Europe and the United States in the immediate post-war period was secured on the basis of what some political economists have characterized as a *Fordist* regime of accumulation. (The name 'Fordism' is derived from the American automobile manufacturer, Henry Ford . . .)" (Lazarus 2004: 21–2). Fordism, being actively promoted by Western powers in recently decolonized countries, indicated an important move from military to economic colonialism. As Michael Rustin points out, one of the main strategies of Western capitalism was "the internationalization of its operations, transferring 'Fordist' forms of production to less developed countries" (Rustin 1989: 55).

13. Full name: *Septimia Zenobia, Aramaic Znwbya Bat Zabbai*, queen of the Roman colony of Palmyra, in present-day Syria, from 267/8 to 272. She conquered several of Rome's eastern provinces before she was subjugated by Emperor Aurelian (ruled 270–275). Zenobia was not content to remain a Roman client. In 269, she seized Egypt, then conquered much of Asia Minor, and declared herself independent from Rome. Marching east, Aurelian defeated her armies at Antioch (now Antakya, Turkey), and at Emesa (now Homs, Syria), and besieged Palmyra (historical facts taken from *Encyclopedia Britannica Online*, available at: http://www.britannica.com/EBchecked/topic/656544/Zenobia, accessed February 5, 2014).
14. A village chief or headman.
15. The naming practices in the Arab world are largely rooted in religious traditions: for example, Islamic names (such as Muhammad, Ahmad, Fatima) or Christian names (Boulos, Girgis). This makes it possible to identify a person's religious affiliation simply by knowing his or her name. However, some names have a shared use across different religious communities, and Rizqallah and Ibrahim belong to this category. "Rizqallah" means "subsistence/fortune from God," and "Ibrahim" is the Arabic version of "Abraham."
16. "Zanuba" is one of the regional variations of "Zaynab" and it is used particularly often in rural areas.
17. All Biblical quotes are taken from the New King James version.
18. These biographical facts are taken from Michael Hall's article, "Leila Abouzeid's *Year of the Elephant*: A Post-colonial Reading" (Hall 1995: 67).
19. Here and further quotes are taken from Barbara Parmenter's English translation of the novel, *Year of the Elephant* (Abu Zayd 1989).
20. "I am not pushing back at French, I am not choosing to write in Arabic. I didn't push French away; it happened to me, it was forced by colonization" (Munro 2003: 5).
21. Quoted from "An Interview with Layla Abu Zayd," in *Ad-Dad: A Journal of Arabic Literature*, January 1993.
22. My italics and my translation of the original text: "*Wa Layla lā tadaʿuka tansa laḥẓah wāḥidah ʾannaka taqraʾu liʾuntha.*"
23. A Middle Eastern loose garment with a hood and with sleeves and skirt of varying length (the description is taken from the glossary to the English translation of the novel: Abu Zayd 1989: 102).
24. Barbara Parmenter's translation says "I'm a guerrilla fighter," but in order to illustrate the gendered discourse on a linguistic level I have translated it closer to the original text.

25. Similar tendencies articulating the need to incorporate Islamic ideology in lieu of purely secular European trends are also characteristic of Middle Eastern feminist movements. In this regard, Sherin Saadallah emphasized that "the impact of Muslim feminism is more comprehensive than secular feminism, which has been resisted in Muslim societies because of its identification as a Western intrusion and thus a threat to 'authenticity'" (Saadallah 2004: 224).
26. These historical facts are taken from the *Encyclopedia of Islam*, New edition, eds. B. Lewis, Ch. Pellat, and J. Schacht, London: Luzac, 1965, p. 895.

2

Writing Selves on Bodies

> "I realized the body has a private landscape without words, and I knew I had to find a language to talk about my scars."
>
> Kim Hewitt, *Mutilating the Body*

1 Autobiographical Bodies: Theory and Practice

Writing about physical human bodies and their sexualities has always been a controversial issue in Arabic literature. Although classical Arabic literature contains a number of exceptions (most remarkable of which is medieval erotic poetry), the love theme – one of the most popular themes in both classical and modern Arabic literature – is, as a rule, highly romanticized and detached from any notion of corporeality. In contemporary Arab narrative culture, some writers took on the challenge of incorporating aspects of sexuality in their works, but in most cases they were careful to avoid graphic depictions. Yusuf Idris, for instance, while bravely focusing his story *ʾAbū al-Rijāl* (published in Arabic in 1987 and translated as *A Leader of Men*) on a homosexual character,[1] still uses the kind of language that renders the physical desires of the body in a rather subtle, veiled manner. Consider, for example, the following excerpt depicting the protagonist's homoerotic fantasy that avoids any references to sexual organs and, instead, focuses on "neutral" body parts such as arms and legs:

> a feverish groping that makes his hands shake and his whole body shiver as he swoops down on the young man, squeezing the powerful muscles of his arms and the bulging muscles of his legs, and inside him yearning howls boldly and madly unleashing a wailing cry that represents his masculinity. (Idris 1988: 5)

Similarly, many Arab and Western scholars of Arabic literature often preferred to investigate the subject of sexuality from a body-less point of view by treating it as an ideological device and utilizing metaphorical language to talk about it, rather than depicting sexual identities through specific physical experiences. For example, Hilary Kilpatrick suggested that in Arabic literature, "the search for love is intimately connected with the individual's desire for freedom and fulfillment, while the frank affirmation of sexuality, of whatever kind, represents a challenge to a rigid and hypocritical social order" (Kilpatrick 1995: 15). Certainly, such attitudes and strategies of effacing sexual bodies from texts are rooted in specific cultural and religious traditions in the Middle East where most schools in theology, philosophy, and related disciplines have valorized the spiritual as a desired core of human agency. Within the framework of conventional discourse, the literary works where sexuality and corporeality are on display are almost unavoidably destined to become either marginalized or to acquire the label of "scandalous" literature.

In autobiographical writing, the tendency to avoid the bodily becomes even more evident, since, with the assumption that authors unveil their personal life stories, the presence of corporeality would mean an exposure of their own bodies and, consequently, could be perceived as an act of exhibitionism. In the past, autobiographical works of those few writers who chose to situate their selfhood in human physicality and sexuality were more often than not stamped as pornographic. Among the most apparent examples of such attitudes is this chapter's case study, Muhammad Shukri's *al-Khubz al-Ḥāfī* (*Bare Bread*), which continues to be banned in some parts of the Arab world. Another representative case is a Francophone work *La Répudiation* (*The Repudiation*, 1969), an autobiographical novel by Rachid Boudjedra where the author "freely discusses homosexuality, incest and rape, all subjects hitherto avoided by Maghrebi writers" (Abu-Haidar 1989: 42). *La Répudiation* was banned in Algeria during 1970s, but was later included in the academic curriculum of the Faculty of Letters at the University of Rabat. However, the eventual acceptance of this novel into official discourse could be explained by its language of composition, French, which entails its inaccessibility to larger Arab audiences. The autobiography of the prominent Arab poet Nizar Qabbani, *Qiṣṣatī Maʿa al-Shiʿr* (*My Story with Poetry*, 1973), greatly contributed to his reputation as the *enfant terrible* of Arabic literature for his "unusually frank and unconventional approach towards love and sexuality" (Wild 1995: 200).[2] Thus, Arab autobiographers who embarked on constructing their narrative identities through bodies, produced works that were unavoidably subversive to preestablished conceptions of self and life-writing.

Nonetheless, literary attitudes toward corporeality and sexuality began to change in the last two decades of the last century. Substantial reevaluation of traditional norms in different spheres of Arab society generated a tendency to incorporate the bodily into both novelistic and autobiographical writing, particularly in the works by women authors (Hanan al-Shaykh and Nawal al-Saadawi are the most obvious examples). Whereas the conventional literary discourse in many ways continues to abstain from depicting physicality – not only sexual, but of *any* kind – the corpus of autobiographical works, where bodies are increasingly visible as sites of identity construction, grows by the day. With that, it is important to bear in mind that these works render the human body in ways that are often markedly different from Western narrative representations and theoretical conceptions of physicality and sexuality.

This chapter investigates two different physiological dimensions of self-referential discourse: one highlighting the body's sexuality and another rooted in the body's aesthetics. I present two case studies: *Al-Khubz al-Ḥāfi* (*Bare Bread*, 1973) by Muhammad Shukri,[3] and *Taqāsīm ʾala Watar Dāʾiʿ* (*Improvisations on a Missing String*, 1992) by Nazik Saba Yarid. My selections of these particular texts – by a male and a female writer – does not offer the familiar framework of the masculine–feminine bipolarity. Instead, I aim to demonstrate a remarkable plurality of the newly emerging corporeal articulations of the autobiographical by discussing the two works that render very different approaches to the human body. In Shukri's text, the autobiographical body is overtly sexual and defined by blatantly graphic depictions of physicality, while Yarid's *Improvisations* emphasizes the body's aesthetics, where identity is formulated through the binary of ugly–beautiful and is outlined by the subject's negotiations with her (imagined) physical abnormality.

An important point of my inquiry is to examine a variety of modes in which these autobiographical novels dialog with and challenge Western concepts and formulae of sexuality. Whereas male and female sexuality are often viewed as two diametrically opposite sources of identity formation in Western theory (for instance, in early feminist criticism), in *Bare Bread* these are not constructed as a conceptual binary, but, rather, are joined into one subversive discourse where the dichotomy is based on body versus mind, physical self versus spiritual self, and not on sexual differences between the two genders. Such a representation of corporeality, I argue, is meant to offer an antithesis to the conventional notion of bodiless and spiritual self, established in traditional Arabic autobiographical discourse as an "appropriate" site for identity formation. Yarid's autobiographical novel offers a different challenge to Western theories by offering a different approach to physical disability and its impact on one's identity. The majority of Western theoretical works that examine the subgenre of life-writing dedicated to stories of disease categorize physical illness as compromising autobiographical identity, and view it as an obstacle that the subject must overcome. In Yarid's *Improvisations on a Missing String*, on the contrary, cancer becomes a *positive* aspect in the autobiographical act since it is utilized as a means of suppressing the subject's ugliness and physical unattractiveness. In other words, by using Muhammad Shukri's and Naqik Saba Yarid's works as examples I will demonstrate some of the internal diversity and unique qualities of the corporeal autobiographical modality.

Discursive avoidance of depicting physicality is not limited to Arabic culture of autobiography. Western life-writing practices, too, have long demonstrated uneasy relationships with the human body. Shirley Neuman wrote in 1989:

> Bodies rarely figure in autobiography. Even movie stars – those icons of an ideal body . . . tend in their autobiographies to minimize the significance of their bodies to their personal and professional lives . . . [they] strive above all to demonstrate *the spiritual quest* behind their culturally produced and idealized bodies. The history of autobiography and its criticism . . . work consistently towards such repression of bodies in autobiography. (Neuman 1989: 1)

Neuman further explains that such "near-effacement of bodies" in life-writing stems from "a Platonic tradition which opposes the spiritual to the corporeal and then identifies 'self' with the spiritual" (*ibid.*: 1). Traditional works of the genre – among them autobiographies of Augustine, Rousseau, Henry Adams, and others – participated in conceptualizing the individual as a fixed and uniform entity, which is preconceived and separated from other entities, with "well-defined, stable, impermeable boundaries around a singular, unified and atomic core" (Smith 1993: 5). The idea of a universal human subject was cultivated through the historical development of Western ideologies and philosophical thought:

> The inaugural moment of the West's romance with selfhood lay in the dawn of the Renaissance, during which time the notion of the "individual" emerged, a universal human subject . . . Subsequently pressed through the mills of eighteenth-century enlightenment, early nineteenth-century romanticism, expanding bourgeois capitalism, and Victorian optimism, the individual came by the mid-nineteenth century to be conceptualized as a "fixed, extralinguistic" entity consciously pursuing its unique destiny. (*ibid.*: 5)

Naturally, one of the central limitations of this traditional conception of selfhood is that it is completely detached from the body. The self's disembodiment was further promoted and theorized by Descartes, who argued that the essential self – the "I" – is a soul fully separate from the body:

> I hereby conclude that I was a substance, of which the whole essence or nature consists in thinking, and which, in order to exist, needs no place and depends on no material thing; so that this "I", that is to say, the mind, by which I am what I am, is entirely distinct from the body. (Descartes 1968: 54)

During the last decades of the twentieth century, this perception of subjectivity as focused on a "unique, unitary, unencumbered" self that "escapes all forms of embodiment" (Smith 1993: 6) was substantially revised and filtered through the newly emerged theoretical and analytical frameworks. When it comes to the now deconstructed bodiless Cartesian subject, which, as Paul Eakin pointed out, presents the "danger of an overly narrow approach to human subjectivity" (Eakin 1999: 8), two main approaches came to light. The first is the so-called neurobiological method: it argues that the life of a self is, above all, the life of a body. In other words, the formation of one's subjectivity is essentially based on tangible – physical and sensory – human life experiences. In his article "Neurology and the Soul," Oliver Sacks suggested the following concept of selfhood: "One is not an immaterial soul . . . I do not feel alive, psychologically alive, except insofar as a stream of feeling – perceiving, imagining, remembering, reflecting, revising, recategorizing runs through me. I am that stream – that stream is me" (Sacks 1990: 49). In their focus on the body as a physiological site of subjectivity and a necessary condition to self's existence, scholars of neurobiological (or neuroanthropological) approach – Oliver Sacks, Israel Rosenfield, and others – maintain that "subjectivity and selfhood are deeply rooted in the body, psychology and physiology are intimately linked" (Eakin 1999: 20). The methodology developed by this theoretical school proved to be particularly important for the rapidly developing critical studies of autobiographies centered on disability and trauma, as it provided evidence of the inevitable connection between authors' physical disabilities and their narrative identities. As Israel Rosenfield pointed out, "if the bodily structure is damaged, so is the sense of self, memory, and consciousness" (Rosenfield 1992: 139).

What is typical of the neurobiological method is that it situates the physiological self against Cartesian bodiless subject without, however, contemplating the body's sexuality. The endeavor to conceptualize considerations of sexuality and gendering of bodies in cultural production was at the core of the second anti-Cartesian approach, and was initiated by students of feminism, queer studies and, more recently, by theorists of masculinity. Feminist scholars argued that the disembodiment of the subject was an ideological strategy of patriarchal systems where men conceive themselves as universal subjects – rational, transcendent, and bodiless – and thus, continuously marginalize women due to their "natural" affiliation with physicality. Discourses of this universal subject, Sidonie Smith suggested, "assign the 'tremulous private body' to marginal status at the periphery of consciousness" (Smith 1993: 11). Another feminist critique, presented by Shirley Neuman, maintains that the patriarchal tactic of stripping identity of its physical quality had a direct impact on autobiographical discourse: "That western cultures assume an analogy between mind, masculinity and culture, and between body, femininity, and 'nature,' only reinforces the disembodiment of the self characteristic of most autobiographies" (Neuman [1991] 1998: 416).

The female body, which is by definition excluded from the official discourse, is nevertheless not entirely absent. First, its existence appears to be a necessary condition for the effective functioning of the mind–body and male–female binary which, from the feminist point of view, is a foundational principle of hegemonic discourse. In Judith Butler's words, "masculine disembodiment is only possible on the condition that women occupy their bodies as their essential and enslaving identities" (Butler [1987] 2004: 23). Second, this female body has a potential to transcend the boundaries and become a legitimate part of the official discourse. By grounding her essence in the bodily, woman can enter the dominant discourse for the very fact that she does establish her selfhood, even if through unconventional practices: "Anatomy becomes the irreducible granite at the core of woman's being. This, then, becomes her essence, and, paradoxically, her route to nonessentiality" (Smith 1993: 12).

Queer studies and recent feminist scholarship continued to further conceptualize the bodily by erasing the male–female binary and proposing to view sexual bodies not as necessarily inhabiting one of the two sides of discursive bipolarity, but rather as continuously creating discourses of plurality and multiplicity. Thus, Andrew Shail offers an example of ambiguous bodies (such as transgender): "bodies that present as neither entirely male nor entirely female expose the complexity of 'sexing levels' and the morphological similarity elided in the penis/vagina 'distinction'" (Shail 2004: 102). Those sexual bodies and sexual identities that reside in an ambiguous territory between traditional male–female gender distinctions are set to destabilize this binary and put it in a state of perpetual fragmentation. As Edward Davies pointed out, contemporary queer theory and transgender studies developed and challenged the second wave feminism's conceptualization of gender and "foregrounded the possibility of new, perhaps undiscovered, genders" (Davies 2004: 115). Moreover, studies of masculinity have substantially revised the preestablished notions of a uniform manhood and of the mighty male body, immune to external and internal disturbances.[4] These newly emerged ideologies and theories have significantly contributed to expanding and enriching the analytical frameworks employed in studies of corporeal and sexual autobiographical subjectivities, and armed students of autobiography with new tools with which to explore self-referential discourse.

So where are Arab autobiographical negotiations of corporeality situated in this complex hierarchy of theories? While rich Western theory offers an analytical framework and an intellectual approach, one should not underestimate region-specific cultural meanings that prompt different interpretations of theory and often challenge it. Muhammad Shukri's *Bare Bread* challenges the popular notion that a marginalized autobiographical body is a prerogative of women's writing. In depicting life in the Moroccan underworld, sexuality and the bodily are fleshed out in a bold and extraordinarily unconventional way for Arab cultural discourses. Most remarkably, the male body here is not measured against or juxtaposed to female physicality, but, on the contrary, both are integrated into one openly subversive discourse in opposition to conventional autobiographical practices of effacing the bodily.

Nazik Saba Yared's *Improvisations on a Missing String* offers, I will argue, an interesting counterpoint to the reading of Kristeva's abject as dramatically endangering identity, proposed by a number of Western feminist scholars.[5] In her examination of Audre Lorde and Paul Monette, Allison Kimmich views abjection in terms of "psychologically or socially diseased body" and explores the ways in which autobiographers embrace their abject bodies – cancerous, homosexual, and so on – in the process of self-definition (Kimmich 1998). Meanwhile, Yared's text, which I approach as an *autopathography*, gives an account of a *deliberate contamination* where the imagined diseasing of the body with cancer is a means to "fix" the autobiographical body and legitimize it as the site of autobiographical construction. In other words, in Yarid's text abjection becomes subjection. If Shukri's narrative defines the subject through his sexuality, Yarid's autobiographical novel explores the aesthetic dimension of the bodily. But both texts, as different as they might appear, illustrate the already remarkable internal diversity within the corpus of works constituting the relatively new corporeal modality of autobiographical transmission.

2 Identity of the Body and the Body of Identity in Muhammad Shukri's *al-Khubz al-Ḥāfi* (*Bare Bread*)

Muhammad Shukri was born into a poor Moroccan family in the Rif in 1935. Illiterate until the age of nineteen, Shukri became one of the most interesting and controversial figures on the Arab literary scene. His autobiographical work *al-Khubz al-Ḥāfi* was written in 1972, and first published in 1973 in its English and French adaptations, while the publication of the original Arabic text appeared only ten years later. Because of its frequent graphic references to sexuality and violence, this book was, and still is, banned from publication in some Arab countries. The author received numerous accusations of promoting pornography, and *al-Khubz al-Ḥāfi* was labeled as "immoral" literature "whose place is in taverns and brothels."[6] Nevertheless, censorship and conservative critics' labeling of the text as overly sexual and pornographic did not prevent Shukri's autobiography from gaining extraordinary popularity with the Arab reading public: it became the first Moroccan literary work to have sold almost 20,000 copies in less than two years.[7]

Bare Bread covers nineteen years of the protagonist's life, from his early childhood to his departure to another city to enter elementary school, and describes his years in the Moroccan underworld, including drug smuggling, prostitution, rape, and other subjects previously unspeakable in Arab public discourse. Shukri suggested an original and very unusual way of telling a life story in Arabic autobiographical discourse and, on a larger scale, this work introduced a discourse of graphic physicality to the Arabic literature proper. In order to illustrate how the bodily functions as a primary site of the autobiographical act, my discussion here focuses on two central features of *Bare Bread*. First, not only does the subject's explicit corporeality signify a critical departure from bodiless, spiritual, and virtuous identity-making of conventional autobiography, but it offers sophisticated mockery and a caustic antithesis to the conventional *Bildungsroman* model. To this end, Shukri employs a number of narrative techniques, such as "telegraphic" language, a straightforward and unembellished imitation of oral speech; the replacement of the traditional "story of education" with the "story of the body"; and thematic novelties, such as the deromanticizing of love and the portrayal of ugly sides of family relationships between parents and children, and between spouses. Second, I will demonstrate the autobiographical narrator's/protagonist's complex relationship with his own and other characters' physicality, where the human body is simultaneously admired and despised, is perceived as both beautiful and ugly, and evokes both feelings of ecstasy and the desire to destroy and obliterate it. What is remarkable about Shukri's narrative is that here the body appears to be an *inescapably* defining aspect of autobiographical identity. Because of the circumstances of his environment and upbringing, the body becomes the only available tool for articulating autobiographical selfhood.

The narrative discourse of *Bare Bread* persistently subverts the conventional parameters of traditional autobiography and shows a break away from the truth-telling mode typical of traditional works of the genre. The very subtitle of *al-Khubz al-Ḥāfī – Sīrah Dhātīyah Riwāʾīyah* (*A Novelistic Autobiography*) – points at the presence of fictional elements (the word *riwāʾī* can mean both "novelistic" and "fictional"). This definition immediately establishes a narrative mode that is different from that of a conventional autobiography. While the latter is, as a rule, characterized by a narrative structure resembling historical non-fiction, with its clearly marked distance from the narrated events and an authoritative presence of the autobiographical narrator, a novelistic autobiography utilizes the narrative techniques of the novel, where *how* the story is told is as important as the story itself. Narrative nuances and detailed descriptions of objects and environments receive particular significance in the text since they highlight the autobiographical subject's physicality. Every single narrative moment, it seems, is rendered in markedly visual and bold terms, relating each and every event of the protagonist's life to his body. The following scene describing young Muhammad's feelings of hunger, when he was forced to eat a rotten fish he found on the beach out of starvation, emphasizes the graphic physicality of this experience:

> I feel severe pain in my stomach as I walk under the burning sun . . . I pick up a small dry fish. I smell it. Its stench makes me want to vomit. I peel off its skin. I start chewing it with disgust. Its taste is rotten. I keep chewing it, not able to swallow. Sharp stones are hurting my feet. I chew the fish like it's a chewing gum. I spit it. The stench stays in my mouth. I'm chewing the emptiness in my mouth. I chew it and I chew it. My insides gurgle. Gurgling and gurgling. I feel drowsy. I feel drowsy and yellow water starts pouring out of my mouth and nose. I take a deep breath. My heart is beating violently . . . Sweat is streaming down on my face. Streaming and streaming. (Shukri 1982: 100–1)[8]

If in a conventional memoir a description of hunger would likely be linked to larger social and economic issues, in *al-Khubz al-Ḥāfī* it is very personal, viewed exclusively in terms of very real, physical experiences of the body. These bodily depictions, graphic to the point of being repulsive, are voiced in a very laconic Arabic, free of any eloquent expressions and often written in a way that resembles the structure and rhythm of a poem. For example, the above excerpt offers repetitions of the final word in each sentence, and some sentences are rhymed: Tanaffastu *bi-ʿumq*. Qalbī yakhfiq *bi-ʿunf* – a feature that does not translate into English (*ibid.*: 101; rhymed words are italicized for emphasis). Thus, the bodily – even its ugly side – is poeticized in the narrative, which could be perceived as ridiculing the conventional valorization of mind, soul, and the morals, typical of traditional autobiographical works.

Another technique utilized in *Bare Bread* which stands in contrast to the conventional mode, is the constant blurring of the borderlines between the real and the imaginary. The narration is not limited to recollections of past events, but it also includes reminiscences of dreams and imaginary scenes and figures in a way that does not clearly set the two apart. For example, the little Muhammad's encounter with a jinn is described as a real event:

> I looked towards the other shore. A ghost figure advanced to the river. I had heard that if you saw a djinn, you must thrust a knife into the ground and then the djinn would be unable to move from his place. I violently struck the knife into the ground. I ran but my knees failed me. I fell and got up. I could not scream nor turn around. I felt that if I only turned and looked back, the monster that I saw would snatch me. (Shukri 1982: 38)

Shukri's text also introduced a markedly different perspective on the formulation of the autobiographical "I". A conventional Arabic autobiographer, as a rule, is preoccupied with describing his or her extratextual personality in a manner that assumes the presence of a self-aware identity outside the narrative – an identity that had been fully formed *before* the process of writing began. Such an autobiography looks back at the author's life with the goal of answering the question "how did I become who I am?" through consciously analyzing certain events and people that influenced the formation and development of this non-narrative autobiographical "I." Hence, in a traditional Arabic autobiography, we usually see the childhood events through the eyes of an adult intellectual who offers a retrospective view on his or her life. Consider, for example, Salama Musa's autobiography where the narrator, having stated that he has seen "the nineteenth century through the eyes of a young child," immediately proceeds to analyze the political situation in Egypt during his early years (Musa 1961: 7).

In *al-Khubz al-Ḥāfī*, in contrast, the narrator's remembrance of his early life is given from the child's perspective, emphasizing events and feelings that are likely to be the brightest memory from a little boy's point of view: not only the major events are important, such as the death of a family member or starvation, but so are minor incidents as well – such as street fights with other boys. Every detail is significant here, and the narrator's early experiences are even reported in a child-like manner. Here is how the narrative begins: "Surrounded by the other children, I am crying because of my uncle's death. Some of them are crying, too. And I only cry when someone hits me or when I lose something" (Shukri 1982: 9). In this very first episode, it feels as if the little Muhammad – not the adult Shukri – tells us his story: it is presented in a matter-of-fact manner, in short sentences imitating speech and lacking any retrospective "mature" viewpoint. He then proceeds to describe the great famine in the Rif province, and rather than analyzing this particular historical moment with its sociopolitical situation, its causes and consequences – as one may expect from a conventional autobiography[9] – we hear the viewpoint of the so-called "naive narrator": "I see other people crying also. The great famine is in the Rif. Drought and war" (*ibid.*: 9). The presence of the naive narrator in the text is emphasized by numerous accounts of childhood feelings, emotions, and fears: we constantly hear the child's voice, such as the previous excerpt depicting an encounter with a jinn, and the storytelling process is not dominated by the adult narrator. Another important notion is that Shukri's work does not have a retrospective view of the past. The story is often told in the present tense, thus, eliminating a clearly defined distance from the past events, as exemplified in conventional works of the genre. Such narrative technique highlights the fact that autobiographical identity is formed in the process of writing, and is not a preexisting conception.

As we have already seen, *Bare Bread* offers plenty of dissimilarities with the established autobiographical tradition. But the most fundamental difference between the two discourses is Shukri's choice of the body as the primary site of the autobiographical act. The text has a strong confessional mode with its blunt display of sexuality and, to some extent, could be compared with

Western canonical works of the genre where, as Michel Foucault argues in *The History of Sexuality*, such confessions had been already established as a discourse – unlike in Arabic literary tradition. There is, however, an important distinction: in *Bare Bread*, the erotic and violent scenes (including rape), as well as other shameful activities, such as drug-taking, stealing, smuggling, and prostitution, are portrayed with no sense of guilt. Shukri's narrator presents them as a matter of fact, as any other life experiences and, therefore, subversively mocking the "spiritual quest" of a conventional autobiography.

Not only is the autobiographical protagonist's sexuality revealed and highlighted, but the majority of other characters are also presented through their sexual experiences and graphic descriptions of bodies. In other words, the emphasis is placed on their physical attributes, rather than on their personalities and human qualities. Everyone's identity is articulated through body language – which, no doubt, introduced a radically new element into Arabic literary discourse. Shukri's self-exposé is also accentuated by a markedly different linguistic mode: sharp telegraphic sentences, detailed graphic descriptions, circular repetitions, short dialogs, and a lack of complex linguistic structures create a language that is stripped of any embellishments, exposed as a naked body. The following fragment depicts a scene unthinkable in the framework of conventional autobiography – a sexual intercourse between the protagonist's parents, where the very graphic and visual language highlights the scandalous exposure of the taboo subject:

> I woke up in the night with a full bladder. The clapping sound of kisses. Continuous panting. Love-whispering. They make love. Goddamn their love. Flesh clapping. Eww! . . . Panting. Kisses. Moaning. Panting. Kisses. Panting. Kisses. Moaning. They are biting each other. They are devouring each other and licking each other's blood. (Shukri 1982: 27)

Most critics hold to the view that Shukri's autobiography is clearly alien and subversive to the canonical works of the genre and represents marginalized discourse. However, a close study of *al-Khubz al-Ḥāfi* shows that it does not simply reject the formal elements established by earlier autobiographies, but rather builds on them, utilizes them in the narrative, and, eventually, deconstructs and reverses these elements in such a way that they end up transforming canonical discourse into subversive. I will present two examples of these deconstructed elements.

One of the typical recurring themes in conventional autobiographical writing in Arabic literature, in particular autobiography of childhood, is a quest for freedom where the autobiographical protagonist is preoccupied with freeing him- or herself from the repressive patriarchal family, which represents an Arab society in miniature and symbolizes the old world order. This conflict is usually reflected in the protagonist's alienation from the father, whose "despotic figure" became an archetype in Arabic autobiography. Whether it is the father's lack of enthusiasm to give his children education (Jurji Zaydan's *Mudhakkirāt*), or, on the contrary, him being overly zealous in forcing his sons to excel in their studies (Ahmad Amin's *Ḥayātī*), or, especially in women's autobiographies (Fadwa Tuqan's *Riḥlah Jabalīyyah*) the father's tyranny toward the female members of the family, he is sharply criticized by the narrator and perceived as an embodiment of the patriarchal system. This alienation from the father is often juxtaposed with warm romantic feelings for the mother, who is a victim of the male oppression in the family. In his study of Arabic autobiographies of childhood, Tetz Rooke pointed out that the narrator's targeted criticism of the oppressive father is often a veiled social commentary and is not at all uncommon in Arabic autobiographical writing: "A negative image of the father figure in the narrative, by extension, tends to be meant/interpreted as an attack on the dominant social order" (Rooke 1997: 239).

In *Bare Bread* the father–son conflict takes on a different level of intensity and becomes mutual hatred. The teenage Muhammad is not simply alienated from his father or wishes to leave the family house to free himself from the despotic rule, but dreams of killing him and recounts this dream in graphic detail:

> In my imagination, my father is the villain in the film. I am the hero. I pulled the trigger: Tra-tah-tah . . . Tra-tah-tah. My father dies. The bullets are cooling off in his heart and brain. And the blood runs from him as it runs from the villain on the screen. His limbs quiver for the last time. My father died in my imagination just like the villain died on screen. This is the way I've always wanted to kill him. (Shukri 1982: 95)

Muhammad's love for his mother is juxtaposed to his hatred toward the father, but this love is anything but romantic or sentimental. If for Jurji Zaydan and Salama Musa the mother is an idealized figure of high morals, purity, and self-sacrifice who, in Musa's words, "instilled in my heart many tender impressions that cause my childhood memories to come back to my mind . . . filling me with a mixture of pleasant sadness and happiness" (Musa 1961: 18),[10] Shukri's narrator sees his mother as, first and foremost, a female *body*, suffering from her husband's physical abuse, hunger, and childbirth. For instance, he describes her pregnancy with a rather obvious disgust:

> My mother's belly is expanding. Sometimes she does not go to the market. She vomits several times a day. She is pale. Her legs are swollen. She sobs. Her belly is getting bigger and bigger. I wonder if it would burst. (Shukri 1982: 24)

Furthermore, Muhammad's feelings for his mother even have an implicit sexual connotation, in his father's words: "You love her. You don't love anyone but her . . . I see this love in your eyes and in hers too. She spoils you as if she is still breastfeeding you. Her milk is still on your teeth . . . The only thing you are capable of is biting your mother's breasts" (*ibid.*: 93). Thus, a seemingly safe traditional theme of family relationships in *al-Khubz al-Ḥāfī* becomes a shockingly subversive element. Shukri elevates the simple binary of father–mother and alienation–love to a much more intense emotional level – the level of violence and sexuality. Alienation from the father metamorphoses into hatred and violent competition for male dominance in the family, while his emotional attachment to the mother is intertwined with feelings of disgust for her body with a hint of Oedipal love.

Another thematic deconstructed element of conventional autobiography is the portrayal of the author's individual life as representational of a larger group. As I pointed out in Introduction, a substantial number of traditional autobiographies show a tendency to present personal life stories within a larger context, as a symbolic mirror of a generation of intellectuals, a particular social class, or the author's environment. Structurally, *Bare Bread* does not deviate from this pattern: numerous secondary characters and the sociocultural environment are active participants in the autobiographical act. As in a conventional autobiography, Shukri colorfully, and with much detail, describes his milieu, but it is precisely this milieu that mocks the official discourse by replacing prominent intellectuals, literary figures, and religious and social reformers with prostitutes, thieves, drug addicts, beggars, smugglers, and madmen.

One should mention that depiction of underprivileged social classes was not completely alien to Arabic literature prior to Shukri's publication, but there have always been strictly defined degrees and levels of marginality. Representation of the low and, in particular, lower-middle classes – impoverished working people struggling for survival in difficult social and political conditions – has long been a favorite tool of Arabic social realism. Some writers even incorporated the characters of thieves and prostitutes in their works (for instance, Naguib Mahfouz in his novel *Bidāyah wa Nihāyah* (*The Beginning and the End*)) to demonstrate the existence of this social phenomenon. However, no Arab writer before Shukri had dedicated the entire book to the history of urban underworld. Not only did he realistically depict these people living on the farthest margins of the Moroccan society, but he also exposed himself as one of them – a beggar, a thief, a prostitute. *Bare Bread* ends on a note that is quite typical for a conventional autobiography of childhood (Jurji Zaydan, Abd al-Majid Bin Jallun, and Tawfiq al-Hakim, among others) – the narrator's departure to Larache to study Arabic literacy. Muhammad's visit to his younger brother's grave before leaving Tangiers symbolizes a farewell to the old life and hope for a new beginning. He is not ashamed, however, of what he is, neither does he directly blame his environment for his miserable early years.

Muhammad Shukri's *al-Khubz al-Ḥāfī* does not simply exemplify Moroccan or Arabic autobiographical anti-discourse. But, comparably to Hanna Minah's and Layla Abu Zayd's voicing of the colonized subaltern, it formulates a marginal(ized) autobiographical identity by manipulating the narrative patterns, structures, and devices of the conventional literature in a subversive manner – and through these discursive practices legitimizes the existence of the corporeal autobiographical subject.

3 The Beauty and the Beast: Reading Nazik Saba Yarid's *Taqāsīm ʿala Watar Dāʾiʿ* (*Improvisations on a Missing String*) as Autopathography

Nazik Saba Yarid, born in Jerusalem, received her PhD in Arabic literature from the American University in Beirut, and published more than fifteen works of both fiction and non-fiction. Her *Taqāsīm ʿala Watar Dāʾiʿ* (*Improvisations on a Missing String*) first appeared in Arabic in 1992, and was translated into English by Stuart Hancox in 1997. Narrated from both first- and third-person point of view, the novel tells the story of Saada and offers a non-linear structure of continuous flashbacks. Saada's stay at the hospital in Beirut, where following a mastectomy she is awaiting yet another cancer surgery, is intertwined with her reminiscences of her life prior to disease – her growing up in Jerusalem, her studies at the university in Cairo, and her life in Beirut as a teacher of Arabic language and literature. Much of Saada's recollections are centered on her complex relationships with her mother and younger sister, whose beauty is juxtaposed with the protagonist's less fortunate – in her opinion – looks. The story ends with Saada's discovery that the tumor removed from her lung was not malignant.

I approach Yarid's work as yet another veiled autobiographical narrative. Although *Taqāsīm* bears the subtitle of a novel (*riwāyah*) and could be certainly read as such, I propose an autobiographical reading of the text. First, the protagonist shares certain facts from her personal history with the author's, such as place of birth, family background, and occupation. Second, the protagonist's (Saada's) appearance, which is described in detail, shows an evident resemblance with the author's photographic images. Finally, the portrayal of the protagonist's mother (her looks, her cancer) is pretty much identical to the way in which Nazik Yarid described her mother in her explicitly autobiographical work *Dhikrayāt Lam Taktamil* (*An Incomplete Memoir*, 2004). I argue that it is precisely the anatomical similarity that constitutes the main autobiographical aspect of *Improvisations*, since physicality is the primary element of identity-making in the text. In comparison with Shukri's very graphic and provokingly sexual autobiographical body, here the function of corporeality takes an essentially different turn: the focus is on the body's aesthetics, where (alleged) unattractiveness is constructed as a site of disability. Therefore, I read *Improvisations* as an *autopathography*. I use the term offered by Thomas Couser, who applied it to a particular kind of life-writing defined by the autobiographer's physical abnormality which plays a crucial role in the articulation of selfhood: "Bodily dysfunction may simulate what I call *autopathography* – autobiographical narrative of illness or disability – by heightening one's awareness of one's mortality, threatening one's sense of identity, and disrupting the apparent plot of one's life" (Couser 1997: 5).

An important aspect of this autopathography is that the source of the subject's sense of bodily abnormality is caused not by a serious illness, but by the innate physical appearance. The fictional contamination of the body with cancer,[11] on the contrary, appears to be a symbolic act of "fixing" the autobiographical body and freeing it of undesired features – whitening of the skin, thinning of the figure, and so on. When ugliness or unattractiveness is an inborn condition, rather than an unnatural change experienced by a normal body (for example, resulting from an accident, an illness, and the like), it seems to be difficult to perceive it as being equal to a more "serious" physical disability, such as blindness, deafness, or loss of body parts. Nonetheless, depending on the degree of traumatic experience that one's dissatisfaction with one's appearance generates and the impact of this trauma on one's selfhood, ugliness can indeed be constructed as disability – even when the actual condition is highly exaggerated, as in the case with *Improvisations*. In other words, the core of the physical disability or deformity lies in the subject's *self-perception*. Bodily defects and disorders take many forms, and so do their representations in autobiographical discourse and their impacts on articulation of one's selfhood.

In his book *Recovering Bodies: Illness, Disability, and Life-Writing*, Thomas Couser points out that "personal narratives of sickness and disability may . . . take forms other than autobiographical accounts. Broadly considered, the category would include journals, essays, and full-life narratives" (Couser 1997: 6); and we should certainly add the autobiographical novel to this list. Besides being a popular form of artistic expression among Arab autobiographical authors, novelistic discourse could be a particularly appropriate medium for a disabled or a traumatized self. Lacking the troublesome directness of a traditional autobiography, where the narrating "I" and the narrated "I" are unambiguously linked to the extratextual author by means of Lejeune's autobiographical pact, the more flexible novelistic discourse offers an opportunity for the autobiographer to create a distance with his or her disabled body. On the one hand, the indirectness of novelistic expression, such as the use of a different name, changes in biographical data, and so on, minimizes the trauma of approaching an already troubled relationship with the autobiographical body. On the other hand, claiming that one's disability belongs to the protagonist or the narrator, and not to the author, helps the autobiographer to engage in a dialog with the defective body and to analyze its impact on the construction of autobiographical subjectivity more objectively.

In the case of Yarid's narrative, Saada's perceived unattractiveness practically dictates the course of her life – her choice of profession, her love relationships, and her national affiliation. The genre of novel makes it possible to emphasize and build on certain biographical facts in order to create a convenient setting for addressing and perhaps resolving the issues of disability. For instance, Saada's stay in Cairo during her college years (Yarid studied in the Fuad First University from 1944 to 1949) provides the protagonist with an ideal setting for her physical defect: in Egypt, her "fat body" and "dark skin" are a norm, she does not feel alienated or othered because of her appearance, as when she is surrounded by her beautiful slim mother, sister, and their friends in Jerusalem and Beirut.

As we have already established, in *Improvisations* the body's ugliness does not comply with the biomedical paradigm of physical disability. Here, the pathological aspect of the autobiographical subject is constructed as a *visual* defect – not functioning strictly as a physical impairment in the way blindness or paralysis do, but mainly producing a significant psychological effect. This certainly does not reduce this disability's role in the autobiographical act. The distorted perception of her appearance forges the autobiographical subject's worldview, frames her relationships with others and her own body, and even causes ambiguity with regard to national affiliation (she calls herself "a chameleon" when talking about national identity). In Saada's words, "Doesn't the way you look affect the way you think and the way you think affect the way you look?" (Yarid 1997: 83).[12] Even the protagonist's name serves as an epitome of her ugliness. Whereas the name "Saada" in Arabic means "happiness," she associates her name with another word of the same linguistic root: *saʿdānah* – "a female ape" – as other children nicknamed her:

> Saada! Did they choose that name because I was ugly, ugly from the day I was born? . . . Did Papa ever hear them making fun of me at school, chanting in the playground: "Saada the monkey, she hops around the pantry."

> I hated my name, I hated my aunt because of that name, and now I hated myself. The right name for the right person! (*ibid.*: 7–8)

In Yared's autopathography, the autobiographical subject's physical disability, which is represented in a psychologically troublesome relationship with her (imaginarily) deformed body, generates a desire and a need to articulate her selfhood. As Thomas Couser pointed out, "whatever form it takes, bodily dysfunction tends to heighten consciousness of self and of contingency" (Couser 1997: 5). Therefore, one may assume that a physical deformity accelerates the autobiographer's urge to explore subjectivity. I will focus my discussion on three central aspects of autobiographical identity in Yarid's text: the initiation of the autobiographical act, prompted by this body's *otherness* with regard to surrounding bodies; the projection of this otherness onto all other, non-physiological aspects of life, as her body becomes the core element of her selfhood; and the body's symbolic "recovery" from ugliness by contamination with imaginary cancer.

The autobiographical subject sees her ugliness as an unfortunate condition she was born with, which means that there is not a clearly delineated split into a "before" and an "after" on her autobiographical timeline – in other words, there is no pre-trauma self to go back to. Saada's distorted perception of her body was gradually constructed by her mother's and later her sister's judgment of it. Her painful awareness of her appearance stems from numerous traumatic experiences with the family, which could be interpreted as a form of an emotional abuse. For instance, both her mother and her sister constantly tried to "fix" her body and mold it to their liking by forcing her to diet: "Take it easy on the bread and the butter, Saada. Don't you see how fat you're getting?" (Yarid 1997: 4). Not surprisingly, this precipitated her compulsive eating habits and an openly hostile attitude toward her torturers:

> They hate me, they hate me. They're trying to starve me. Food – my only pleasure! I felt the saliva gathering in my mouth, covering inside my cheeks, my tongue, the back of my throat – the taste of butter and apricot jam, the bread and the fruit tartness softening the sweetness of the sugar. And eating, how could I not love it! (*ibid.*: 5)

Saada's physical features stand in sharp contrast with her mother's: "Mama was tall, slender. Her coal-black hair accentuated her pale skin and green, almond eyes. She was a queen. And when age began to streak her black tresses with grey, it only made her more majestic" (*ibid.*: 5).[13] Suha the younger sister – in Lebanese Arabic her name means "a star, a princess," quite fittingly – inherited her mother's appearance: "she turned to look at herself in the mirror. She took in her slim figure, her long, slender neck, her attractive features, green eyes, and upturned nose" (*ibid.*: 8). These two iconic beauties frequently and openly express their disappointment with the older daughter's appearance, and so do their friends and relatives. It is not Saada's body *per se* that makes it a disappointment, but it is this body's *dissimilarity* with the mother's and sister's bodies that construes it as deformed. Thus, the autobiographical body exhibits a *relationally constructed* disability where the subject's realization of her deformity is initiated and shaped by others:

> [I] stood before the mirror, examining my reflection: medium height, slightly plump; sleek black hair gathered in two braids; olive complexion; small, dark, sparkling eyes; a small, snubby nose; and average-sized mouth with full lips . . . "Am I beautiful? Ugly? Plain?" So I was ugly. Sitt Widad thought I was ugly. Mama thought I was ugly. I scrutinized the image reflected in the mirror: my ugly face; my short, fat, ugly body. (*ibid.*: 7)

An object of ridicule and humiliation at home and among her friends, Yarid's Saada strives to find a place where her appearance would be interpreted as "normal", which appears to be possible only by physically distancing herself from her mother and sister – her beautiful antipodes who play the crucial role in the ugly–beautiful dichotomy. Saada travels to Cairo to study at the university, just like Nazik Yarid did, and Egypt becomes a place where she truly feels at home: "Since nobody at the university knew my mother or sister, no one could compare me to them. Dark-skinned? The Egyptian women were dark-skinned. Fat? No one disapproved of obesity in Egypt" (*ibid.*: 24–5). Not only does her body make her an insider, but she also adopts the Egyptian accent when speaking in Arabic and, as a result, she is mistaken for an Egyptian girl by fellow students: "you look Egyptian and you have an Egyptian accent" (*ibid.*: 24).[14]

The problematic nature of bodily difference constructed in her native

Jerusalem is that it generates an augmented sense of isolation. Saada's disability, being a social construct rather than a medical condition, marks her as a social outcast – she sees herself as "a stranger among my people" (*ibid.*: 30).[15] These feelings of alienation intensified during her stay in Egypt. Here she attempts to erase her otherness by any means, and to completely assimilate with the society that does not see her as an outsider: "Saada the monkey? No, the chameleon . . . I had only spent three months in Cairo and already I had an Egyptian accent" (Yarid 1997: 24). She goes as far as wanting to dissolve her individual self in a collective identity, which she tries to achieve by participating in Egyptian student demonstrations. Instead of being completely different, she desires to be absolutely identical:

> I concentrated all my strength in my throat, erasing the physical, sexual, and cultural differences between me and them. *I wasn't Saada – my own individuality was lost, dissolved in that awe-inspiring and tumultuous sea.* I repeated the slogans without thinking, moved along without thinking, knew nothing but the fanaticism that grew stronger and stronger and the fire in my voice, our voice. (*ibid.*: 25)[16]

However, the autobiographical subject's self-identification as "different, not like everybody else" – a label she continues to apply to herself – proves to be impossible to escape. Saada eventually comes to the realization that difference provides her with a solid core around which she can assemble her (disfigured) identity. It is an essential element of her self, which cannot be erased no matter how hard she tries: "I thought of myself as one of them because I was estranged from my family. I laughed at my stupidity – did I really know [what] 'here' [means]? Did I really fit in 'here'? The chameleon, after all, can change only its color" (*ibid.*: 41). Saada's (imagined) deformity, articulated through the beautiful–ugly binary, imposes difference onto autobiographical identity as its fundamental attribute. Yarid's autobiographical narrator makes an attempt to come to terms with her bodily image by assigning a positive meaning to her dissimilarity – she begins to compare it with "naturalness":

> Should I put on lipstick? Eyeliner? . . . It wouldn't be me. They would know that I was trying to copy them . . . I didn't need that. I replaced my feelings

> of inferiority with an outlook which would restore my self-confidence. I was different: I was natural . . . I was the odd one out, a stranger, the one who's different because she's natural. (*ibid*: 9–10)

The beautiful–ugly visual dualism is now substituted by a more substance-based binary of artificial–natural. Saada's association of her unattractiveness with naturalness implies that beautiful equals artificial (fake, superficial), and the mother is a vivid example of these qualities – she is physically beautiful but she also is a shallow hypocrite: "I couldn't understand my mother's inconsistent attitude: she associated with the poor and needy, yet she forbade me to make friends with a girl whose father was a laundryman?" (*ibid*.: 5)[17]

Another strategy to resolve the autobiographical body's unattractiveness is her persistent application of the cultural stereotype where "ugly" equals "smart" and "beautiful" equals "stupid." This semantic relationship is established through Suha's voice when she defines Saada's difference not through her unappealing looks, but through her intelligence which stood in sharp contrast with Suha's underperformance at school:

> "Saada Rayyis's sister?" I nodded in reply; then came the familiar response . . . "Are you intelligent and hardworking like her?" Like her? Intelligent? . . . [She is] so arrogant! How I hated her! Our teachers – it never occurred to any of them that comparing me with Saada only increased my contempt, loathing, and resentment . . . As usual, Saada's grades were excellent. As usual, my grades were dismal. (Yarid 1992: 56–7)

An important consequence of physical disability or defect is that it also determines the configuration of one's identity, including all its non-bodily aspects as well. Thomas Couser argued that the subjectivity's relationship with an abnormal body is at the core of autopathography, which challenges and broadens our understanding of human selfhood:

> life-writing about illness and disability promises to illuminate the relations among body, mind, and soul; indeed, it is significant not just because it represents a relatively new category of life stories, but also because it promises to foreground somatic experience in a new way by treating the body's form and function . . . as fundamental constituents of identity. (Couser 1997: 12)

As I argued earlier, the distorted autobiographical body in Yared's narrative defines its experience in juxtaposition with "normal" bodies, and situates dissimilarity at the core of identity. The autobiographical subject "Saada" projects her physiological difference onto all aspects of life – it becomes a lens through which she views her self. Thus, her dark skin generates a sense of national consciousness: her physical feature is seen as an authentic, defining element of her ethnicity which sets her apart from foreign European – colonial – bodies. When her mother's English friend, Mrs. Setney, treats Saada as a servant, she explains such behavior as caused by her physical appearance: "Did they treat me like that because I was ugly, dark-skinned, because I wasn't blond like her, like my friend Kristel?" (Yarid 1992: 14). Similarly, when her German schoolmate Kristel chooses a blonde girl over Saada as her best friend, the protagonist sees this as also stemming from her *ethnic* ugliness. Therefore, the autobiographical subject's physical deformity gives her a heightened sense of national and ethnic belonging. She recognizes her body as different from blond and fair-skinned foreigners, just like her Arab identity is different from that of European colonizers:

> But as time went by, I started to become aware of something that went beyond my ugliness . . . I knew that my country, Palestine, had a British ruler and Arab subjects . . . Were ruler and subject equal? My maturity helped me forget the pain and insult to my pride Mrs. Setney and Kristel had made me feel, but it could not wipe out the insult to my national pride. My passion grew with the way that this nationalism was expressed, in my language, then by the literature of that language. (*ibid.*: 16)

One more episode that illustrates Saada's projection of her physical dissimilarity onto national affinity is a discovery that her European classmates completely misunderstand modern Arabic poetry and Tayyib Saleh's novel *Season of Migration to the North* – literary works that she picked for class discussion. Her difference, initially established as the essential attribute of the body, transcends physical boundaries and manifests itself in a fundamental dissimilarity from Westerners – not only visually, such as their complexion and hair color, but most importantly, *in substance* – their worldview, traditions, culture. Saada comes to realize that difference occurs not only on a physical level, but it also frames her national identity, and, in turn, initiates her self-awareness as a colonized subject:

> It all came back to me: the history lesson about Clive of India, the image of Kristel and Mrs. Setney, the pain of humiliation and degradation that not even long years had been able to wipe out, and the deep hatred I had buried deep inside because the weak have no other recourse but to bury their hatred. "Because I'm not one of you." (*ibid.*: 22)

Gradually, all other aspects of autobiographical identity become defined through difference, including her religious affiliation. Saada is Christian and she grows up in Jerusalem and Beirut – both cities having substantial Christian populations, but she does not see her religious affinity as a category of belonging. Instead, it is constructed in a way that, once again, emphasizes her essential and absolute difference. Ali, the man she fell in love with, is a Muslim. When he leaves her and gets engaged to another woman, Saada cannot explain his choice by her unattractiveness because the other woman is not beautiful either. Nevertheless, Saada insists on rationalizing Ali's rejection as stemming from her dissimilarity – if not physical, then religious:

> Like me she is a teacher of Arabic language and literature. Like me she is neither rich nor beautiful. But unlike me she isn't a Christian. The difference in religion doesn't stop us becoming friends . . . I didn't realize that religion might prevent love or marriage . . . Naïve and idealistic. Ali is right. How he has changed! Or perhaps he hasn't. (*ibid.*: 97)

Saada's choice of profession, too, is essentially dictated by her body's abnormality. Despite her mother's insistence that she studies medicine – a science that is most closely related to human anatomy, Saada decides to become a teacher of Arabic language and literature – a much more abstract discipline. Even when she reads books on the history of medicine, brought to her by the mother, Saada is preoccupied with the intellect of scholars who contributed to the evolution of sciences, rather than the composition of the human body, which, despite her thirst for knowledge, she persistently avoided studying during her school years:

> *The Medicine of the Ancient Egyptians*, *The History of Arab Medicine*, *Magic and Medicine*. I read them furiously. I read them because they talked about man's intellect, his beliefs, his imagination. Mama didn't know that I had never read one book in school about the human body, chemistry, or the

> other sciences which served as a grounding for studying medicine . . . The result was that I got my high school diploma without ever knowing what oxygen, carbonic acid, virility, the collarbone, or the jugular vein were. (*ibid.*: 13)

Later, Yarid's narrator clearly indicates that literature and, with it, the spiritual (read body-less) nature of this discipline reflected her self-perception: "Wasn't the reason I loved literature because it mirrored my inner self?" (*ibid.*: 85).

However, numerous efforts to free her self from the deformed physicality do not seem sufficient, and in order to take control over her body and erase its abnormality a radical step is taken: the autobiographical body becomes contaminated with breast cancer. The significance of *Improvisations on a Missing String* in its treatment of the autobiographical somatic self lies precisely in its unorthodox approach to a cancerous body. Unlike many Western self-referential narratives of illness written by women,[18] where cancer is viewed as polluting the body and compromising the female identity, here the disease has an opposite meaning: the cancering of the autobiographical body aims to fix it by ridding it of ugliness. The disease makes it slim and gives the dark skin the desperately desired whiteness. This new body is so different from the old one that she approaches it in the third person: "Her frail hands perfectly still on top of the bedsheet – they seem so pale . . . Her face haggard, translucent, and the cheekbones so prominent above sunken hollows which, perhaps only recently, were two plump cheeks" (*ibid.*: 3).

Such a fundamentally different perception of cancer with respect to the female body perhaps lies in the fact that in Yarid's text cancer does not reference a real-life medical condition experienced by the autobiographer. Rather, it functions as a metaphorical tool, utilized to erase the undesirable qualities of the autobiographical body. But even taking into consideration that in *Improvisations* the autobiographical subject's disease is a rhetorical framework, the way in which breast cancer participates in the identity construction is remarkable nonetheless. When the disease affects such a distinctly feminine organ, it is usually perceived as an imminent danger to female subjectivity. Having examined many autobiographical narratives of cancer, Thomas Couser points out that "in addition to breast cancer's threat to life, its striking an organ distinctive of women makes it a potential threat to a woman's identity. Cancer – and the usual surgical 'treatments,' lumpectomy and mastectomy – can literally and symbolically disfigure a woman" (Couser 1997: 36). On the contrary, when Yarid's Saada falls ill, her cancer becomes instrumental in the identity-making process by eliminating the physical abnormality. Here it functions, paradoxically, as means of *purification* – as opposed to the expected contamination of the body. Whereas in the rest of the narrative Saada speaks in the first person, here she addresses herself as "the patient," "it," "she," and even "a stone," stressing the fact that it is specifically her body (an "it") that is affected by and must go through cancer in order to overcome its deformity. In addition to that, it brings Saada closer to her mother, who suffered from the same disease: cancer finally makes their appearances identical.[19]

In conclusion, Nazik Saba Yarid's autopathography shows that the autobiographical body's deformity can take various forms: it does not necessarily have to be a biomedical condition, such as a missing limb or deafness, in order to have a fundamental impact on one's selfhood. The degree of trauma behind physical abnormality and its role in the autobiographical act are defined primarily, if not exclusively, by the subject's self-perception. Finally, Yarid's text offers a different conceptualization of otherness – one rooted in the human body. As the author pointed out in one of the interviews, "I chose the title of my *Improvisations* because I felt I was the missing string. I identify with something that others don't identify with."[20]

4 Conclusion: My Body is My Own?

Both *Bare Bread* and *Improvisations on a Missing String* put autobiographical bodies on display and root identities in corporeality. These negotiations of identity illustrate that in contemporary Arab self-referential discourse the bodily is no longer silenced: on the contrary, it is gradually becoming a distinct marker of personal identity and an expanding category within Arab autobiographical production. But at the same time, the authors Muhammad Shukri and Nazik Yarid configure their autobiographical bodies in distinctly different ways. In addition to offering two different modes of corporeality – sexual and aesthetic – these autobiographical narratives also have different takes on the semantic relationship between the private and the collective.

As we have seen, Shukri's work offers a radically subversive take on the genre – not only by means of graphic depictions of sexuality, but also on a deeper discursive level by deconstructing and mercilessly mocking the fundamental elements of the conventional discourse – the coming-of-age story, family structure, and representation of "group identity," among others. Although the individual and private autobiographical body is front and center in the narrative, Shukri's autobiographical identity still has a very strong notion of the collective, resembling – ironically – the identity-making processes in autobiographical works that focus on nationalism. If Minah's and Abu Zayd's self-representational discourse includes Syrian and Moroccan national narratives and voices the colonized subaltern, Shukri weaves the story of the Moroccan underworld and voices its inhabitants – prostitutes, thieves, drug dealers, and other invisible outcasts of the society proper. Shukri talked about his "message" in an interview with Idwar Kharrat:

> The characters of my autobiography are not content with their immoral condition. They are not being corrupt out of pleasure. They do not rejoice in being corrupt, but they become so through horrible social oppression. Their life is turned into a commodity and that is why they lose their humane values. And my life among them could be considered an example [of such]. (Shukri 1986: 73)

Nazik Saba Yarid's *Improvisations on a Missing String*, on the other hand, presents a very different autobiographical paradigm in its focus on the subject's individuality and uniqueness with regard to bodily features. If Shukri's book, however subversive and outrageous a discourse it may formulate, still heavily incorporates the collective in the identity-making process, then, Yarid employs autobiographical body to establish the subject's individualism. The protagonist's desire to establish any semblance of belonging – either with her family, or her local community, or her nation – remains unfulfilled, which, according to her, is rooted in her physical dissimilarity. While initially being the source of a painful identity crisis, this bodily distortion is elevated to a discursive tool and a signifier of an overtly individualist selfhood. The examples of Muhammad Shukri's and Nazik Saba Yarid's very different uses of autobiographical body illustrate that corporeality has not only entered the realm of contemporary Arab autobiographical discourse, but it also demonstrates different dimensions (sexual versus aesthetic) and representational qualities (collective versus individual).

Notes

1. Ramzi Salti argues that in Arabic literature it was "the first published work in many centuries to address homosexuality in such a blatantly noncloseted manner" (Salti 2001: 255).
2. Qabbani's erotic poetry was continuously censored for his refusal to comply with the norms of conventional romanticized Arabic poetry. One of his *qaṣā'id* (poems) – *'Inda al-Jidār* (*At the Wall*) – was banned from Egyptian textbooks as late as 1990 (Wild 1995: 252 fn. 5).
3. Paul Bowles translated Muhammad Shukri's autobiographical novel into English under the title *For Bread Alone* (1993). However, I use my own English version of the title, which is closer to the Arabic original – *Bare Bread*. The English translation was criticized in Arabic literary circles because Bowles made some modifications to the original text, which, besides the creative freedoms he took with the Arabic original, could be rooted in orientalist ideologies. For example, there is evidence of Bowles' exoticizing of the text in line with the audience's typical expectations from a "third-world" literary piece and which sustains the mystical otherness of Oriental narratives. Nirvana Tanoukhi noticed that differences between the Arabic and English texts "recur in recognizable patterns and point to the diverging horizons of expectations" (Tanoukhi 2003: 129). Therefore, I provide my own translations of the Arabic text. Meanwhile, an exploration of divergences between Shukri's and Bowles' texts could be an interesting subject of study elsewhere.
4. For instance, in his seminal work *Masculinities*, R. W. Connell identifies four categories of masculine discourse – hegemonic, subordinate, complicit, and marginalized – rooted in established societal patterns (Connell 1995: 76–81). Lawrence R. Schehr explores "the figure of the vulnerable white male body" (Schehr 1997: 4) in his book *Parts of an Andrology: On Representations of Men's Bodies*, where he indicated that his research aims were to "to provide a counterpoint in gender studies to readings of the representation of the female body" (*ibid.*: 4).
5. Judith Butler, Elizabeth Grosz, and Allison Kimmich, among others.
6. Quoted from Ahmed Shiha's speech (a member of the education committee in the People's Assembly) during the meeting on March 2, 1999, on the

matter of banning *al-Khubz al-Ḥāfi* from educational curricula in Egypt. For more, see Samia Mehrez's *Egypt's Culture Wars: Politics and Practice* (Mehrez 2010).

7. This fact is taken from Civantos (2006: 39).
8. The translation of this and all subsequent passages from the novel are my own. I provide the Arabic original of this fragment to illustrate Shukri's telegraphic style:

   أحسست بوجع قاس في معدتي ماشياً تحت شمس كاوية ... التقطت سمكة صغيرة جافة ومُداسة. شممتها. رائحتها مقيئة. سلختها. مضغتها باشمئزاز. طعمها نتن. أمضغها وأمضغها دون أن أقوى على بلعها. حجارة ناتئة تؤلم أخمص قدمي. أمضغ السمكة كعلكة. تفلتها. رائحتها بقيت في فمي. ألوك فراغ فمي. ألوك وألوك. أمعائي تبقبق. تبقبق وتبقبق. دخت. دخت وتدفق الماء الأصفر من فمي وأنفي. تنفست بعمق. قلبي يخفق بعنف ... العرق يسيل على وجهي، يسيل ويسيل.

   (Shukri 1982: 100–1).
9. Many contrasting examples can be found in traditional Arabic autobiographies. For instance, in Ahmad Amin's *My Life*, childhood memories are intertwined with scholarly examinations of particular social conditions: "The birth rate in our neighborhood was conversely proportionate to the wealth of the classes, the poorest one having the most . . . the death rate was high like the birth rate. Health conditions were as bad as could be" (Amin 1978: 30). In other words, in conventional autobiographical works, the "adult narrator" dominates and leads the story.
10. In Hanna Minah's *Baqāyā Ṣuwar*, discussed in Chapter 1, the protagonist's mother is pictured in a similar manner: she is a Christ-like figure who lives for her children.
11. Having consulted all available biographical sources, I did not find any references indicating that the author Nazik Saba Yarid had herself had such experiences with an oncological illness.
12. This and subsequent quotes are taken from Stuart Hancox's English translation of *Taqāsīm ʿala Watar Dāʾiʿ*.
13. There is a striking similarity in the description of the mother's physical features in *Improvisations on a Missing String* and Yarid's autobiography *Dhikrayāt Lam Taktamil* (*An Incomplete Memoir*) (the latter describes the mother's looks in her later years). In fact, the autobiography begins with a very detailed portrayal of the mother's appearance, which only highlights the importance of both the mother–daughter relationship and the author's relationship with the physical aspect of identity. I provide both excerpts in Arabic for comparison, as well as my English translation of the *Dhikrayāt Lam Taktamil* fragment.

From *Improvisations on a Missing String*:

الماما: قامة طويلة ممشوقة، شعر أسود فاحم يلفت النظر إلى بشرتها البيضاء وعينيها اللوزيتين الخضراوين. كانت ملكة. وحين بدأ الزمن يمزج خيطانه البيضاء بخصل شعرها الأسود ازدادت جلالاً.

(Yarid 1992: 9).

From *An Incomplete Memoir*:

أمامي صورة امرأة في العقد الثاني من عمرها: الشعر بُنّي أجعد قصير، الوجه جميل جداً، صافي البشرة، دقيق الأنف مستقيمه فوق فم رقيق الشفتين، تعلوهما ابتسامة خفيفة. ويبدو الحاجبان كأنهما رُسما رسماً... ثم العينان! عينان خضراوان واسعتان ثاقبتان تشعّان ذكاء وعزيمة...

In front of me is a picture of a woman in the second half of her life: curly short brown hair, a very beautiful face, glowing skin, straight thin nose above the mouth of delicate lips, elevated in a light smile. And the eyebrows look like they have been painted on . . . And then the eyes! Piercing green wide eyes radiating intelligence and determination' (my translation). (Yarid 2008: 15).

14. The author also talks about her experiences of assimilation with the Egyptians in her autobiography *An Incomplete Memoir* (Yarid 2008: 95–6).
15. Here I modified Hancox's translation which says "a stranger in my own family," and made it closer to the Arabic original "*gharībah bayna ʾahlī*" (Yarid 1992: 41), where the word *ʾahl* has a broader meaning than "family" and could also mean "people" or "nation."
16. My emphasis.
17. This particular episode – the mother forbidding Saada to be friends with the laundry ironer's daughter – is repeated word for word in Yarid's autobiography, which once again points to the autobiographical nature of *Improvisations*: "I was confused. My mother who runs to any opportunity to help the poor, enters their homes, and makes remarkable efforts to help them, forbids me to befriend a girl because she is an laundry ironer's daughter!" (Yarid 2008: 24); my translation of the following excerpt from the Arabic text:

    ذهلت. أمّي التي تركض لخدمة الفقراء، تدخل بيوتهم وتبذل جهوداً فائقة لمساعدتها، ترفض أن أصادق فتاة لأنها ابنة كوّاء!

18. Arabic literature also has examples of autobiographies that are centered on experiences with breast cancer: for instance, *Fa la Tansa Allah* (*Do Not Forget God*) by the Moroccan writer Layla Hulw (for a detailed study of this work, see Fedwa Malti-Douglas' *Medicines of the Soul*).

19. Nazik Saba Yarid's mother did suffer and die from cancer, as the author wrote in her autobiography (Yarid 2008: 32–3).
20. The quote is taken from the following online source at: http://arablit.wordpress.com/2012/12/21/lebanese-novelist-nazik-yared-on-starting-late-and-writing-with-honesty, accessed July 22, 2012.

3

Mapping Autobiographical Subjectivity in the Age of Multiculturalism

> With their memories perpetually on overload, exiles see double, feel double, are double. When exiles see one place they're also seeing – or looking for – another behind it. Everything bears two faces, everything is shifty, because everything is mobile, the point being that exile, like love, is not just a condition of pain, it's a condition of deceit . . . exiles can be supremely mobile, and they can be totally dislodged from their original orbit, but in this jittery state of transience, they are thoroughly stationary
>
> Andre Aciman, *Letters of Transit*

1 Hybridity and Polyphony of a Multicultural Selfhood

Jamal Mahjoub, the award-winning British Sudanese novelist, wrote in his *Travelling with Djinns* about the struggles of living between the cultures:

> I sometimes think I envy those people who know where they belong; writers who have a language and a history that is granted them with no catches, no hooks . . . Along with a nation of willing accomplices, compatriots who see their own fate and that of their nation's history and literary tradition reflected in the mirror of the writer's labor. It is all so neatly sewn up. Of course, I enjoy no such privilege. I belong to that nomad tribe, the great unwashed, those people born in the joins between continental shelves, in the unclaimed interstices between time zones, strung across latitudes. A tribe of no fixed locus, the homeless, the stateless. I have two passports and quite a variety of other documents to identify me, all of which tell the world where I have been, but not who I am, nor where I am going to. My language is a bastard tongue of necessity, improvisation, bad grammar and continual misunderstandings. I am a stranger wherever I go. (Mahjoub 2004: 4–5)

The Russian American writer Vladimir Nabokov, who created two versions of his autobiography – in English and then in Russian – shared with his Russian reader the pain behind his bilingualism:

> When in 1940 I decided to switch to English, my difficulty was that previous to this, for more than fifteen years, I was writing in Russian and during all these years I left my own personal imprint on this instrument of mine, my facilitator. When transitioning into a different language, I therefore rejected not just the language of Avvakum, Pushkin, Tolstoy or Ivanov, my nanny, Russian journalism – in other words, I did not simply abandon the common language, but my individual, intimate dialect. The long habit to express myself in my own fashion left me unsatisfied with the patterns of the newly chosen language. The horrible difficulties of the upcoming metamorphosis and the terror of separation from the living domesticated pet have at first put me in a state of being that I cannot even talk about. (Nabokov 1954: 7–8)[1]

Indeed, those torn between places, cultures, and languages are destined to experience the most torrid and intricate negotiations with their inescapably fragmented, polyphonic selves. A lack of a singular space to situate one's subjectivity and a singular language to articulate this subjectivity, forces one's selfhood into a permanent state of exile. In our times of multiculturalism, massive migrations, and global economic, political, and technological transitions, the binary of homeland and exile is becoming increasingly vague. As Magda Stroinska points out, exile could be "any kind of displacement, voluntary departure or compulsory expulsion, from one's native land, expatriation, or simply finding oneself outside the borders of one's native country, not because one had moved abroad but because the borders were moved" (Stroinska 2003: 95). Naturally, such a broad variety of displacement scenarios produce diverse autobiographical representations of cultural displacement. In this chapter I examine three literary works that illustrate a remarkable plurality of Arab autobiographical narratives of exile, informed by cultural exchanges between East and West: Sumayyah Ramadan's *Leaves of Narcissus* (2001); Batul al-Khudayri's *A Sky So Close* (1999); and Ihab Hassan's *Out of Egypt* (1986). The state of exile is a state of perpetual transit where the displaced subject is forced to cross borders – be it geographic, cultural, or linguistic. To be in exile means to live on the edges between different cultures, peoples, societies, and languages. Autobiographical texts analyzed in this chapter offer three distinct types of *borderline* and fragmented identity, generated by different forms of displacement.

Drawing on Mikhail Bakhtin's theories of hybridity and polyphony, I explore the multiplicity of narrative voices in the context of fragmented autobiographical identity. According to Bakhtin, hybridization is "a mixture of two social languages within the limits of a single utterance, an encounter, within the arena of an utterance, between two linguistic consciousnesses, separated from one another by an epoch, by social differentiation or by some other factor" (Bakhtin 1981: 358). I propose to situate the "social languages" in the framework of the author's multiculturalism and multilingualism, where a separation between linguistic consciousnesses is a separation between fractured autobiographical selves, and where the autobiographical act performs as an utterance. An exploration of such a hybridity would offer an insight into different modes of multicultural and multilingual selfhood and its articulation through the medium of autobiographical narrative.

Bakhtin's concept of polyphony, based on his reading of Dostoyevsky, also offers an interesting and useful framework for studying the phenomena of multicultural selfhood:

> *A plurality of independent and unmerged voices and consciousnesses, a genuine polyphony of fully valid voices is in fact the chief characteristic of Dostoyevsky's novels.* What unfolds in his works is not a multitude of characters and fates in a single objective world, illuminated by a single authorial consciousness; rather *a plurality of consciousnesses, with equal rights and each with its own world,* combine but not at all merged in the unity of the event. (Bakhtin 1984: 6)[2]

Projecting the Dostoyevsky polyphonic model onto autobiographical discourse offers a method of approaching the fragmented types of selfhood as composed of separate selves – each offering a distinct voice, each claiming "equal rights" on autobiographical identity.

Keeping in mind these conceptualizations of hybridity and polyphony, the subsequent sections of this chapter will demonstrate the articulation of displaced, bicultural and bilingual subjectivities in Ramadan's, al-Khudayri's, and Hassan's texts. My aim here is to examine how the notions of exile and displacement – be it physical or psychological – shape the articulation of selfhood for those situated between Arab and Western cultural terrains. Given the many differences between Arab and European or American contexts, what consequences do they entail for the formation of a borderline identity? In what ways do autobiographers choose to negotiate these cultural tensions? Finally, what are the types of texts that accommodate the culturally and linguistically fragmented identities? These questions are central to my critical inquiry in this chapter.

2 Shifting Spaces, Languages, and Identities in Sumayyah Ramadan's *Awrāq al-Narjis* (*Leaves of Narcissus*)

Sumayyah Ramadan's autobiographical novel *Awrāq al-Narjis* was first published in Arabic in 2001, and translated by Marilyn Booth into English as *Leaves of Narcissus* in the following year. The novel won one of the most prestigious literary awards in Egypt – the Naguib Mahfouz Prize. This, however, did not stop many Egyptian critics from attacking its author "as elitist and Westward-gazing" (Booth 2003: 48). Ramadan, who received her PhD in English from Trinity College, Dublin, centers her novel on Kimi – the autobiographical protagonist born into a well-off Cairene family. Numerous facts from the author's life point to the autobiographical nature of this novel: her background and growing up in Cairo; her bilingualism and Arabic–English translation work; and, finally, her graduate studies in Ireland. Moreover, Sumayyah Ramadan indicated in one of the interviews that she is the central subject of this work:

> The time had come when I could write about myself. The nineties provided the time and the place for people to write about their individual selves. So I became more confident that what I had written would not be strange or inappropriate. (Mehrez 2001)

One of the central features of Ramadan's autobiographical novel is its highly fragmented narration, constructed through a series of rapid shifts: temporal, from childhood to adulthood; spatial, between Cairo, Dublin, London, and Belfast; and narrative, between first and third person. With regard to spatial shifts, Kimi's border-crossing between Egypt and Ireland, and constant relocations from her parents' home in Cairo, to Belfast, to student dorms, and finally, to a mental hospital in Dublin generate autonomous selves in each of these locations, whereas antagonistic relationships between these multiple selves make it impossible to formulate a uniform identity.

In addition to that, the kaleidoscopic nature of Ramadan's narrative is emphasized by another type of border-crossing – the linguistic shifts between two languages, Arabic and English. Although the narrative is composed in Arabic, the English language also plays an important role in the text, mainly taking the form of intertextuality since the author uses numerous references to Western cultural contexts in general, and English and Irish literatures in particular. The autobiographer's two linguistic identities – or, in Bakhtin's terms, "linguistic consciousnesses" – stand in tense opposition, endlessly clashing and silencing each other. "All languages are mine and so I have no language," says Kimi (Ramadan 2002: 63).[3] These narrative shifts outline the protagonist's quest to situate her ruptured identity between the clashing categories of home and exile, where the two do not constitute an expected clearly defined binary but are fluid and constantly alternating elements. Here, the linguistic hybridity is semiotically damaging to the autobiographical subject as it imposes alienation and lack of belonging. *Leaves of Narcissus* is a narrative of an *absolute* exile where the autobiographical subject is unable to develop a sense of homeland either spatially or linguistically. Standing on the borderline between different places and cultures and torn between multiple selves, the autobiographical subject questions her very existence. The subject's displacement appears to be her permanent *state of being*, an essential quality of her selfhood.

In *Leaves of Narcissus*, Bakhtin's polyphony of voices translates into autonomous pieces of a fractured identity. This polyphony is problematized by the fact that the impossibility of merging these pieces into unity undermines the autobiographical act and threatens to erase the autobiographical subject. On the one hand, there is a nostalgia for a solid identity – "memory of oneness with the whole, and of being: before I became me and you, you became you" (Ramadan 2002: 26) – even though the desired uniformity is just an illusion. But, on the other hand, there is a realization that human selfhood is a fundamentally unstable category, lacking clearly defined boundaries:

> How do we shape limits for ourselves – edges to our beings – that will let us know, at their merest recollection, that each of us can assume our own clearly etched self, an inside and outside, knowable confines for the endurable – the possible – beyond which we cannot, need not, go? . . . I have no edges, no borders to separate my aches from the pain of others. (*ibid.*: 18)

This conflict between the desire to formulate a uniform identity and the impossibility of fulfilling such a desire culminates in the autobiographical subject's mental illness. The irresolvable polyphony of selves causes insanity, just like Kimi's Egyptian nanny warned her: "Don't look at your *nafs*[4] in the mirror too much, it will make you mad" (*ibid.*: 52).

Assigning a separate self to each of Kimi's locations – Cairo, Dublin, and the St. Patrick's mental hospital – systemizes the polyphony of autobiographical selves. Ramadan's autobiographical protagonist lives in the state of perpetual departure: "your room in your father's house is but a momentary dwelling that you do not own, and it is yours only until your departure is arranged" (*ibid.*: 73), and it is precisely the differences in sociocultural environments in all these places that inform stark dissimilarities between these autobiographical selves. When in her childhood home, Kimi is a shy introverted girl whose identity is defined through her fundamental differences with family members and through her desire to associate with her nanny Amna. Her childhood story alternates between the first and third person, and therefore the narrative becomes a dialog between the narrating "I" and the narrated "I." Recollections of childhood events are intertwined with the narrator's analysis of how these events affected Kimi's sense of displacement. She feels like she has nothing in common with her father, mother, and her siblings, and her alienation from family members is most obvious when she pretends not to be her father's real daughter: "my father – who raised me among his daughters as if I were one of them – felt pity for me" (*ibid.*: 24). She keeps coming back to this topic over and over again throughout the narrative, emphasizing that she is a stranger in her family home. She sees herself a different species – a "Medusa":

> They did not realize that I had begun to care for the boulder that filled me, such that I would sleep and sense the weight of my brain on the pillow. I would run my fingers carefully over my face, probing its features, knowing

> that as I slept it would change into the face of a statue carved from stone: a Medusa. Upon awakening, I would be instantly afraid for my eye to fall upon them. (*ibid.*: 10–11)

The only person in their household whom Kimi feels connection to is Amna – her illiterate but very outspoken nanny. Moreover, Kimi wants to *be* Amna. The narrator's reminiscences about her childhood are intertwined with her nanny's childhood story in a manner that makes their identities inseparable: "I have no edges, no borders to separate my aches from the pains of others. I am Amna, and I am her tale" (*ibid.*: 18–19). There is an interesting aspect to Amna's character: she is portrayed as basically stripped of human qualities, a bodiless spirit, an idea, rather than a person: "I don't remember seeing her eat, ever, except on very rare occasions. She ate as if she wasn't eating. She lived in our midst and I never knew when she used the bathroom and when she changed her clothes" (*ibid.*: 18). I believe that such references are not incidental, suggesting that Amna is nothing but a layer of Kimi's Cairene self.

In Dublin, we encounter a very different Kimi, now a graduate student. Her relocation to a different place generates a complete remaking of identity. The impulsive, stubborn, and rebelling girl metamorphoses into a cold, lonely, and eccentric woman. The narrator describes her in the third person with much detail:

> Here lived, for an entire and consecutive four years, an eccentric woman. One who didn't make overtures to anyone, nor did they to her. She imprisoned herself in her room, emerging only to answer a nightly telephone call – always precisely at eleven o'clock – from Beirut. On Mondays she received a bouquet of roses . . . She was a cold, distant, self-protective woman, yet on occasion a bout of human warmth would overpower her aloof demeanor . . . And then, all of a sudden she would draw back as if she regretted having made any overtures toward friendship. (*ibid.*: 29–30)

This woman – the "Dublin" autobiographical self – lives next door to the house where Oscar Wilde was born, and just like the Irish writer she dedicates herself to writing: "Inside, for days on end the lamp hardly ever went out. She was writing" (*ibid.*: 30). In fact, the multilayered and fragmented autobiographical constructed in Ramadan's novel resembles the Irish author himself since, in Jonathan Freedman's words, "there has been no figure of the past century so insistently multiple as Oscar Wilde" (Freedman 1996: 1). One may notice how Ramadan's perpetually metamorphosing autobiographical selves resonate with the Wilde-ian anti-essentialism: "the only thing that one really knows about human nature is that it changes. Change is the one quality we can predicate of it."[5] The autobiographical narrator's quest to find and establish her subjectivity seems to support Wilde's claim, formulated in his *The Soul of Man Under Socialism*, that "it is the realization of the self that serves as the true fulfillment of life's aim" (Roden 2004: 1). The autobiographical subject's search for selfhood in her mirror reflections – "all your life, you've spent your time staring into mirrors" (Ramadan 2002: 110) – and her subsequent insanity brings to mind Wilde's conception of self-destructive narcissism. These implicit references to Oscar Wilde indicate the presence of English-language discourses, which are likely to be inaccessible to the majority of Arabic-speaking readers, and, thereby, using Bakhtinian terminology, the presence of at least two "social languages" in the text.

Despite her psychological alienation from Cairo and her hopes of finding a home elsewhere, Kimi's feelings of displacement only intensify when she becomes an Egyptian expatriate in Ireland. She is emotionally isolated from her Irish peers and begins an affair with a Lebanese expatriate – yet another displaced character. To her own surprise, at some point she finds herself defending Arabs in response to her foreign friends' sarcastic comments about Libya. At the beginning of her stay in Ireland, Kimi attempts to construct a national identity for herself, notwithstanding her mockery of Egyptian heritage when living in Cairo – such as laughing at her father for organizing "authentic Egyptian lunches" for foreign delegations. But now that she is in Ireland, she is longing for a *concrete* homeland to fulfill the need to belong. However, soon enough she realizes that that homeland is nothing but an abstract concept, an illusion made up by people "to reflect affectionate yearning for a homeland of imagination" (Ramadan 2002: 32). Therefore, Kimi's attempts to formulate a clearly demarcated national identity are hopeless, especially since the country with which she is so desperately trying to associate[6] is as fragmented as her own self:

> Between the passages and the arteries of her heart a civil war rages among all Egypts. And she *is* all of them: if she rings her eyes with kohl, so, and

> becomes Nefertiti; if she plants fenugreek and lentils in anticipation of Eastern Easter; if she recites Arabic poetry; if she longs for her father's house in Alexandria; if she recalls her mother's tales of the trousseau of her Turkish mother-in-law, and her father's derisive words about al-Azhar, the venerable Muslim university in Cairo, and its families of adherents. (*ibid.*: 34)

When Dublin-based Kimi fails to Egyptianize herself, she takes on constructing an Irish identity. With this goal in mind, Kimi takes a white lover with a "long pale languid body," a man "untouched by the purifying blade of circumcision" (*ibid.*: 39). She also becomes close to her roommate Mary who embodies Kimi's Irishness – just like Amna was a representation of her Egyptian selfhood in Cairo. But when Kimi leaves Dublin, she also leaves this newly acquired white identity behind: "I left Mary behind – or perhaps I threw her out, and she complied without question" (*ibid.*: 38).

St. Patrick's mental hospital becomes yet another site of identity construction. At the hospital, the autobiographical narrator makes another attempt to (re)create an Egyptian identity: she pretends to be "Amna," a poor illiterate woman, and detaches herself from "Kimi," which was now "a name I recognized, though it lacked the ring of my own name in my ears" (*ibid.*: 23). She performs her Amna role to a tee: she refuses to read or write, and treats the foreign doctors as arrogant, educated representatives of a privileged social class – in spite of her actual belonging to upper-class society in Egypt: "[the doctor's] smile struck me as mocking, superior, arrogantly dismissive of the wretched daughters of the poor who have nothing to say about anything and whose families prevent them from attending school" (*ibid.*: 22–3). Nevertheless, she once again fails to establish a solid sense of identity and, completing the full circle of her spatial shifts, leaves to go back to Cairo. The autobiographical act in *Leaves of Narcissus* highlights the impossibility of delineating identity within the dimensions of physical space. In striking contrast to Hanna Minah's and Layla Abu Zayd's autobiographical narratives discussed in Chapter 1, Ramadan's autobiographical subject strongly resists the collective that she associates with belonging to a particular place. Thus, the impossibility of Kimi's acquiring a national identity is rooted in her strong sense of individualism: "We Egyptians. 'People in my country' . . .

Who is that 'we'? Precisely which 'people' in that country? I am them, and I'm not them. I am that 'we' and I'm also 'I' – just 'I'" (*ibid.*: 45).

So where can one find a site for identity construction if physical space is irrelevant? The autobiographical narrator is very well aware of the subject's fragmentality – "I cut Kimi into fourteen equivalent parts and threw her limbs into the waste bin" (*ibid.*: 45) – and strives to reconcile different pieces of her self on the leaves of paper, writing becoming the only place with a promise to solidify her identity: "The point at which one blade edge intersects the other requires something more than itself to attain its full identity: to make it cut. It needs paper" (*ibid.*: 65). She hopes that writing would give her "the joy of life," and would become a site of harmony where "equivalences of time, correspondences of place, find completion in a third roster" (*ibid.*: 66). But even this symbolic space is a zone of death where the two languages – English and Arabic – erase and silence each other. As Kimi laments to the reader, "all languages are mine and so I have no language" (*ibid.*: 63).

As I pointed out earlier, Ramadan's narrative is characterized by the autobiographical desire to formulate a solid, homogeneous identity. However, the shifting categories of physical and symbolic space, and the irreconcilable tension between the two "linguistic consciousnesses" lead to the ultimate failure to fulfill such a desire. Here the autobiographical act takes place between "writing and erasing," between life and death, between voicing and silencing, in a continuous process of killing and regenerating itself: "This self of yours is a thing you craft constantly. You carve it out, if need be, from nature, from the world around you" (*ibid.*: 102). In Paul de Man's words, autobiographical discourse is a means of a writer's "self-murder," *prosopopeia* being a defining trope of autobiography: "the dominant figure of the epitaphic or autobiographical discourse is . . . the *prosopopeia*, the fiction of the voice-from-beyond-the-grave" (de Man 1984: 77). In *Leaves of Narcissus*, this "grave" is exactly the location where the autobiographical resides. Death being the necessary final step in the autobiographical process, it is the only way to reach the ultimate completeness of selfhood. Louis Marin wrote about this paradox in his "Montaigne's Tomb, or Autobiographical Discourse":

> It is not possible to write, to transmit, to communicate death as one's own death. It is impossible and yet it is essential, for it is the ultimate experience

> in which each man singularly identifies himself in his particular truth, in his propriety. (Marin 1981: 55)

As if echoing de Man, Ramadan's autobiographical narrator, too, comes to recognize that only in dying, in killing and erasing her self – *all* her selves – can she attain the absolute wholeness of her selfhood:

> How can something be complete unless it dies? This is self-evident . . . we're made complete when we kill ourselves having so liked to claim that we were in this shape, or that, or that we still are. For there is something enticing about endings. The temptation to set in place the final endpoint, with our own hands, we kill ourselves, all by our selves. (Ramadan 2002: 111)

Death as a central trope of identity construction is highlighted for it is a recurring theme in the narrative. First, *Leaves of Narcissus* begins with the autobiographical narrator's announcing that she must kill herself in order to free her conflicting "I"s. Attempting to assemble the dispersed pieces of her selfhood into one uniform entity, she sentences all of her Kimis to death:

> As I prepare myself for death, I – little body – this one or that, or all of them in one, become one with me, inseparable; and I am faced with an awesome, fearful process. I must free them one from the other, and all from the inner spaces of my body and spirit. My self, upon which that voracious, duplicate, multiple devil feeds: she is me and she is not me . . . I must kill her and preserve my soul . . . How can I allow her to pass and endure her death rattles, and not die with her? (*ibid.*: 6)

Second, the narrator gradually obliterates each of the separate identities that Kimi formed in different locations – sometimes physically, sometimes metaphorically. The Cairene self of her childhood, represented in Amna, gets erased upon her relocation to Dublin: "I silenced Amna, nine-year old Amna, after I had given her a voice, I stifled and strangled her" (*ibid.*: 45). The embodiment of Kimi's Irish self Mary, too, cannot survive the process of autobiographical self-defacement: she commits suicide in Dublin. Third, the death of the subject is implied in the allegorical tale that Amna tells to little Kimi – the story of the king of the Atlas Mountains. When the king fell ill, a nameless physician cured him, and the latter's only request for compensation was a promise never to search for the physician's true identity. But the king's curiosity "kept him sleepless at night," he became obsessed with finding the physician's name – reiterating Kimi's obsession with finding her own "true self." The king's search resulted in his death on the doorstep of the physician's house: "when the King attempted his passage upward through the pipe, the shattered glass assailed his body . . . until blood ran along every inch of his body" (*ibid.*: 20).

Death renders the completeness of selfhood, and writing is the killing site of fragmented autobiographical selves. Leaves of paper – also representing leaves of narcissus[7] – constitute a symbolic location where autobiographical identities reside in a perpetual process of death and (re)creation. The polyphonic autobiographical "I" – Kimi-the-narrator, Kimi-the-protagonist, the autobiographer herself – writes only to erase and then to write again. Writing can never reach completeness, and neither can her selfhood:

> I write, I erase, I write. What if someone reads these leaves of paper before they're . . . complete? Writing is never complete and yet people manage to read it! . . . being demands that we never end . . . never. Being demands that we erase and return to writing and life once again, a writing and a life that might be. (*ibid.*: 111)

I argued that the function of writing as a site of death is also rooted in the autobiographer's bilingualism. Her two languages, Arabic and English, are entangled in a tense, painful relationship: "the words, Arabic and English, nouns and names, exerted a mutual pull from mere echo and assonance . . . then they distended, doubled back, collided, crashed, like ellipsis-tracings of atoms in orbit" (*ibid.*: 50). The very fact that the autobiographical operates in two languages undermines the effort to attain uniformity: if language and identity are inseparable, then the presence of more than one language inevitably means the presence of more than one identity. In Magda Stroinska's words, "the ability to speak several languages . . . implies access to multiple identities and more than one way of self-representation, suggesting that a multilingual and multicultural individual has several *faces* and wears several hats" (Stroinska 2003: 97).[8] Other Arab writers and intellectuals have also pointed out the problematic nature of bilingualism for the construction of autobiographical identity. In his article "No Reconciliation Allowed,"

Edward Said wrote about his difficulties in using Arabic and English simultaneously:

> Arabic, my native language, and English, my school language, were inextricably mixed: I have never known which was my first language, and I have felt fully at home in neither, although I dream in both. Every time I speak an English sentence, I find myself echoing it in Arabic, and vice versa. (Said 1999: 96)

For Kimi – Ramadan's autobiographical narrator-protagonist – the irresolvable tension between the two languages is, as in Said's case, brought about by her permanent state of displacement. *Leaves of Narcissus* is composed almost entirely in Arabic, for as Kimi puts it, "English was not fit . . . for telling of truth or for lying. For it is my language, and it is not my language" (Ramadan 2002: 45). But it certainly does not mean that English is absent from the text. On the contrary, it is integrated into the Arabic text in many different ways: the narrative offers numerous instances of intertextuality, most of which are foreign to Arabic cultural contexts. Among these are the imaginary dialogs with Joyce, translated fragments from his *Sirens*, parallels between Ramadan's autobiographical subject and Oscar Wilde, references to Salvador Dali's artwork *Narcissus* and to Sylvia Plath whom the "Irish Kimi" sees as a role model.

Since the narrative is written in Arabic, English-language discourses primarily function on the level of a separate cultural consciousness. But at times, the English language does communicate with the reader in a linguistically direct way: for instance, when the narrator talks about home by means of a popular English idiom: "and one of us said, in English, '*There's no place like home*'" (*ibid.*: 79),[9] which is a rather ironic allusion given that Kimi was talking about her *Egyptian* home. Indeed, "when you move between two languages, your odds of stumbling upon word affinities increase twofold" (*ibid.*: 50). This textual bilingualism poses an important question: who is the target audience of this autobiographical narrative? The Arabic–English hybridity seems to call for a reader who – like its author – is also situated on the borderline, trapped between two worlds, two cultures, and two languages.

3 Brown versus White: Reconciling Arab and English Identities in Batul al-Khudayri's *Kam Badat al-Samāʾ Qarībah (A Sky So Close)*

Kam Badat al-Samāʾ Qarībah, published in Arabic in 1999 and translated into English by Muhayman Jamil as *A Sky So Close* in 2001, was the first novel of Batul al-Khudayri, born in Baghdad in 1965 to an Iraqi father and a Scottish mother. The unnamed heroine-narrator of this autobiographical novel, like al-Khudayri herself, grows up in a family of mixed ethnic and linguistic background: an English mother and an Iraqi father. The linear narration, told from the first-person point of view, begins with the narrator's childhood in a small village near Baghdad and ends with her mother's death of breast cancer in London during the First Gulf War. In addition to numerous biographical similarities between al-Khudayri and her protagonist, the writer said in one interview that writing *A Sky So Close* was her way of reconciling herself with and accepting her bicultural subjectivity:

> I transformed my contradictions into words on paper and I produced my first novel *Kam Badat Al Sama Qareeba*. Instead of fighting the differences, I tried to mesh and to benefit from both cultures. One learns from experience and with time you learn how to make the most out of it. In the end, it is about bridging between cultures rather than denying them. (Khudayri 2005)

The autobiographical protagonist's complex relationship with her bicultural identity is at the core of the narrative. She finds herself on the borderline between her two languages and two ethnic identities: her Iraqi father's and her English mother's. Like Ramadan's Kimi, al-Khudayri's autobiographical subject also strives to stabilize her identity through the desired uniformity. To this end, she makes a conscious choice to prioritize her Iraqi self and attempts to erase any traces of Englishness. An interesting aspect of the autobiographical in *A Sky So Close* is that an affiliation with one national group and a separation from another are primarily based on physical markers, more specifically color, where brownness is constantly juxtaposed with whiteness. Al-Khudayri's protagonist identifies herself with the Iraqi environment and traditions and, showing resentment toward her mother's customs, refuses to accept (or at least, attempts to do so) everything associated with the "white"

English culture. Nonetheless, even as she chooses to self-identify with the Iraqi culture, to embrace her brown skin, and to communicate exclusively in Arabic, the white color is not completely absent from the identity-making process. She is yet another hybrid subject, unable to overcome her hybridity. Like in *Leaves of Narcissus*, the question of belonging appears to be at the center of the autobiographical act and, likewise, the autobiographical subject comes to understand that "it is a foolish notion, this question of belonging. We only belong to the shadows of our bodies which follow us around as long as we're alive" (Khudayri 2001: 201).[10] In this part of the chapter, I will argue the autobiographical hybridity in *A Sky So Close* as formulated through color-coded ethnicity (brown and white) and language (Arabic and English).

The representational discourse includes a clearly delineated binary between the protagonist's parents. Representing the conflicting ethnic and linguistic identities of the subject, the two are situated as polar opposites in all their characteristics – from skin color to eating habits. Naturally, these differences translate into deep and constant disagreements about everything, where the autobiographical protagonist always finds herself in the middle of their quarrels: they argue about her looks, her language, her manners, and her future education. Every single detail referencing the parents seems to reinforce their dichotomy: "My mother has toast with jam and butter. You chew on a small piece of brown *khubuz* – our local round, unleavened bread . . . As you lift your cup of tea, she lowers her cup of instant coffee" (*ibid.*: 15). The mother–father binary is so transparent and confrontational that one wonders if the two are constructed as antipodes on purpose, as a way to highlight the irreconcilable differences between the subject's Arab and English selves.

The protagonist's father appears to be imposing the Iraqi identity on his daughter by vigorously eliminating any signs of Englishness – including language and cultural customs – from her character and surroundings. He establishes her identity as affiliated with his *exclusively*. He tells his wife during one of their arguments: "don't you realize, woman, that we're now in the Arab, Islamic world, and she and I are Muslims?" (*ibid.*: 10). He sees the narrator as a successor to his – and only his – traditions and heritage, and excludes his English wife from her daughter's cultural upbringing: "woman, let her mingle with the peasants' traditions, there's no harm in that. Let her bond with the land, with the people and their animals, the way we were raised. For God's sake, let her see what you can't see!" (*ibid.*: 10). Likewise, he completely forbids the narrator to speak English at home, insisting that the mother teaches her to converse *only* in Arabic – ironic, considering that the mother hardly knows any Arabic at all:

> I said: – "Mummy, give me a plate and a 'spoon.'" As I said the word 'spoon' in my mother's language, I noticed the snarl coming from you [the father] . . . On another occasion, I made the mistake . . . of saying the word 'door' in English . . . You glared at me, then slammed it hard . . . [Father speaking to mother] "Have I not asked you time and time again to remind her to speak only in Arabic? . . . Why can't you teach her to say 'Shukran' instead of 'Thank you?'" (*ibid.*: 20–1)

Unsurprisingly, the protagonist comes to associate her cultural identity solely with the father's and begins to view her English mother as a cultural outsider – an alien element in her and her father's shared Iraqi environment: "[she] chuckled at the way she's expressed herself in broken Arabic" (*ibid.*: 60). English receives the status of "my mother's language," never referred to as a native tongue: "I finished reading my storybook about Alice in Wonderland. I had read it in my mother's English" (*ibid.*: 50). As she gradually distances herself from the mother's culture, she begins to project these attitudes onto other English people she encounters. For instance, she perceives her mother's friends, Millie and David, as foreigners and always addresses them as "they," never as "us": "How her [mother's] mood and tone of voice change as she welcomes them! She calls me over to greet them, asking me to shake hands and say hello in their language" (*ibid.*: 27). Everything about these British people is incomprehensible to her: she finds their customs of exchanging kisses between men and women odd, and she does not understand their humor. Eventually, the mother, too, completely withdraws from her daughter's upbringing, surrendering to the latter's dominant Arabness. She even gives up on teaching the narrator her native language: "My mother no longer insists that I learn her English" (*ibid.*: 60). And when, years later, the First Gulf War began and the two of them were living in London, the mother sees her daughter as an Iraqi – a foreigner in England: "I know it's an especially bad time for you now, when you're so worried about the news from your country" (*ibid.*: 193).

Therefore, it seems as if the autobiographical subject utterly adopts a singular solid Iraqi identity, having successfully erased all English affiliations. However, such uniformity is nothing but an illusion. This is a *desired* outcome of identity formation, attempted by the narrator and her father who fears that his daughter's "confusion" would make her a "laughingstock" (*ibid.*: 21). But in actuality, the efforts to rid the autobiographical subject of all cultural markers that would prevent it from solidifying its Iraqi self – the English language and customs – are unable to eliminate the subject's inherent hybridity. Although she self-identifies as Arab, it does not mean that others perceive her as such. In fact, she appears to be always seen as a foreigner, a *perpetual outsider* – both in London and in her Iraqi village.

Tormented by her parents' endless squabbles at home, the autobiographical protagonist finds comfort in her friendship with little Khaddouja, a girl from a very poor family of villagers who seem to have accepted her as one of their own. This friendship, rooted in their common "brownness," becomes a rebellion against her mother who, rather derogatorily, calls her little friend a "filthy lice-bearer." However, despite her resentment of her mother's disdainful attitude, the protagonist herself is not completely free from a certain sense of superiority over Khaddouja and she gradually begins to realize the cultural divide between the two of them. Thus, she cannot explain her mother's tales to Khaddouja, while the latter's grief over a dead cow is incomprehensible to her:

> I found it impossible to explain to Khaddouja the idea of the moving flock of sheep, or the thought of the suckling chickens. I also found out that what made me laugh meant nothing to her, and what hurt her was alien to me. When their cow Najma – "star" – died, the whole family grieved for it. I felt sorry that they had lost one of their miserable animals, but I couldn't understand how a cow could mean so much to them . . . I realized that things had started to change. (*ibid.*: 56)

These differences indicate that the autobiographical protagonist is, after all, as much an outsider to the villagers as she is to her mother's English friends. Although Khaddouja's family has always received her very warmly – "I never felt like a stranger when I was among them," apparently – that was nothing but a sign of villagers' traditional hospitality. They, too, perceive her as an alien because of her English mother: "They called us 'the foreign woman's family'" (*ibid.*: 7).

But perhaps the most important signifier of the subject's difference is her skin color. For instance, children at school always make fun of her because her skin is too dark: "The other children pinch me from behind the seats. They make fun of the darkness of my skin, saying, 'Here comes the black girl!'" (*ibid.*: 32). Gradually, color becomes the primary marker of belonging to a particular group – be it national, ethnic, or linguistic. In *A Sky So Close*, whiteness and brownness are not viewed as merely a physiological identification of racial identity, but they serve as visual symbols of culture. Here color defines everything: emotions, habits, speech patterns, and cultural affiliations. A clear differentiation between "white" and "brown" reinforces the irresolvable conflict of English and Arab. When it comes to the protagonist's parents, even their voices are defined by skin color: "Your deep voice that resembles your dark skin – somebody once asked you if you borrowed your skin color from the Indian market – mingles with my mother's high-pitched tone" (*ibid.*: 19).[11] The father – a trader in food flavorings – is himself an embodiment of color and teaches his daughter how to recognize different shades and how to name them, letting her "imagination go free, to the end of the rainbow" (*ibid.*: 84). In his view, color equals life – filled with vivid images, tastes and flavors, shades and nuances. Colors represent Arabness, they symbolize the magical, mysterious, and seductive Orient:

> I never thought that I could imagine the color pink as Cherry Gel, or that I could call the color green a Lazy Forest, a Fermented Apple Skin, or a River Pebble. How do you come up with such magic, Father? Is this what my mother meant when she said that you seduced her with your descriptions of the East? (*ibid.*: 86)

The father's colorful identity is juxtaposed with the mother's bland whiteness. This dichotomy between "colorful Arab" and "colorless English" is constructed as a tense relationship between native and foreign. Her own dark skin helps the autobiographical protagonist to distance herself from mother's Englishness, manifested in the latter's fair complexion, her "long white rubbery neck" and exotic, from an Iraqi point of view, beauty: "They say she's beautiful. I suppose they're dazzled by the whiteness of her skin" (*ibid.*: 39). The mother is the embodiment of the color white, from her skin to her surroundings: "She keeps her lips splayed apart to avoid smearing the white cigarette holder with her lipstick. She chose it in white to match the white towel and the white bathroom slippers" (*ibid.*: 32–3), and even her tears are colored in white: "maybe her tears are white, like the color of her skin" (*ibid.*: 48). With that, white becomes representative of everything English, including the language: "She answers me in English as white as her skin" (*ibid.*: 8). What is interesting in the configuration of whiteness here is that while it is equated with "British" and "European," it generally lacks a negative connotation of colonial language. In other words, it does not represent the "white man's" oppression but, rather, is synonymous with color-*less* – something bland, cold, and void of emotions. For instance, the protagonist compares her mother with a Chinese doll – a beautiful, but artificial and cold thing. Later on, when she meets three half-French sisters in her ballet classes, she describes them and their whiteness in similar terms, emphasizing their emotionless and inhuman qualities. Like her mother, they are objectified as cold dolls:

> Her delicate bones protrude from underneath her pale skin. Her voice is so soft it can barely be heard . . . Her twin sisters follow behind her. They compete with her in their pallor and skinniness, like a pair of flattened fish . . . Their eyes . . . are free of expression . . . Sara and her twin sisters resemble Pinocchio in triplicate. They come down the stairs like puppets, moved along by their strings . . . If the three sisters stood in a straight line, all I could see from the side would be a column of hair, curled in the shape of blond buns. (*ibid.*: 126–7)

Therefore, whiteness, as well as Englishness, is constructed as lacking any emotions and feelings. The autobiographical subject's brown color, operating as a visual marker of Arab identity, also translates into other anti-English qualities, such as her passionate and temperamental personality. The mother's phlegmatism remains a mystery, and once again situates her as a cultural Other with respect to the autobiographical subject. When the mother is diagnosed with breast cancer, the narrator is perplexed with the former's lack of emotion: "I couldn't figure out if her coolness was a sign of resignation, or a self-enforced measure to cool down the fires in her breast, or if it was merely her English way to hide her emotions" (*ibid.*: 155). The human-less quality of white, contrasted with the autobiographical subject's animate Arab brownness, is particularly evident in the final scene of the novel. The mother achieves her absolute, fully manifested whiteness in death, "her skin is whiter than ever" (*ibid.*: 240). Evidently, the subject's rejection of whiteness symbolizes her rejection of Englishness. In addition to that, the white color also participates in formulating a uniform English cultural identity. All English characters in the novel are depicted from the perspective of their *sameness*: they are nothing but clones of her mother, who "all laugh in the same way" and inhabit identical bodies, with "their fingers seeming to blend together in their whiteness" (*ibid.*: 28–9).

In contrast, brownness is conceived as a positive signifier of the Arab self. It visually links her to her father and their generational heritage; it helps her to find friendships (as with her dance teacher, "Madame"); and, most importantly, it generates a sense of *belonging* to her land and her people, making her a part of the Iraqi collective:

> Khaddouja's family is always rushing to and from, blending into the color of their background. Even their complexions are brown, like the mud around them. They're all part of the same brown family, a coloring they've inherited unfailingly for generations. I feel so amazed[12] when they welcome me as one of them: "Here comes the girl with the round face the color of baked bread!" (*ibid.*: 38)

If in her childhood al-Khudayri's autobiographical protagonist felt uneasy about her dark skin, as an adult she completely embraces her brownness as a defining element of her identity: "For the first time in my life I was pleased by the reflection I saw before me . . . my skin color no longer displeased me" (*ibid.*: 112).

Thus, one may assume that by consistently rejecting and erasing any traces of the white color and, correspondingly, her Englishness, the autobiographical subject adopts a solid and clearly delineated Arab Iraqi identity. However, her acceptance of dark skin cannot prevent her from secretly *desiring* whiteness. Her first love affair is with Saleem, a Christian Iraqi who looks very European, with his fair complexion, Greek nose, and blond mustache. She ends up losing her virginity to him, symbolically surrendering to whiteness: "His smooth blond body is dripping beads of sweat that have melted the walls of my palace. I'm swimming in a milky white fluid. I can't escape; I surrender" (*ibid.*: 165). This affair undermines her Arab, Muslim, brown identity which she has been working to solidify her whole life. She betrays her father's dark skin, his religion, and customs that he so tirelessly tried to make his daughter accustomed to during her childhood. The disloyalty to her father's identity becomes particularly obvious when Saleem reveals his superior and arrogant attitude toward dark-skinned people with a story about the African boy Mambo who "the Lord forgot in the oven for a few minutes too long" (*ibid.*: 151–2).

The autobiographical subject's visual brownness, which serves as a principal indicator of her Arab identity, cannot entirely erase her *internal* whiteness, manifested in the narrator's recognition of her cultural differences with the brown Khaddouja and in her attraction to Saleem's whiteness. The seeming solidity of the Arab self begins to break down. Her father dies and so does Khaddouja, the former being the preserver of cultural traditions and the symbol of Arab and Iraqi nationalism, and the latter representing an idealized image of the Iraqi countryside. Thus, the autobiographical protagonist loses both of her close personal connections to her Arabness, and realizes that these losses will have a crucial impact on her identity: "Khaddouja's death and the deterioration of your [father's] health had changed me into a different girl" (*ibid.*: 67). Moreover, just when she finally accepts her Englishness as an indispensable element of identity, she also loses her mother – the embodiment of the subject's English self – to cancer.

These deaths threaten her both identities and destabilize her selfhood, especially when she finds herself in London – doubly displaced, since she is physically away from the Iraqi homeland and psychologically disconnected from the surrounding English environment despite her native fluency in its language. The conflict between two ethnic – cultural, linguistic – selves particularly intensifies with the mother's progressing disease and the outbreak of the First Gulf War. The balancing act between the two identities – one at war and the other succumbing to cancer – becomes more intricate: "I breathe in the days with anticipation; in one hand I hold all the analyses of the current situation; in my other hand, the latest results of my mother's medical tests" (*ibid.*: 189). This is also the time when the protagonist realizes that, paradoxically, her mother experiences the same identity conflict as the protagonist. Displaced from her home country, but unable to assimilate in Iraq, the mother, who she used to see as the ultimate epitome of Englishness, in reality is a borderline self as well:

> I stopped belonging here when I left England and decided to try and belong to the East. In spite of all my efforts, I could not belong there either, and now that I'm back here again, I find that I no longer belong to my original homeland. (*ibid.*: 201)

As the protagonist goes through the deterioration of her two identities, she has a yet another failed affair – now in London. Arnaud, her new lover, is himself a product of ethnic and cultural hybridity. A child of an African mother and a French father, he is virtually the narrator's male twin with regard to their antagonistically mixed ethnicity: "That explains the combination of your [Arnaud's] dark skin with your aquiline nose. Anyway, you can say that I too, am the product of a contrasting mixture" (*ibid.*: 197). Their shared hybrid nature is highlighted in the scene describing their first sexual encounter. Although strangers, the sameness of their selfhood translates into the sameness of bodies and creates a sense of quintessential familiarity. However, when the protagonist discovers that she is pregnant, she decides to have an abortion, unwilling to bring another cultural and ethnic hybrid into the world. The narrator's two failed love affairs symbolize that a culturally hybrid autobiographical body is unable to situate itself firmly on either side of the borderline. Neither the Iraqi Saleem – the "white Arab" – nor the foreigner Arnaud, with his mixed ethnic background, can offer her stability.

The autobiographical act in *A Sky So Close* illustrates the impossibility of achieving homogeneity for al-Khudayri's biethnic, bilingual, and bicultural subject. Despite the efforts to affirm her cultural identity as singularly and uniformly Arab, the autobiographical self is permanently ruptured and alienated, unable to firmly establish its cultural and ethnic belonging. Her desired Arab brownness is repeatedly diluted by the whiteness of her English self. The subject experiences the state of irreconcilable *inbetweenness* with respect to both of her homelands, and there is an ultimate realization that her exile is a permanent one: "I am not from here, nor am I from there" (*ibid.*: 197). The protagonist's swinging between the two worlds is metaphorically illustrated in the episode, referencing the title of the book, where she tries to reach the sky on a swing: "I kick the air with my feet . . . I rise upward . . . I kick harder . . . I rise higher toward the heavens . . . I breathe in the horizon . . . A sky so close! . . . Suddenly the rope breaks. I'm lying on the ground on my back" (*ibid.*: 16–17). The sky is so close, yet impossible to reach – just like the singularity of one's identity.

4 Pyramids versus the Statue of Liberty: Ihab Hassan's Negotiations of American Egyptian Identity in *Out of Egypt*

When Ihab Hassan, a prominent Egyptian American intellectual and distinguished scholar of postmodernism, published his *Out of Egypt: Scenes and Arguments of an Autobiography* in 1986, it received an array of mixed reviews. Many criticized Hassan for evoking orientalist visions and stereotypes about Third World countries in general and Egypt in particular. Among the harshest critics who talked about the contradictions between Hassan's autobiographical writing and his scholarly work was Wail Hassan:

> It would be warranted to dwell on ironies involved in the fact that Orientalist stereotypes are recycled by one who fled Egypt because he could not liberate it from the colonizers, or that Manichean metaphysics is trumpeted by one of the prophets of postmodernism. (Hassan 2002: 15)

Other reviews emphasized the orientalist aspect of Hassan's autobiography in terms of its acceptance and affirmation of hegemonic white masculinity and the author's desire to be included in this discourse:

> Hassan's journey . . . exemplifies the way in which masculine severance readily cooperates with the politics of neocolonial imperialism. By representing himself as the self-made man who leaves the claustrophobic, constricted East to find success and prestige in the free, promised land of the West, he reaffirms the Orientalist pattern. (Coleman 1993: 66–7)

Some critics complained that Hassan did not elaborate on his transition into American culture (Beard 1987; Falcoff 1987), and criticized his exaggerated, utopian idealization of the United States, depicting it as a "promised land" and completely disregarding negative aspects of American society. Yet others gave a positive affirmation that Hassan's autobiography should be seen through the perspective of his scholarly writing. Thus, Jerzy Durczak suggested that this work is not "a merely literary exercise, nor it is a self-advertisement or a narcissistic self-examination. It is rather yet another attempt by Hassan to present his vision of the changing civilization – this time through an even more personal and universal medium" (Durczak 1992: 6).

The general consensus (often expressed in an openly blaming fashion) was that by means of his autobiography a successfully "Westernized" Ihab Hassan persistently establishes his American identity, void of any traces of Egyptianness or Arabness. These views were also reinforced by the author's own rather blunt statements elsewhere, where he identifies himself as first and foremost American: "born in Egypt I have lived all my life – so it seems – in America . . . I regard my birth in Cairo as . . . an accident, not a destiny" (Hassan 1993: 453). Moreover, he rigorously refused any affiliation with the Arab diaspora: "Arab-American is to me redundancy, pleonasm" (*ibid.*: 460).

Despite such prevailingly unfavorable views, Hassan's work is a remarkably interesting example of a representational discourse where the multicultural–multilingual autobiographical identity is purposefully and comfortably established as linear and uniform – standing in sharp contrast to the often painful negotiations of the fractured self in Ramadan and al-Khudayri. In *Out of Egypt*, Hassan's borderline subject, it seems, makes every effort to assert its complete and permanent crossover into the "Western land." Nevertheless, despite attempts to utterly disassociate himself from Egyptian culture and to define his masculine "I" strictly in terms of American identity, I will demonstrate that the Egyptian self is never completely erased, never fully invisible. Although the Bakhtinian hybridity and polyphony are certainly much more subtle here than in *Leaves of Narcissus* and *A Sky So Close*, Hassan's Egyptianness does register on several levels in the text – thematic, psychological, and, at times, linguistic. Consequentially, it undermines and destabilizes the hegemonic autobiographical discourse, a part of which *Out of Egypt* seemingly strives to become.

My discussion of Ihab Hassan's work centers on two aspects of the autobiographical act. First, we will investigate how a multicultural (read: inherently diverse) subjectivity translates into a decidedly uniform identity in the text. Second, I will illustrate how the Egyptian voice still manages to pave its way through the (seeming) solidity of the American self. Although *Out of*

Egypt renders a different mode of articulating a multicultural selfhood, it does have certain common elements with the two works discussed earlier, the most important of which being the unavoidable fragmentality of the borderline subject, as I intend to demonstrate.

The autobiography focuses on the first twenty-one years of Ihab Hassan's life – his childhood and adolescence in Egypt – and ends with his departure to the United States to study engineering. The published full title of this work is *Out of Egypt: Scenes and Arguments of an Autobiography*, but Hassan later mentioned that he wished he had called it "Fragments of a Memoir," emphasizing the difference between an autobiography and a memoir in that "the former attempts to recount a whole life without succeeding, the latter succeeds, with luck, in telling about a fragment of life" (Hassan 1998/9). He also gave reasons for selecting a period of his life, rather than producing a fully-fledged autobiography: "I resist writing a full autobiography . . . I believe that the most personal elements in one's life should find expression in oblique forms, say in art, or teaching, or the quality of a person's love" (*ibid.*).

Hassan, born into a wealthy Cairene family during the colonial period in Egyptian history, was surrounded by multilingualism from early age, including his Francophile mother and college friends, many of whom could barely speak Arabic.[13] Therefore, it is not surprising that Hassan's autobiographical narrator more often than not offers a distinct *cultural outsider's* view of his home country. He talks about the Pyramids using the words of Flaubert (Hassan 1986: 2–3), and he quotes a *New York Times* article to describe Egypt's social crisis: "I perceive the changes from afar, in the tales of travelers, in news reports . . . Cairo itself has become a place of unspeakable pollution and occlusions, 'crumbling under the weight of its people,' the *New York Times* reports" (*ibid.*: 13–14). At times, Hassan goes as far as sharing openly Western-centric, even orientalist, opinions: "this . . . is the paradox of 'developing countries': they seem hardly to develop at all" (*ibid.*: 14). Predictably, when he compares American and Egyptian systems of education, he accuses the latter of fundamentalism and lack of aesthetic values: "In the New World, the educational premise sustained the American Dream for two centuries . . . And in 'developing' countries? The mandate remains practical, technological, illiberal – or else fundamentalist, sweeping away knowledge in the name of Allah, a jihad against history" (*ibid.*: 63).

These uncompromising views on Egyptian social conditions are highlighted by the autobiographer's unorthodox attitudes toward colonialism. Although Hassan admits the negative impact of the colonial system and tells the reader that he "like every schoolboy . . . grew up with fierce fantasies of liberating Egypt" (*ibid.*: 24), there is still a certain justification of the British, since he suggests that British colonialism was "more civilized" in comparison with the Spanish, French, and Portuguese, and contemplates whether Egypt's backwardness is its own people's fault: "I wonder: had Britain brought illiteracy and disease to Egypt in the first place? . . . Who makes imperialism possible? And how healthy, free, or affluent are Egyptians thirty years after their liberation?" (*ibid.*: 25). Hassan also revealed his sometimes positive opinions of the British occupation in other writings. Thus, in an autobiographical essay "Maps and Stories: A Brief Mediation," he implies that he personally benefited from it:

> Sometimes, as a child in Egypt, I hid in an unused, shuttered room in the house. Maps piled there on sagging wooden shelves . . . The prevailing color on those maps was red, a kind of pink. That was the color of the British Empire, on which the sun never set. Many years later, I wondered if the fact that I speak English now, speak and count and dream in English, had something to do with those pink-colored maps in a darkened room in Egypt. (Hassan 2005: 751)

Although Hassan's categorical opinions on Egypt and British colonialism might provoke condemnation and criticism, I argue that in *Out of Egypt*, the valorization of the West serves a very specific purpose: it is utilized as a tool to formulate an autobiographical identity that would fit into the Western framework of a masculine uniform subject. In many ways, Hassan's autobiography conforms to the conventional mode of exemplary life stories, with particular emphasis on masculinity and the logical self. Thus, the autobiographical subject asserts his masculine identity on several levels simultaneously. He is attracted to the sense of authority contained in the English language. He is fascinated with the army and his father's guns – a typical attribute of a manly man. Finally, he displays his democratism as a truly Western man's quality: he claims to have never been "cynical" with his female cousins, and always liked to spend time with his family's cook, butler, and chauffer (*ibid.*: 83). As he is growing up, Hassan's autobiographical protagonist contemplates different *types* of masculinity. He goes through a brief stage of dandyism, constructing a visual identification with Western manhood: "I dressed like a dandy less to please others than to distance, even alienate – and so re-create? – myself, as dandies since Brummel and Baudelaire have intuitively known" (*ibid.*: 85). Later, as he enters a new phase in his intellectual quest, he reformulates his identity through the markers of male asceticism: "I think of myself as puritan, monotheist, somewhat stoical" (*ibid.*: 73). Even his sport of choice – fencing – is viewed through the prism of masculinity: "fencing compounded violence and ceremony, instinct and skill, engagement and distance . . . men acknowledged in that instant their capacity to deal and receive death" (*ibid.*: 76).

When it comes to the autobiographical body, Hassan's narrator is preoccupied with constructing a spiritual and disembodied Cartesian subject. When young Hassan's sexuality is concerned, it takes a form of very innocent and platonic affections. He is appalled by public displays of "erotic urgencies" and sees it as yet another reason to disassociate himself from the "vulgar" Egyptian environment: "nothing seems to me now more preposterous than the strut of sex in Egypt" (*ibid.*: 83). Ultimately, he makes a conscious decision to suppress all bodily desires and to concentrate on the intellectual aspect of his selfhood in order to achieve his biggest goal – completing his higher education with honors which, he is hoping, would open a path to America:

> I turned to work, sensing that my Great Escape from Egypt depended on professional achievement more than on existential quests . . . At eighteen, I began to reproach myself for all the time I lost in erotic fantasies . . . "You will never become a scientist or engineer that way," I admonished myself at least once a day. (*ibid.*: 87)

In his insistence on subscribing to Western manhood, the autobiographical narrator clearly distances himself from Egyptian masculinities – be it his cynical uncle Mahmoud with his backward attitudes toward women, or other manifestations of the Egyptian machismo: "their conversation turned to sex and money, about which they divagated in witty, obscene, and exhausting detail. Their paths crossed briefly mine. But their paths finally led deep into the rank corruption of Egypt, which I abhorred" (*ibid.*: 85). Yet the young Hassan cannot help but show superiority to women who, with the sole exception of his wife Sally, failed to understand his desire for knowledge. He goes as far as questioning whether women generally lack creativity and, consequently, are unable to participate in human evolution: "The Imagination is the teleological organ of evolution. It predicts change, it directs change, it fulfills change . . . The women in my life – mother, grandmother, some others – have always wanted me to stop reading. Is woman hostile to Imagination? (Not Sally)" (*ibid.*: 57).

Unlike the agonizing negotiations of culturally hybrid autobiographical subjectivities in Ramadan's and al-Khudayri's narratives, Hassan does not seem to have any misgivings about completely separating his American and Egyptian selves. It looks like the American "I" takes an absolute victory over the forgotten and erased Egyptian identity, which was left behind without regrets a long time ago – or rather, as Hassan tries to convince his reader, he never really had it in the first place. It is as if his coming to the United States was first and foremost a matter of survival, a matter of removing his intellectual self from the land of irrationality and absurdity embodied in the bizarre figures of Hassan's uncles. However, a closer analysis of *Out of Egypt* reveals that the Egyptian self does have a presence in the text. Indeed, despite the autobiographer's vigorous attempts to establish his cosmopolitanism, the Egyptian voice finds its way into the narrative. The apparently successful implantation of the autobiographical subject into an American milieu is destabilized by a number of factors – from autobiographical fragmentation to the occasional use of Egyptian colloquialisms.

From the beginning, the narrating Hassan acknowledges the fragmented nature of memory, and he warns the reader that his remembrance of past events is "like the scattered bones of Osiris" (Hassan 1986: ix). Moreover, he recognizes the presence of multiple voices: "The reader may encounter here other distractions: quotations, brief interludes. In this time of immanent media, minds blend into minds, voices into voices" (*ibid.*: x). But most importantly, there is an evident split of the autobiographical subject into two selves, who carry different names – "I. H." (the initialized name he assigns to the Egyptian self) and "autobiographer" (the American self) – while the two engage in a dialog. It is as if the underlying objective of the autobiographical act in *Out of Egypt* was an attempt to reconcile the tension between the two consciousnesses.

Notably, the process of autobiographical writing takes place in Munich – a "neutral" third place. By physically distancing himself simultaneously from Egypt and the United States, Hassan attempts to look at his selfhood objectively and to reconstruct the deeply buried Egyptian identity: "I return to Germany to worry this dismal query, and construe the deep grammar of my heart. But perhaps I return also, in this reflexive year especially, to recover my own youth in Egypt" (*ibid.*: 27). Germany is where he approaches his selfhood as an observer, an objective outsider. For example, there are several meditational entries dispersed throughout the narrative: most of them are titled "Munich" and they are short narratives within the narrative, telling the reader *about* writing autobiography. These excerpts indicate yet another split of the autobiographical subject: the Munich narrator is different from both the narrating American and the narrated Egyptian selves. There is even an open confession of the autobiographical subject's triangular nature, and a suspicion that such heterogeneity is characteristic of human selfhood in general:

> Home, they say, is where the heart is. But three hearts beat in me. One existential, a little Faustian; one utopian though politic; one Orphic, almost mystic. Those three hearts, I suspect, beat in us all, pumping blood into the near, the middle, and the far distance. (*ibid.*: 27)

The American narrator persistently tells us that all his memories of Egypt are gone. He cannot (does not want to?) even remember the house in which he was born and wants to erase every memory associated with his parents – witnesses to his Egyptian roots: "the reality of my parents, long dead – dead to me perhaps before they entered their grave – must evade me just as I have tried to escape Egypt" (*ibid.*: 31). Nevertheless, Hassan's memories of Egypt are not easy to erase: his recollections of childhood and adolescent years are vivid, precise, and full of detailed descriptions of the colorful personalities and the environments he encountered. These unexpected remembrances and flashbacks surprise the narrator and make him speculate what effect these may have on his seemingly solid American self:

> Still, my feelings run strong, flow in channels surprising in their twists: anger here where I expected none, reconciliation there where I thought least to find it, bemusement veining a mental landscape like the delta of the

Nile. And I wonder how all these emotions touch my American career as "teacher," "critic," "humanist." (*ibid.*: 14)

From the linguistic point of view, *Out of Egypt* is filled with textual markers of doubt – numerous question marks and heavy use of "yet," "still," "but," "I wonder if," and "who knows." This evident uncertainty of the narrating voice proves that the autobiographical act here is not as straightforward and uncomplicated as it appeared to be initially. Textual ambiguity displays the autobiographer's hidden nostalgia for the country he left and subverts his anti-Egyptian statements. For instance, having defined "Eternal Egypt" as "something closer to a curse," he immediately recalls "a landscape breathtaking in its spare beauty, a strip of green winding with the Nile through endless sand" (*ibid.*: 16). He harshly criticizes the country's backwardness, yet he longs for the desert, which for him is a symbol of his solitary nature: "A part of me has always longed for . . . the fierce solitude of the nomad, moving across timeless sand . . . I have always returned. The desert waits" (*ibid.*: 41).

The text of *Out of Egypt* is composed in an impeccable, beautiful English, yet it still shows an interesting tension between Arabic and English discourses – or, using Bakhtinian terms, "social languages." Hassan talks about his uneasy relationship with Arabic and his preference for English as a favorite vessel of communication: "French and Arabic were my first languages; but I liked far more another which I now write" (*ibid.*: 3). He sees English as a source of power and an entry ticket into the dominant, hegemonic discourse. Meanwhile, Arabic represented everything he wished to leave behind, it was the "battered native tongue" that Hassan fiercely resisted. After years of living in America and writing scholarly works in his beloved English, Hassan claims to have completely lost his knowledge of Arabic, to not know how to "'speak Egypt' anymore" (*ibid.*: 12). English emerges as the only linguistic medium through which Hassan can communicate his identity. Sometimes the valorization of English even takes a comical turn – for example, in his choice to voice an Egyptian peasant (*fallāḥ*), who would normally speak in a heavily accented colloquial Arabic, in archaic English: "the fellah sings mournfully in the fields: Hast thou resolved upon strangling me, O Allah? Loosen the noose!" (*ibid.*: 42).

Nevertheless, in spite of Hassan's obvious preference for English, the narrative stability is being constantly undermined by numerous Egyptian colloquialisms. It is true that many orientalist records and recollections of the Middle East, composed by European travelers, usually contain a number of Arabic words in order to exoticize the narrative and to give it a certain "indigenous flavor." But in the case of *Out of Egypt*, the difference is that the autobiographical voice has a native-speaker knowledge of Arabic. Many of transliterated Egyptian words and expressions are followed by English equivalents in parentheses, but one might wonder why employ colloquialisms in the first place? Yet a number of words are left untranslated – sakiah, baksheesh, baladi, shadouf, ezbah – hence, concealing certain images and meanings from an English-speaking reader. Therefore, this occasional use of the Egyptian colloquial illustrates the impossibility of completely obliterating the Egyptian linguistic consciousness.

In addition to the frequent use of colloquialisms, Hassan's autobiography contains other indications that the language question remains unresolved. The narrator suspects that his rejection of Arabic does not completely free him from his native tongue, and does not give him full authority over a foreign language either: "Who reckons the deep declensions of Desire, inflections of the Logos, or denials of a Mother's Tongue? Does 'matricide' free men into alien speech?" (*ibid.*: 3). Furthermore, he suggests that language by itself does not completely reveal one's identity, there is always something unspoken and hidden:

> And my parents, my own parents? Who will recall them now, if not I, their sole son? Who will speak them? In their case, I do not know – *will* not know? – whereof I speak . . . Only language, simulacrum of our presence, speaks. But really: *only* language speaks? I have never quite believed it. (*ibid.*: 10–11)

In conclusion, the autobiographical act in Ihab Hassan's *Out of Egypt* demonstrates that an effort to synthesize the subject's plurality of cultural identities is doomed to fail. Although Hassan's Egyptian self is decidedly silenced, there is a realization that it will always remain an essential element of his hybrid identity. The "Eternal Egypt"[14] is a curse, but also an inescapable destiny, and although suppressed and concealed deep inside, it will continue to threaten to take over the seemingly invincible American identity: "For a long time after leaving Egypt, I had a bad, recurrent dream. I dreamt that I was compelled to go back . . . There was terror in that banal dream, terror and necessity" (*ibid.*: 108).

5 Conclusion: Multicultural Selves – Reconciliation Impossible?

Autobiographical texts discussed in this chapter demonstrate that the categories of multiculturalism and exile take various meanings and representations. Besides producing literary accounts of a displaced selfhood, this diversity gives us an insight into how conceptions of self, incorporating elements of more than one culture and language, are disseminated in the contemporary Arab world. The complexity of narrative identities formulated in *Leaves of Narcissus*, *A Sky So Close*, and *Out of Egypt* illustrate the fundamental complexity of a multicultural subjectivity. What all these texts have in common is a clearly articulated desire to reconcile their borderline subjectivities by generating a stable uniform identity with a singular cultural and linguistic belonging. However, the notions of hybridity and polyphony undermine every attempt at unification of the autobiographical identity. Here, exile and displacement – both physical and metaphorical – are central sites of autobiographical construction.

Another common feature of the case studies in this chapter is the problematics of bilingualism (more specifically, Arabic–English bilingualism), which in all three texts is a projection of intercultural relationships. In Sumayyah Ramadan's narrative, the Arabic text is continuously disrupted by multilayered English intertextuality, and this creates an antagonistic polarity between the two languages and, in turn, destabilizes the autobiographical subject. The text itself – the *territory of writing* – serves as a metaphorical place of belonging, but the hostile relationship between Arabic and English makes it a site of death. In *A Sky So Close*, bilingualism is informed by a different kind of dichotomous relationship: language is tied to physical markers of ethnicity, where the brown color represents Arab and English equals whiteness. Just as brown and white belong to the opposite sides of the color spectrum, so the two languages of al-Khudayri's autobiographical subject do not blend with one other. The "confusion" between Arabic and English signifies the ambiguity of her ethnic belonging. Notwithstanding a determined choice of the father's Iraqi identity, the subject's Englishness does not – cannot

– completely disappear. Ihab Hassan's subject seems to have successfully resolved the problem of multilingualism by selecting English as an exclusive language of autobiographical communication. However, Arabic is never fully absent: it repeatedly surfaces in the text in the form of numerous Egyptian colloquialisms and indicates the presence of an inerasable Egyptian self.

In all three texts, exile and displacement define the autobiographical act. For Ramadan's Kimi, exile is a highly abstract category, detached from any specific physical place. Being in exile constitutes a particular state of being, a state of mind, rather than a geographic relocation. Displacement equals perpetual alienation and indicates the autobiographical subject's inability to belong. In contrast, exile in *A Sky So Close* is a physical displacement from Iraq, constructed as cultural and ethnic homeland, to London – a metropolis of white Englishness. This relocation makes the autobiographical subject realize that homeland is an illusory category and leads to her accepting her permanent foreignness. Unlike Ramadan's and al-Khudayri's narratives, Ihab Hassan's autobiography constructs exile as a *positive* category. His displacement is voluntary, and the United States is perceived as an ideal location for his intellectual self, unlike his native "backward" Egypt. In other words, categories of home and exile are reversed. Nevertheless, the very process of autobiographical writing initiates the long suppressed nostalgia and constructs Egypt as an inescapable homeland.

In conclusion, the three texts examined in this chapter illustrate a distinct mode of autobiographical transmission in recent works of Arab authors: the one articulating multilingual, multicultural, and displaced forms of selfhood. The hybridity of different linguistic consciousnesses that speak different "social languages" – representing ethnic, cultural, linguistic, or other duality of the subject – in the same autobiographical utterance proves to be impossible to overcome. Neither can one resolve the polyphony of autobiographical selves, each claiming their own rights for existence, which points at the unavoidable and permanent rupture of a multicultural subject. Therefore, the autobiographical articulations of multiculturalism attest to the presence of necessarily fragmented subjectivities, even when such fragmentality is rejected and concealed. The subjects that are split between cultural and linguistic universes do not only live on borderlines, permanently displaced, but they are set to endlessly negotiate and renegotiate their hybrid selfhoods.

Notes

1. The excerpt is taken from the introduction to the Russian version of Vladimir Nabokov's autobiography, which is missing from the English version. Besides being written in different languages, the two texts also show some narrative dissimilarities, even in the titles. The English autobiography, titled *Speak, Memory*, was published in a single volume in 1951, while the Russian text *Drugiye Berega* (*Other Shores*) appeared in 1954. I provide my own translation of the excerpt into English.
2. The italics appear in the original text.
3. Here and in what follows I use quotes from Marilyn Booth's translation, *Leaves of Narcissus*.
4. Marilyn Booth left the word "nafs" untranslated, perhaps because of its range of meanings in Arabic: personal identity, self; soul; psyche; spirit, mind; human being, person, individual. Interestingly, in Arabic this word is of feminine gender.
5. The quote is from Wilde's *The Soul of Man under Socialism* (p. 284), taken from Freedman (1996: 41).
6. The importance of the Egyptian identity is accentuated in the choice of the autobiographical protagonist's name, "Kimi," which is associated with Pharaonic Egypt. According to the ancient Egyptians, the oldest version of the name "Egypt" is "Keme," which means "black." Kimi is one of its derivatives that continue to circulate in the contemporary version of the Coptic language.
7. In Arabic the word *ʾawrāq* ('leaves'), as in English, refers to both pages of paper and foliage.
8. Italics are in the original text.
9. The linguistic hybridity in the text also includes different registers of Arabic. For the most part, the text is written in *fuṣḥā*, the Arabic formal language, but some dialogues and parts of direct speech are composed in Egyptian colloquial, which creates a distinct voice (a separate "linguistic consciousness") within the Arabic discourse – a feature invisible in the English translation. The following example illustrates this element textually:

   أمّها تلهث قليلاً وعندما تدخل عليها الفتاة لا تراها بداية ثمّ تسأل : – ماعندكيش بلوفر تاني غير اللي انت لابساه ده؟

   "Her mother panted a little, and when the girl entered she did not see her at first, then she asked: 'Don't you have a different sweater, instead of this one you are wearing?'" (Ramadan 2001: 18). Here I provide my own translation, closer to the Arabic text.

As for the English linguistic discourses, they are presented mainly in the form of numerous instances of intertextuality referencing English and Irish literature. There are also some short fragments actually written in English in the midst of the Arabic script (on pp. 52, 54, 82, 98 of the Arabic text: Ramadan 2001), such as the following quote with the English idiom: "fa qāla ʾaḥadunā: There is no place like home" (Ramadan 2001: 82).

10. Here and subsequently I use quotes from the English translation by Muhayman Jamil of al-Khudayri's autobiographical novel, *A Sky So Close* (2001).
11. Here the narrator demonstrates her closeness to her father by addressing him in the second person while simultaneously distancing herself from her mother by referring to her in the third person.
12. I modified Muhayman Jamil's translation here. The Arabic original says "*kam ʾaʿjab*," which I translate as "I am so amazed," rather than Jamil's "I feel so strange."
13. The narrator mentions, for example, that all his friends at the fencing club "spoke French more fluently than Arabic" (Hassan 1986: 76). In another episode, he talks about his peer Riaz who was unable to even ask a simple question in Arabic correctly: "Gentle Riaz, Francophone and Francophile, could barely speak Arabic when we met. 'May I sit with you in the same drawer?' he asked me on our first day at the Faculty of Engineering" (*ibid.*: 90).
14. Hassan refers to Egypt as "she," therefore transferring an Arabic grammatical structure into English: Arabic has two genders, masculine and feminine, and the word "Egypt" is feminine.

4

Visions of Self: Filming Autobiographical Subjectivity

1 Theorizing Cinematic Autobiography

As the technological revolution of the last forty years has made, and continues making, fundamental changes to the culture of perception, and has initiated an array of new art forms, it is not surprising that representational discourse is expanding exponentially and now includes a wide range of visual and performative genres, of which cinema is perhaps the most influential one. Taking into account this and the rising quality and affordability of filmmaking equipment, contemporary autobiographers increasingly choose a moving image over a pen to articulate their selfhood. YouTube, home videos, shorts, autobiographical documentaries, and autobiographical motion pictures – these videographic and cinematic self-referential genres are as diverse and complex as their literary counterparts. As the famous French film director François Truffaut famously predicted in 1957:

> The film of tomorrow appears to me as even more personal than an individual and autobiographical novel, like a confession, or a diary. The young filmmakers will express themselves in the first person and will relate what has happened to them . . . The film of tomorrow will resemble the person who made it. (Truffaut 2008: xi)[1]

For the purpose of this study, I am particularly interested in full-length motion pictures that are autobiographical in that they reference the life of the film director (scenarist, producer).[2] In Western cinema, examples of such works are Federico Fellini's *8½* (1963) and *Fellini's Roma* (1972); Bernardo Bertolucci's *Before the Revolution* (1964); Ingmar Bergman's *Fanny and Alexander* (1982); Andrei Tarkovsky's *The Mirror* (1979); Bob Fosse's *All*

That Jazz (1979); and several of Woody Allen's films, especially *Deconstructing Harry* (1997), *Stardust Memories* (1980), and *Anne Hall* (1977). The narrative structure of a motion-picture autobiography is comparable to a literary work: in a general sense, there is an autobiographical author, an autobiographical narrator, an autobiographical protagonist (or protagonists), a plot, and (more often than not) a range of other characters. Therefore, these basic similarities allow us to situate filmic autobiographies within the same typology that embraces nationalist, corporeal, and multicultural modalities, as discussed in previous chapters. In other words, the current study focuses on *autobiographical storytelling*, which I define as a category of autobiographical material that necessarily contains an act of written, verbal, performative, or visual storymaking, including a plot, a sequence of events, a narrator(s), a protagonist(s), and a temporal dimension that locates the story within the "beginning" and "end" boundaries. From this point of view, autobiographical novels, poems, diaries, graphic novels, motion pictures, some subgenres of documentary film,[3] television series, stage plays, web blogs, as well as more conventional autobiographies and memoirs belong in the category of autobiographical storytelling. On the other hand, such self-referential material as sculptures and images (paintings, drawings, photographs, and so on) lie outside this group, considering their status as singular autobiographical acts, or autobiographical artifacts, which do not contain a tangible and narratively articulated story. This type of material, however, often offers incredibly interesting modes of autobiographical identity and warrants exploration in its own right.

The cinematic autobiographical mode is an important element in my discussion, taking into consideration that in the last fifty years, film has gradually become one of the most popular media of cultural expression in the Arab world. Andrew Hammond accurately pointed out that:

> Cinema has a hallowed place in Arab culture, in both a physical and metaphysical sense. The huge billboards that dominate the urban landscape in a city like Cairo are a reflection of the space cinema occupies in the cultural psyche of the Arab world. (Hammond 2005: 112)

Being perhaps more attuned to the opinions, feelings, and expectations of its audience than a literary work, Arab film became a vehicle of social and political commentary, and a mirror of political and social life in Arab societies.

Therefore, an exploration into Arab cinematic autobiographies not only highlights the filmic dimension of individual autobiographical identity, but also exposes – in a particularly vivid manner – the environment that influenced the identity-making practices in a particular historical moment. This chapter discusses Youssef Chahine's (Yusuf Shahin) autobiographical trilogy, composed of *Iskandariyah . . . Leh?* (*Alexandria . . . Why?*, 1979), *Ḥaddūtah Miṣriyyah* (*An Egyptian Story*, 1982), and *Iskandariyah Kamān Wa Kamān* (*Alexandria Again and Forever*, 1990).[4] Chahine's stature in Egyptian and Middle Eastern cinema is comparable to the American Francis Ford Coppola and the Italian Federico Fellini. His cinematographic oeuvre had an impact on Arab film similar to Naguib Mahfouz's influence on Arabic literature: the two have given the world the trilogies of their respective cities.[5] But most importantly, Chahine was the pioneer of the autobiographical genre in Arab cinema, and his films, while drawing some interesting analogies with the works of European and American auteurs of self-referential film, have influenced other Arab directors who took on articulating their selfhood through film.

Youssef Chahine is certainly not the only Arab filmmaker who crafted his work autobiographically. Muhammad Malas' *Aḥlām al-Madīnah* (*Dreams of the City*, 1983) and *Al-Layl* (*The Night*, 1992), Ziad Doueiri's *Bayrūt al-Gharbiyyah* (*West Beirut*, 1998), Khalid al-Hagar's *Aḥlām ṣaghīrah* (*Little Dreams*, 1993), Farid Boughedir's *Halfaouine: A Boy of the Terraces* (1990); these and other films from different parts of the Arab world offered interesting and diverse accounts of cinematic autobiographical storytelling. However, none of them was so explicitly labeled and perceived in the framework of filmic autobiography as Chahine's trilogy. Although Lejeune's autobiographical pact is once again not strictly followed – the protagonist carries a different name, Yahya – Chahine never hesitated to emphasize on numerous occasions that Yahya is the director's cinematic alter ego. To give a very typical example illustrating the discourse surrounding the trilogy, Chahine said in one of his interviews: "What connects *Alexandria . . . Why?* and *An Egyptian Story* is Yahya, who is Youssef, who is me. And the life trajectory of this personality – this is what I talk about in these two films."[6]

With regard to theory, assessing cinematic autobiography is no easy task. Scholars of film studies, literature, cultural studies, and other relevant fields, interestingly enough, remain wary of autobiographical film, and the majority avoid considering it within the framework of autobiographical production altogether. Despite a notable number of such films in American and European cinema, theoretical and critical works assessing this filmic genre remain scarce. Having researched this phenomenon in Italian cinema, Clodagh Brook offers the following explanation:

> In recent years, the autobiographical in cinema has been subject to neglect or attack by critics, a treatment at odds with its reception in the field of literary studies . . . Many critics appear uneasy with the implied narcissism of an autobiographical film . . . This suggests that there is something in the nature of autobiographical film that, unlike literary autobiography, makes us – as spectators and critics – uneasy. (Brook 2005: 27–8)

But even when scholars take on the challenge to theorize about autobiographical filmmaking, their stance is often predominantly negative. Philip Lejeune, a major theorist of autobiography, took on the subject of cinematic narratives in his article "Cinèma et Autobiographie" (1987), where he "declared the impossibility of autobiographical film, claiming that the concept of autobiography could not be translated from written to filmic narrative" (Gabara 2006: 68). Even the always-daring Roland Barthes, whose *Camera Lucida* has in many ways revolutionized our perceptions and understanding of the relationship between subjectivity and visuality, did not favor the medium of film: he states at the very beginning of the book that he "liked Photography in opposition to the Cinema" (Barthes 1981: 3). Elizabeth Bruss, among the first to begin conceptualizing autobiographical film in the 1980s, wrote rather uncompromisingly in her article "Eye for I: Making and Unmaking Autobiography in Film," that:

> the unity of subjectivity and subject matter – the implied identity of author, narrator and protagonist, on which classical autobiography depends – seems to be shattered by film; the autobiographical self decomposes, schisms, into almost mutually exclusive elements of the person filmed (entirely visible; recorded and projected) and the person filming (entirely hidden; behind the camera eye). (Bruss 1980: 297)

Moreover, she even proceeds to claim that filmic discourse would eventually kill autobiography as a genre:

> If film and video do come to replace writing as our chief means of recording, informing, and entertaining, and if . . . there is no real cinematic equivalent for autobiography, then the autobiographical act as we have known for the past four hundred years could indeed become more and more recondite, and eventually extinct. (*ibid.*: 296–7)

The answer to concerns and suspicious attitudes toward film lies precisely in what I see as the central issue of Elizabeth Bruss' argument: it is "classical autobiography" that cinematic practices supposedly undermine. However, the neat structure of traditional autobiography has long been broken apart, deconstructed, and sewn together in a kaleidoscope of clashing pieces of narrating and narrated, self and other, individual and collective, and so on. With the growing variety of art forms and means of self-expression, and with the unprecedented technological revolution that both authors and audiences have experienced in the last decades, a paper-based written text has lost its hegemony when it comes to articulating human subjectivity. As Linda Rugg points out, "it is precisely the impossibility of cinematic autobiography . . . that aids in the discovery of a more implicated, complex, and unrepresentable subject" (Rugg 2006: xiii).

As I have already mentioned, Roland Barthes has been suspicious of cinema and he talked about it in several of his works even before *Camera Lucida*. Thus, he explained his "resistance to cinema" in *Barthes by Roland Barthes*:

> The signifier itself is always, by nature, fluid here, despite the rhetoric of shots; it is, without remission, a continuum of images; the film (the French word for it, pellicule, is highly appropriate: it is a skin without puncture or perforation) follows, like a talkative ribbon. (Barthes [1975] 2010: 54–5)

However, Barthes' theories on photography could be approached as an analytical framework, separately from his preferences for one medium over another. After all, the very conception of the photograph has markedly changed since the publication of *Camera Lucida* in 1980: our present-day understanding of a photograph as a digital image – the fluid form that can receive endless alterations – is ontologically different from Barthes' printed photo of his mother.

A crucial point for my approach to autobiographical film is Barthes' conceptualization of the photographed self as the Other. He clearly identifies the three separate participants in the photographic act:

> I observed that a photograph can be an object of three practices (or of three emotions, or of three intentions): to do, to undergo, to look. The *Operator* is the photographer. The *Spectator* is ourselves, all of us who glance through collections of photographs – in magazines and newspapers, in books, albums, archives . . . And the person or thing photographed is the target, the referent, a kind of little simulacrum, any *eidolon* emitted by the object, which I should like to call the *Spectrum* of the Photograph. (Barthes 1981: 9)

When we extend this argument to self-referential visual discourse, if there is an autobiographical aspect to this process – for instance, the observer and the observed reference the same person outside the discourse – the functional difference between the Spectator and the Spectrum constructs them as separate entities. Furthermore, Barthes establishes photographic image as a tangible proof of the identity's essentially fragmented nature: "Photography is the advent of myself as the other: a cunning disassociation of the awareness of identity" (*ibid.*: 12). This split is permanent and irreconcilable, notwithstanding our desire to be one with our photographic self:

> What I want, in short, is that my (mobile) image, buffeted among a thousand shifting photographs, altering with situation and age, should always coincide with my (profound) "self"; but it is the contrary that must be said: "myself" never coincides with my image. (*ibid.*: 12)

In the context of an autobiographical film, such as Chahine's (as opposed to an autobiographical documentary), where a chosen actor is cinematically impersonating the person behind the film director, this element of otherness is particularly emphasized because the fragmentation of identity is *performed* by actually different people. In other words, autobiographical filmic discourse is a medium where the lack of subject's uniformity becomes especially obvious.

Chahine's autobiographical work, too, received mixed reviews. One of the criticisms is on a par with an earlier presented example regarding the Italian cinema culture that looked at such efforts as a symptom of the artist's egotism: "As with any autobiographical work, [Chahine's] movie tends to err on the narcissistic side" (Bechara 2004). While many were impressed with the quality of the Alexandria trilogy, a number of critics questioned its artistic value in comparison with other films by Chahine:

> One might wish for a different trilogy of Chahine films as an introduction to his oeuvre. With the exception of "Alexandria . . . Why?", this trilogy does not showcase the best of Chahine's talent, nor give a sense of his range and variety. (Nice 2000)

But whether or not one's cinematic tastes are in favor of the trilogy, this work is crucial not only for the regional Arab cinema, but for theorizing self-referential filmic discourse. Chahine's trilogy offers an excellent example of an autobiographical subjectivity that can project a series of different autobiographical identities, as I proposed in the Introduction. The three films, made within three to six years of one another, render very different cinematic constructions of selfhood. If *Alexandria . . . Why?* is a coming-of-age story of young Chahine, highlighted by his fascination with his city of birth and its history, *An Egyptian Story* offers an intriguing exploration of an autobiographical body, while *Alexandria Again and Forever* is a highly complex take on the fragmental nature of human subjectivity. While different aspects of Chahine's trilogy have already received substantial attention from a number of scholars,[7] my analysis in this chapter will focus on the ways in which each of the three films articulate the autobiographical with regard to its narrative, audiovisual, and performative aspects. As I outlined earlier in the Introduction to this book, I am particularly interested in discovering the distinguishing elements of the cinematic autobiographical text and forms of identity formulated through this medium.

2 Youssef Chahine's Cinematic Alter Ego and the Memoiristic Discourse of *Alexandria . . . Why?*

The first part of the Alexandria trilogy was released in 1978 to very favorable critical reviews both in Egypt and abroad: it received the Silver Bear – Special Jury Prize at the 29th Berlin International Film Festival. The film takes place during the Second World War in Alexandria and offers a mosaic of subplots, one of which centers on the teenage version of Youssef Chahine's alter ego,

Yahya Mourad, and his coming-of-age story. Although cinematic discourse is by definition an innovative and unorthodox medium for self-representation, in *Alexandria . . . Why?* the narrative framework resembles a rather typical structure of the Arabic literary *Bildungsroman*. Here we have a close connection between the autobiographical protagonist's life and national history; a familiar image of a passionate, but constantly struggling, middle-class Egyptian family; a quest for a better life; and even the last scenes of the film bring to mind the typical "departure ending," characteristic of an autobiography of childhood: as Tetz Rooke points out:

> The most characteristic ending of the Arabic "Childhood" is a scene of departure. It pictures the child's farewell to the familiar environment in which he grew up. When the story ends, the reader often finds the hero boarding a train, a ship or an airplane departing from his home. The scene represents the cutting of ties with the well-known reality and going towards a mysterious future. (Rooke 1997: 136)

Yahya's plotline is not the central one; rather, it is one of several key stories in Chahine's narrative. In fact, we meet the protagonist only after a long sequence about the city of Alexandria and its history, and there are sequences throughout the film (at times as long as 15–20 minutes) where Yayha is completely absent from the narrative. Here we have a range of colorful characters, each telling a story of love and loss, and each connected to Alexandria. There is a tragic love story between the Egyptian Adil (Yahya's uncle) and the British soldier Tommy who eventually dies while defending Alexandria against the Germans. There is another tragic romance between Ibrahim, a member of the revolutionary group, and Sara from a rich Jewish family, who, while bearing Ibrahim's child, is forced to leave the city of her birth in the face of the approaching Nazi troops. Her father's heartbreaking words to Alexandria as they sail away underscores one of the film's meanings as Chahine's love letter to his city:

> For me, Alexandria is my whole life. Not just my family and the generations that lived here through the centuries, but also my childhood, my thoughts – all of these are rooted here. My mother is buried here. So how could I be asked to cast my life here and all my memories behind me to wander in foreign lands?![8]

Chahine's Yahya is not the central character in the film, Adil, Tommy, Ibrahim, and Sara are also principal figures in the film. So is the city of Alexandria, which serves as the canvas for every character's story, and so is the world of cinema, which defines Yahya's existence and is the connecting thread between Youssef Chahine-the author and his autobiographical protagonist. Therefore, *Alexandria . . . Why?* is truly a *filmic memoir* where the memoir mode is "a mode of life narrative that situated the subject in a social environment, as either observer or participant . . . directs attention more towards the lives and actions of others than to the narrator" (Smith and Watson 2010: 274).

A plurality of narrative voices further emphasizes the memoiristic element in *Alexandria . . . Why?* Besides the autobiographical narrator, who in the voice of Youssef Chahine appears only in the very beginning of the film, we have Ibrahim, Sara, and Sara's father narrating different fragments of the story. Our knowledge of Yahya-the-autobiographical-narrator is based on what we hear from other characters about him, especially his parents and Uncle Adil. Yahya never talks about himself – or his self – which, as I will illustrate further, stands in sharp contrast to the second part of the trilogy, *An Egyptian Story*. Furthermore, the polyphony of voices is highlighted with frequent news reports, scenes from American musicals, and American music in the background.

Another "conventional" element that related *Alexandria . . . Why?* to traditional Arabic memoir is presenting the autobiographical protagonist as an exemplary persona, emphasizing his high morals, his intellect, dignity, and other positive characteristics that fit into the sociocultural model of "an outstanding individual." Yahya is portrayed as an excellent and very talented student, a leader among his peers, a good son, and a loving brother. There is a characteristic scene that highlights the autobiographical protagonist's high morals: when his friends picked up a prostitute from the Corniche,[9] Yahya was the only one disgusted with the situation and voiced his disapproval to others.[10]

An important element of the autobiographical act here is its connection to history. Although the narrative timeline is generally linear (with only a few flashbacks to Yahya's childhood years and the death of his older brother), there is filmic intertextuality that consistently disrupts the main narrative

Figure 4 Young Yahya (Muhsin Muhieddin) is fascinated with the Alexandrian cinema house in *Alexandria . . . Why?*

All images from Youssef Chahine's films courtesy of MISR International Films.

in the form of historical documentary. The very first sequence consists of rapidly changing segments of full-color beach scenes and black-and-white Nazi broadcasts, including fragments from Hitler's speech on his intention to occupy Alexandria, with the jazzy American music of the 1940s in the background. Further on, British, American, and Russian war chronicles continue to be woven into the filmic fabric of Chahine's autobiography. As a result, there is a very visual sense of one's life as a part of history. This audiovisual technique[11] accomplishes an important task: the "real" documentary fragments situate Chahine's autobiographical protagonist in a "real" timeline and space which, in turn, assigns authenticity to his individual life story and writes it into official history. Going back to the audience's expectations of finding "truth" in an autobiography, Chahine's incorporation of documentary certainly generates an effect of "truth telling" and legitimizes his narrative as *genuine*. Another interesting instance of intertextuality is Chahine's inclusion of fragments from American films – mainly musicals of the 1940s. This filmic intertextuality would become a defining feature of the whole trilogy, as I will demonstrate in the discussion of the second and third parts.

Despite an evident visual split between the autobiographical author, narrator, and protagonist typical of filmic discourse, in *Alexandria . . . Why?* this split is linear and straightforward. We are very aware of the extratextual persona of Youssef Chahine and the biographical facts that are followed almost precisely; there is one autobiographical narrator in the voice of Chahine himself in the very first scene of the film, and there is only one autobiographical protagonist, Yahya, a cinematic reincarnation of a teenage Youssef Chahine (Chahine does make a brief appearance at the very end of the film). In other words, although the viewer experiences a visual rupture of the autobiographical subject, there is a certain *singularity* to each of the participants of the autobiographical act. This linearity is accentuated in a very fitting casting of Muhsin Muhieddin as Yahya, who at the time was a 20-year-old student of filmmaking. Discovered by Chahine, Muhieddin did his very first acting work in *Alexandria . . . Why?* Some might question the famous director's choice of an unknown and untrained actor for a key role,[12] but he was likely looking for a close enough representation of his young self – an amateur actor-director, inexperienced, naive, and passionately in love with cinema, who dreams of studying at the Pasadena Playhouse. Even when it comes to physical resemblance, young Chahine and Muhsin Muhieddin do look alike. However, I should mention that the film contains a minor attempt to complicate the autobiographical process by creating a "doubled" autobiographical act: there is a scene where Yahya screens a short film, which he directed and played a role in, to his friends and one of them recognizes the young filmmaker on the screen. This is an important detail, since Chahine will really begin improvising with multidimensional autobiographical representation in *An Egyptian Story* and even more so in *Alexandria Again and Forever*.

Another important aspect of autobiographical identity as formulated and performed in *Alexandria . . . Why?* is Yahya's/Chahine's deep connection with his city. As I pointed out earlier, Alexandria is indeed one of the central characters in the film, and not just its famous history and its cosmopolitanism, but the physicality of this place: the bright colors, the legendary Corniche, the coffee shops, the openness and wideness of the sea, the big ships and the small fishing boats. On the one hand, it is not unusual for Arab authors to relate their coming-of-age stories through stories of their cities. Modern Arabic literature has numerous examples of such autobiographical works: Murid Barghuthi's *Ra'aytu Rām Allāh* (*I Saw Ramallah*), Aliyah Mamduh's *Ḥabbāt Haftālīn* (translated as *Naphtalene: A Novel of Baghdad*), Samar Attar's *Līnā, Lawḥat Fatāh Dimashqīyah* (*Lina – A Portrait of a Damascene Girl*), and Muhammad Hamzah Buqari's *Saqīfat al-Ṣafā* (translated as *The Sheltered Quarter: A Boyhood in Mecca*), among others. On the other hand, one cannot help but notice an interesting trend among other autobiographical film directors to celebrate their cities in their self-referential works: *Fellini's Rome* and Woody Allen's films immediately come to mind. With regard to Arab cinema, a similar pattern can be found in Muhammad Malas' *Dreams of the City*, as well as in Ziad Doueiri's *West Beirut*. This phenomenon could indicate that cinematic negotiations of identity perhaps have more profound connections to space.

3 Chahine, Deconstructed: Reading *An Egyptian Story* as a Self-Exposure

The second part of Chahine's autobiographical oeuvre *Ḥaddūtah Miṣriyyah* (*An Egyptian Story*) came out in 1982 – only three years after *Alexandria . . . Why?*, but it offered a radically different approach to both the autobiographical narration and conceptualization of the subject. Released shortly after Chahine's open-heart surgery, the film was evidently a more conscious attempt on the director's part at producing cinematic legacy. He said in one of the interviews:

> As for *Ḥaddūtah Miṣriyyah*, the idea of this film came to me after I discovered that I had to undergo an open-heart surgery. I learned that I was very close to dying, and all those questions came to me: What is it that I've done in my life before today? And as a rule, a filmmaker does not like to leave this world without leaving behind the last building. Just like Khufu who built the Pyramids to immortalize the memory of himself, or like the neighbor who believes in the saying "Those who have offspring, do not die." I do not have a son, nor was I able to build pyramids. So what do I leave behind? A few films.[13]

Yahya returns as a middle-aged man, played with much intensity by Nour El-Sherif – a big time jump from the teenage version of Muhsin Muhieddin, and the two cannot be more different in every way. El-Sherif's Yahya is a

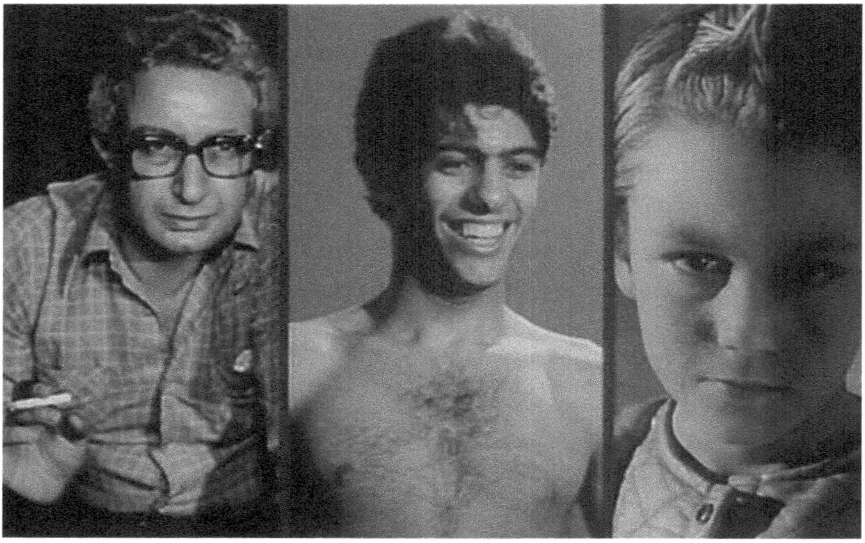

Figure 5 The opening credits of *Egyptian Story* feature the three personas/ages of Yahya: child (Oussama Nadir), teenager (Muhsin Muhieddin), and middle-aged man (Nour El-Sherif)

All images from Youssef Chahine's films courtesy of MISR International Films.

famous film director who, just like Chahine himself, suffers a heart attack as a result of a workaholic lifestyle and heavy smoking, and goes to London to undergo bypass surgery. In sharp contrast to the memoiristic realism in *Alexandria . . . Why?*, its linear narration, and its numerous shots of the city's open spaces, *An Egyptian Story* – likely inspired by Bob Fosse's *All That Jazz* – is a cinematic fantasy, most of which takes place inside Yahya's body during the surgery, with chopped flashbacks to the early days of Yahya's/Chahine's film career, into the *Alexandria . . . Why?* storyline, and into some of his childhood moments.

Starting with *An Egyptian Story*, Chahine's autobiographical project renders an increasingly intricate fragmentation of the subject. Here we are faced with three separate versions of the autobiographical protagonist: El-Sherif's (adult) Yahya, Mohieddin's (teenage) Yahya, and Oussama Nadir's (child) Yahya, not to mention an appearance by an actual Youssef Chahine. The connection among the Yahyas is established from the opening credits of the film where the three are identified as different ages of "Yahya Mourad" – the three images are shown simultaneously on the screen, while at the same time establishing continuity with the first part of the trilogy (see Figure 5). Chahine's entrance into the film is as brief as it was in *Alexandria . . . Why?*, but unlike his appearance at the very end of the narrative in the first movie, here he comes in right after the opening credits, with the camera immediately shifting to Nour El-Sherif's Yahya, where the latter is pictured on a movie set. Thus, the visually constructed continuity between the two reinforces, and quite candidly for that matter, the connection between the real-life director and his cinematic version, where El-Sherif resembles Chahine physically and is also in possession of the latter's famous attributes: thick-rimmed glasses and a cigarette permanently attached to his hand. This scene is crucial with regard to the representational discourse it illustrates. The real-life Youssef Chahine is performing a fictional character in the same filmic narrative where the actor Nour El-Sherif is performing Chahine's alter ego Yahya, while both performances are orchestrated by the real-life Chahine in the extratextual space on the other side of the camera. Such an intricate cinematic trick blurs the boundaries between the real and the fictional, and questions the very existence of self outside its performative function. This, of course, reminds us, in a very literal way, of Judith Butler's theories on the performative nature of sex – and, in more general terms, the performative nature of subject:

> within the inherited discourse of the metaphysics of substance, gender proves to be performative – that is, constituting the identity it is purported to be. In this sense, gender is always a doing . . . There is no gender identity behind the expressions of gender; that identity is performatively constituted by the very "expressions" that are said to be its results. (Butler 1990: 25)

If we give a broader application to this theory and project it onto subjectivity, Chahine's autobiographical act becomes a vivid visual demonstration that the subject does not exist outside the discourse, but rather, discourse is what generates the subject.

The main plot of *An Egyptian Story* takes place inside El-Sherif's Yahya as he is going through his heart surgery. The fact that a significant part of the film happens inside the autobiographical body, on the one hand, reinforces the physicality of the subject and establishes identity as a perishable matter. There is much talk of death and focus on the adult Yahya's self-destructive obsessive behavior with his chain-smoking and workaholic lifestyle that takes a toll on his body. On the other hand, the entering of the autobiographical body symbolizes the journey into the depths of selfhood and offers a convenient medium for the subject's split into a series of identities. The metaphorical trial that takes place within Yahya/Chahine puts the separate fragments of autobiographical subjectivity face to face: the adult Yahya is confronted with the child Yahya inside Yahya's metaphysical body. And, as if this fragmentation were not enough, the Yahya of the "present" (that is, the trial storyline) also communicates through a series of flashbacks with the younger version of the adult Yahya at the dawn of the filmmaker's career and Mohieddin's Yahya from *Alexandria . . . Why?* The number of the ruptured subject's pieces is truly dizzying.

Chahine's merciless fragmentation of identity prompts a take-no-prisoners approach to portraying different pieces of himself. Indeed, there is barely anything attractive in any of these Yahyas, perhaps with the only exception of the teenage version played by Mohieddin – the version that for Chahine, it seems, is gradually becoming an idealized model of his identity (more on this in the discussion of *Alexandria Again and Forever* that follows). Nour El-Sherif's intense, at times even agonizing, performance paints his two versions of Yahya (an ambitious start-up filmmaker and an accomplished director) as constantly agitated, nervous, hysterical, restless, angry, and rude to pretty much everyone around him, with all his bad traits and bad habits exposed to the audience. He is also very aware of his shortcomings: "You should keep in mind that I am complicated and short-tempered, and often childish. And I love to be spoiled"[14] – he warns his future wife Amal (played by the royalty of the Egyptian cinema, Yousra). The child Yahya, too, is portrayed in a rather brutal light – the angry and cunning kid seems to be lacking any emotion and attempts to kill the adult Yahya by blocking his heart arteries. Notably, Oussama Nadir's appearance is drastically different from all other performative manifestations of Chahine's autobiographical body: the blond, fair-skinned, and clothed in bizarre futuristic garments child is a sharp contrast to the "typical Egyptian" complexion of El-Sherif, Mohieddin, and Chahine himself. This obvious visual dissimilarity emphasizes the essential complexity of one's identity, which is composed of necessarily contrasting fragments.

At the same time, there is a sadness to all of Chahine's Yahyas, a sense that, despite the obvious professional success, none of his selves is happy or able to love. The adult Yahya tells us that his heart problems are rooted in his deep dissatisfaction with his being. "What has blocked [the veins]? – 120 cigarettes. Cholesterol lines artery walls from inside. This is because of your highly excitable temper. – Life is all repression: from childhood to college years to the present. As for my own needs, I have always put them off"[15] – he tells his doctor, and the audience recognizes his dissatisfaction when they see Yahya's coldness and indifference to his wife, Amal, or the (implied) secretive affair with the English cab driver in London. He sees himself as stripped of his "real" identity and objectified by the public and fame, as he explains to the cab driver:

> Actor, writer, director, what more? You are a star in your country! – Never use this word with me! A star is a consumerist product. Like a chair, tennis shoes. Buy them, use them, throw them. I hope I have avoided at least that.

There is also an awareness that it is impossible to reconcile these fragments of self with one another, impossible to change things. "I'm unable to even quit smoking – how can I be expected to get rid of my complexes and change the past?",[16] El-Sherif's Yahya asks Amal. Despite the autobiographical desire to attain the self's completeness, despite the alleged happy ending when the child and the adult Yahyas merge through a cinematic trick of the child's image visually dissolving into Nour El-Sherif's body, and despite the newly "complete" Yahya's claim that he is "not alone anymore," the complex and antagonizing structure of Chahine's filmic narrative does not make this claim very believable.

The difference between autobiographical discourses in the first and second installments of the trilogy is highlighted throughout the film. Perhaps one of the most effective illustrations of these contrasts is a very different portrayal of the protagonist's family. In *An Egyptian Story*, Chahine is as representationally ruthless to his family members as he is to himself: long gone is the idyllic Mourad household of *Alexandria . . . Why?* The compassionate and self-sacrificing mother, the loving sister, and the righteous father are replaced with a bickering squad of selfish and miserable people. The mother's character in particular is so fundamentally different from the earlier version

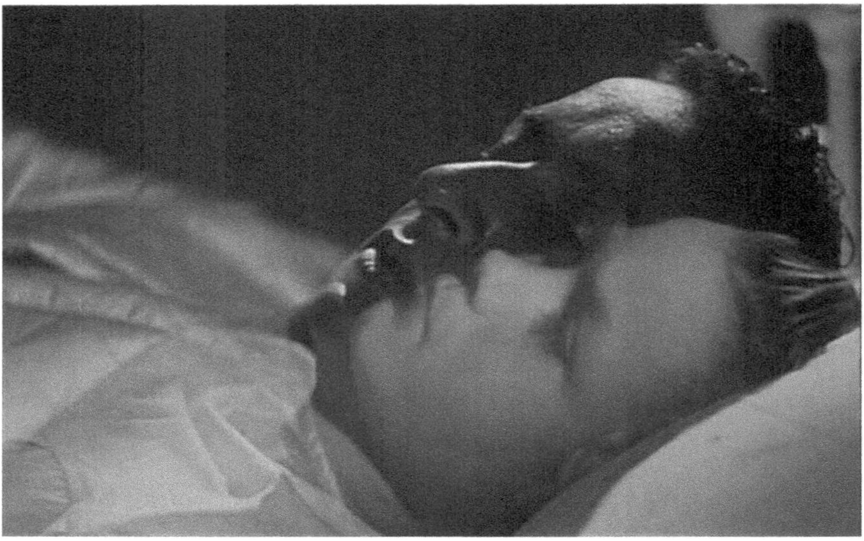

Figure 6 Final scenes in *Egyptian Story*: The images of young Yahya (Oussama Nadir) and adult Yahya (Nour El-Sherif) are merging into one another on screen

All images from Youssef Chahine's films courtesy of MISR International Films.

– she is now a self-centered and angry woman, who flirts with other men and who marries off her daughter at a very young age to a rich older man – that a different actress was cast to play this role (Suhayr al-Babli). These examples prove furthermore that each separate autobiographical act produced by the same author generates a different discourse and a different identity – or a set of identities. All in all, *An Egyptian Story* is a much more blunt, mocking, and self-deprecating autobiographical portrait than the first part of the trilogy. Chahine's raw method of self-representation makes it truly a *self-exposure*. Nothing is concealed, not a single thing is embellished, everything is exposed: bad traits, vulnerabilities, secret desires, and the insides of the autobiographical body.

There is a scene in the film where Yahya the film director is very closely compared with Gamal Abdel Nasser. When Yahya considers quitting his career after an unsuccessful attempt to get his movie script approved by the censorship committee, we hear a fragment from the famous resignation speech by Nasser in the background,[17] quickly shifting to a documentary segment chronicling mass demonstrations protesting the resignation. While some might consider Chahine's apparent self-association with Nasser,[18] who many still view as a sanctified figure of modern Egypt, an arrogant move, he mocks himself mercilessly in the next scene and accuses himself of egoism (for instance, the child Yahya is accused of "egoism and self-indulgence" at the inside-the-body trial). Even the title of the film *Ḥaddoūtah Miṣriyyah*, a closer translation of which is *An Egyptian Tale*, could be interpreted as a sarcastic take on the concept of the American Dream and the impossibility of realizing such a dream in Egypt – partly political commentary, partly self-ridicule referencing his obsession with international awards and impressing American critics and audiences. These contrasting shifts from self-praise to self-deprecation and back are the core of the autobiographical identity in the film, since they display, along with the multilayered fragmentation of the autobiographical subject, the conflicting nature of human subjectivity.

Intertextuality is evermore present in *An Egyptian Story* than in *Alexandria . . . Why?*, and it is becoming more complex structurally. In addition to the already familiar excerpts from historical documentaries (chronicles of the Cannes Film Festival, footage of anti-British riots, nationalization of the Suez Canal, Nasser's resignation speech), we are presented with numerous excerpts from Youssef Chahine's earlier films and imitation movie sets: *Ibn al-Nīl* (*Son of the Nile*, 1951), Chahine's first nomination in Cannes; *Djamīla Bouḥerīd* (*Djamila, the Algerian*, 1958); *Al-Nāṣṣer Ṣalāh al-Din* (*Saladdin, the Victorious*, 1963); and one of his finest works, *Bāb al-Ḥadīd* (*Cairo Station*, 1963). Chahine's inclusion of his earlier works – as if directed by Nour El-Sherif's Yahya Mourad – into the current narrative – certainly supports an autobiographical reading of *An Egyptian Story*. But most importantly, such intertextuality forms an elaborate relationship between Youssef Chahine's subjectivity and his multiple narrative selves. It is as if the filmic Chahine–Yahya communicates with the real Chahine and vice versa through the medium of film, blurring the boundaries between the signifier and the signified. There is a truly remarkable scene where, in a flashback to Chahine's early days, El-Sherif's Yahya performs Chahine on the *Cairo Station* film set, where in real life the latter performed as both the director and the main character.[19] Here we encounter a chain of self-referential performances: Youssef Chahine directs the performance of the actor Nour El-Sherif, who acts as Chahine's

Figure 7 In one of the most remarkable scenes from the identity-making point in *Egyptian Story*, Nour El-Sherif's fictional Yahya reenacts the real-life Youssef Chahine's performance in *Cairo Station*

alter ego Yahya, who on the set of Chahine's *real* film *Cairo Station* directs his own performance in the acting role of Qinawi – Youssef Chahine's most celebrated *real-life* role. Indeed, *An Egyptian Story* offers an autobiographical puzzle, rather than an autobiographical narrative. Such a performatively and visually complex self-representation, I argue, is possible only in the cinematic medium. This, as I call it, "nesting-doll" autobiographical representation, on the one hand, illustrates the fragmented nature of human subjectivity. On the other hand, it challenges the fundamental paradigm of autobiographical narrative by erasing the boundaries between the author, the narrating self, and the narrated self. Chahine continues to explore the nesting-doll representational method in the subsequent installment of the trilogy, *Alexandria Again and Forever*.

4 Chahine and His Doppelgängers in *Alexandria Again and Forever*

The final installment of the trilogy, *Iskandariyah Kamān Wa Kamān* (*Alexandria Again and Forever*, 1990), features – finally – Youssef Chahine himself, who steps into his own frame to play his alter ego, Yahya Mourad. The film centers on Yahya's obsession with the young actor Amr, who is a cinematic representation of the real-life actor, Muhsin Mohieddin, after his successful turn in *Alexandria . . . Why?* Indeed, the fragmentality of the autobiographical subject is front and center in *Alexandria Again and Forever* even more so than in the first two films. In a peculiar casting, Yousra is also back – not as Yahya's wife, but as a young actress and activist, Nadia, with whom Yahya becomes obsessed toward the end of the film.

In his usual manner, Chahine is uncompromising in his bold depictions of controversial themes – from homosexuality to political commentary on the country's corruption, to an exploration of his own successes and failures in both his professional and personal life. Not surprisingly, the film received an array of conflicting reviews, raging from "a dazzling installment, one of the most passionate celebrations of bisexuality ever filmed",[20] to "as far as I could understand the movie as movie, it was a mess."[21] These comments aside, it is perhaps the most elaborate – from the performative point of view – autobiographical piece by Chahine. Amr, played by Amr Abd El-Gelil, is at the core of the nesting-doll autobiographical act in the film. While he performs as the actor Muhsin Mohieddin in a fictional account of the latter's life after *Alexandria . . . Why?* – where Mohieddin performed as a young Chahine – El-Gelil's Amr is an alter ego of an alter ego. Therefore, the boundaries between the autobiographical author, the narrator, and the protagonist are even more ambiguous here than in *An Egyptian Story*. As Chahine's Yahya says in response to his friend's suggestion that Amr looks like him during his school years, Chahine's Yahya says: "When he was performing me, I got confused. I could not figure out which was me and which was him. Perhaps he too got confused."[22] Likewise, there is an ambiguity in the film's representational discourse. Is Chahine performing himself? Or is it Yahya performing Chahine? Or it is Amr performing both Chahine and Yahya? The make-up of the autobiographical act in *Alexandria Again and Forever* could not be more confusing. This ambiguity is an excellent visual-performative demonstration of the inherent complexity of human selfhood. The intricate and nonlinear relationships between different characters in the film and different actors who play them replicate the intricate relationships between different pieces – selves – of a fragmented subjectivity.

One of such examples is the onscreen relationship between Yahya and Amr. On the surface, it is a passionate affair between the two men: in the very first scene of the movie they squabble like lovers; there is a long dance sequence with the two of them performing as partners; and there are numerous shots of their eye contact and body language suggesting that their relationship is much more than friendship or a bond between the director and his favorite actor. But on the other hand, Yahya's obsession with Amr may as well be his being in love with the younger version of himself. Or is it Chahine's obsession with the autobiographical subject of *Alexandria . . . Why?* who gradually becomes, as we have seen in *An Egyptian Story*, an idealized version of Chahine's autobiographical identity? The self-referential narcissism is further highlighted in occasional Pygmalionian connotations: "I still love him until now. But go ask him – does he love the real me? Or the image that he made up in his head?!" Amr tells Nadia.[23]

In the third part of the trilogy, Chahine continues to fluctuate between self-praise and self-ridicule. While in *An Egyptian Story* he compares himself to Gamal Abdel Nasser, here he adopts an array of prominent personalities – from Mark Anthony to Alexander the Great, to the great English actor John Gielgud, famous for his brilliant performance of Hamlet. Moreover, throughout the narrative, Yahya–Chahine metamorphoses into Hamlet himself, completing the subplot he drew through all films of the trilogy.[24] In addition to that, there are occasional self-praising speeches, usually voiced by Nadia, either in reference to his character ("People often think that you are a monster. But the truth is – you are transparent"),[25] or complimenting his talents (for example, the constant mentioning of his brilliant performance of Hamlet). Even the song recurring throughout the film, which praises Alexander the Great in Amr's performance, does sound like an ode to himself: "Look at him through my eyes: you will find him beautiful from inside."[26] While one may find such self-flattery narcissistic, Chahine does not seem to take himself too seriously. We as the audience find out that Yahya's "movie" *Alexander the Great* is in actuality a musical parody of period dramas, which also offers a humorous pastiche of various filmic genres from cop movies to Chaplin physical comedy. As for Amr's performance of Alexander, with his brigandine and now lightened hair, which visually references the blond Yahya-child of *An Egyptian Story*, it is nothing but self-mockery.

With respect to Chahine's self-inclusion into the long list of prominent Alexandrians – "Sostratus, Alexander the Great . . . they say that even Jesus studied in Alexandria"[27] – this is likely an indication of going back to his roots and reconstructing his Alexandrian identity, which he departed from in *An Egyptian Story*. In fact, his return to the Alexandrian discourse – in the film's title, setting, and numerous references to the city's greatness – indicates the completion of his cinematic life-circle, on the one hand, and, on the other hand, it may as well be a therapeutic narrative – his healing himself after the unforgiving self-exposé of *An Egyptian Story*, where the latter is never mentioned in this film, in sharp contrast to frequent references to *Alexandria . . . Why?* and the metatextual continuity created with the first autobiographical film.

Chahine continues his experiments with intertextuality in the last installment of the trilogy, and here it takes on truly epic proportions. Not only does Chahine continue to interject, in his typical manner, the documentary footage into his narrative, but there are also fictional "movie inside the movie" pieces – fragments of films that Yahya had either created already or imagines directing in the future: *Hamlet*, *Alexander the Great*, and *Cleopatra*. Moreover, *Alexandria Again and Forever* offers a homage to a wide range of cinematic genres: the Gene Kelly-style musicals, French musical films, Batman movies, cop movies, cartoons, Chaplin physical comedy, spy movies, and period drama, and this structural intertextuality often offers a light-hearted approach by parodying the above genres. These constant narrative shifts stress the highly fragmented nature of his autobiographical identity, and could be seen as a cinematic technique that helps to formulate the identity's perpetual fragmentation both narratively and visually. On a larger scale, Chahine's intertextuality helps to construct an autobiographical reality that is a hybrid of "cinematic reality" (the life of Chahine's cinematic alter ego Yahya) and "real reality" (the life of the filmmaker Youssef Chahine). The constant mixing of filmic (fictional) characters with real personalities, films made by Chahine in real life with films "made" by Yahya in the course of *Alexandria Again and Forever*, and continual inclusion of documentary footage and photographs – all in the same discourse – makes it difficult to separate real from cinematic. In one such scene, Yahya and Nadia's mother watch *Cairo Station* on TV while arguing about which of Yahya's films is his best work: Yahya suggests that it was *Alexandria . . . Why?*, but Nadia's mother says that *The Land* was his best film (all three aforementioned films have been created by Youssef Chahine). In another scene that blends the two realities, Yahya tells Amr that he looks exactly like a young Yahya: "Gigi [Yahya's wife] has known me since we were young . . . When she saw the film, she felt like you are me exactly. Meligui looks exactly like my father, and you look exactly like me as a young boy. The same look in our eyes."[28] Mahmud el-Meligui is the real actor who played Yayha's father in *Alexandria . . . Why?*,[29] while both Amr and Yayha are fictional characters, and by placing them in one cinematic place Chahine creates his own autobiographical reality where both the real and the imaginary are equal participants in the autobiographical act.

Taking into account the complex, multilayered texture of the film, who then is Chahine's "target audience"? Resembling Sumayyah Ramadan's multilayered intertextuality, discussed earlier and which required an informed reader, Chahine's intertextual puzzle mandates not only a close familiarity with the first two films in the trilogy, but also a solid knowledge of various cinematic genres. Moreover, Chahine's closeness to his viewer is revealed, I argue, in his demonstration of the texture of his cinematic narrative. For instance, at the very beginning of the film there is a scene where Yahya directs Amr in his performance of Hamlet with repeated cuts, highlighting the roles played by the actor, the director, and the camera in composing a story on screen. Chahine illustrates the mechanism behind a cinematic performance and the texture of the cinematic discourse, and therefore shows his viewer the *making* behind his autobiographical narrative. Thus, Chahine's audience also becomes a participant in his autobiographical act.

Finally, *Alexandria Again and Forever* offers an interesting synthesis of the performative and the autobiographical, even in comparison with the first two films. If we define *Alexandria . . . Why?*, *An Egyptian Story*, and *Alexandria Again and Forever* as performative autobiographies – that is, an autobiographical story related by means of cinematic, theatrical, folk, or other performance by one or more actors[30] – then, the last film in the series is perhaps the most intricate of the three because it includes a performance by Chahine himself. In other words, in *Alexandria Again and Forever* we encounter a performative autobiography with an element of autobiographical performance. This synthesis highlights the subject's fragmentality even fur-

Figure 8 *Alexandria Again and Forever*: Youssef Chahine stepping into the role of older Yahya and Amr Abd El-Gelil in the role of Muhsin Muhieddin who played young Yahya in the first installment of the trilogy, *Alexandria . . . Why?*

All images from Youssef Chahine's films courtesy of MISR International Films.

ther, especially since Chahine-the-author contemplates his two professional identities: the filmmaker (accomplished) and the actor (unfulfilled). There is a recurring message throughout the film implying that Yahya–Chahine could have had an outstanding acting career, were he to have followed his brilliant performance of Hamlet in his youth (featured extensively in *Alexandria . . . Why?*) or his breakout role in *Cairo Station*. Thus, the fragmentation of autobiographical identity in *Alexandria Again and Forever* occurs on every level of the cinematic narrative: performatively, visually, and content-wise.

5 Conclusion: Youssef Chahine's Filmic Selves

I believe that despite the many discussions dedicated to the Alexandria Trilogy, Chahine is underappreciated and still largely unstudied when it comes to his contributions to the Arab autobiographical discourse, and, in more general terms, to the development of cinematic autobiography. I also believe that other Arab directors of autobiographical film have been influenced by Chahine's vision in the making of their own filmic life stories. One such example is Ziad Doueiri's *West Beirut*, where occasional interjections of documentary, its memoiristic mode, and its focus on the city of Beirut in many ways resemble *Alexandria . . . Why?* Beyond doubt, Youssef Chahine's trilogy adds a new dimension to the Arab autobiographical discourse. His experimentations with the self-referential narrative using the cinematic medium offer novel methods of articulating personal selfhood, where performative and visual elements highlight the highly complex nature of human subjectivity. Each of the three films offers a different mode of autobiographical representation. If *Alexandria . . . Why?* is a relatively straightforward coming-of-age story composed in a strong memoiristic mode, *An Egyptian Story* is an elaborate attempt to articulate a fragmented subjectivity, while the last film of the trilogy offers an interesting take on the relationship between the autobiographical and the performative.

Intertextuality appears to be a crucial element in all three installments of the Alexandria trilogy. Fragments of documentary chronicles, Chahine's other films, and borrowings from various cinematic genres – all interwoven with the main story – create an uneven, multilayered narrative that seems to imitate the intricacy of a human life. Moreover, the increasing fragmentation of the autobiographical subject throughout the trilogy offers an insight into the nature of fragmented subjectivities. However, despite the multidimensional intricacy of Chahine's autobiographical acts, there is still a desire – nostalgia? – for a uniform self, especially in the last two films. *An Egyptian Story* ends with the child Yahya dissolving into the adult Yahya on screen, suggesting the "happy-ending" unification of the subject. While the final scenes of *Alexandria Again and Forever* seemingly focus on the political as Yahya puts himself behind the camera to film the assembly of the actors guild, their chanting for unity – "One voice! One heart!" – could be also interpreted as Chahine's wish for uniformity of his split self. Echoing Sumayyah Ramadan's, Batul al-Khudayri's, and Ihab Hassan's longings for autobiographical uniformity, discussed in the previous chapter, Chahine, too, does not seem to be content with a fragmented self. And, just as in these narratives that negotiate (irreconcilably split) multicultural identities, Chahine's autobiographical fragmentality remains a condition never to be overcome. If anything, Chahine's autobiographical trilogy displays the complexity of human agency.

Notes

1. Truffaut himself created a number of cinematic autobiographies: a series of films centered on his alter-ego character Antoine Doine, the most well known of which are *The 400 Blows* (1959), and *The Man Who Loved Women* (1977), reflecting on the filmmaker's complicated love life.
2. An important subcategory of a motion-picture autobiographical film that deserves a separate study is cinematographic adaptations of literary autobiographies. In American cinema, there are numerous examples of such works, such as Jean-Jacques Annoud's *Seven Years in Tibet* (1997), based on Heinrich Harrer's autobiography, and *The Boy's Life* (1993), a coming-of-age story of the writer Tobias Wolff.
3. Documentary as a genre resists concrete definition. In Bill Nichols' words, "our own idea of whether a film is or is not a documentary is highly susceptible to suggestion" (Nichols 2010: xii). In addition to that, its internal diversity of form makes a generalizing analysis even more difficult. "Documentary is what we may call a 'fuzzy concept.' Not all films that count as documentaries bear a close resemblance to each other, just as many disparate sorts of transportation devices can count as a "vehicle" (Nichols 2010: 21). With regard to autobiographical documentaries, they indeed call for an inquiry of its own because of the peculiar status of documentary film as representing "reality," and because of its intricate relationship with "truth."
4. In actuality, Chahine's autobiographical oeuvre is a quartet, the fourth installment of the series being *Alexandria . . . New York* (2004). But because the last film represents a significantly later period in the author's life and body of work, which took a different direction from his cinematic style of the 1970s and 1980s, it is not included in this discussion.
5. Here I refer to Mahfouz's legendary *Cairo Trilogy*, which he wrote in the 1950s (the novels constituting the trilogy are *Palace Walk*, *Palace of Desire*, and *Sugar Street*). Moreover, the two giants of the Egyptian cultural scene of the twentieth century have collaborated on two very successful film projects: *Saladin* (1963) and *Al-Ikhtiyār* (*The Choice*, 1970).
6. My translation. The Arabic text available at: http://www.elcinema.com/person/pr1009693/biography, accessed September 30, 2012.
7. There are numerous monographs and articles in Arabic and Western languages about different aspects of Youssef Chahine's work, including: Malek Khouri, *The Arab National Project in Youssef Chahine's Cinema* (2010); Ibrahim al-Aris,

Yūsuf Shahīn: Naẓrat al-Ṭifl wa Qabḍat al-Mutamarrid (2009); Walid Shamit, *Yūsuf Shāhīn: Ḥayāh lil-Sīnimā* (2001); Muhammad Sawi, *Sīnimā Yūsuf Shāhīn: Riḥlah Aydiyūlūjīyah* (1990). For more see the Bibliography.

8. Here and subsequently I provide my own translation (and not the English subtitles on the officially released DVD) of all quotes from the Alexandria trilogy, for more accuracy.

إسكندريه بالنسبة لي كل حياتي. مش بس أهلي والناس إللي عاشوا هنا من قرون، لكن طفولتي وأفكاري، كله نابع من هنا. والدتي مدفونة هنا. وأنا – زيّ إللي مطلوب منّي إنّي أرمي حياتي وذكرياتي كلها ورايا وأسرح في البلاد؟

9. The famous waterfront promenade in Alexandria.
10. Yahya says: "Oh boy, [they act] like animals! I would never be able to act this way!"

الحيوانات يا أخي! بالطريقة دي مش حاعرف أعمل حاجة!

11. A literary example of a similar type of narrative versus documentary intertextuality can be found in Ibrahim Sonallah's *Zaat* (1992), where the main text of the novel is interjected with news headlines, advertising, and captions.
12. Following their collaboration in *Alexandria . . . Why?* and *An Egyptian Story*, Chahine continued casting Muheiddin in major roles – the latter starred in *Adieu Bonaparte* (1984) and *Al-Yawm al-Sādis* (*The Sixth Day*, 1986).
13. My translation. The Arabic text available at: http://www.elcinema.com/person/pr1009693/biography, accessed September 30, 2012.
14. Translated from Arabic:

بس لازم تعملي حسابك : أنا معقد وعصبي وتفكيري زي العيال. وأموت في الناس تدلعني

15. إيه إللي سدّها؟ – ميّة وعشرين سيجارة. – دي طبقة من مادة بتبطّن جدران الشرايين من جوا. ده لأنك عصبي. – الحياة كلها قمع في قمع، من صغري للجامعة لدلوقتي. وكل احتياجاتي دائما أؤجّلها لبكره.

16. الواحد مش عارف يبطّل سيجارة حيقدر يغيّر عقده وماضيه ؟

17. Assuming responsibility for not being able to defend the country effectively during the Six-Day War with Israel, Nasser announced his official resignation on Egyptian television on June 8, 1967. This generated massive anti-resignation demonstrations both in Egypt and throughout the Arab world, and resulted in Nasser retracting his decision on the following day.
18. In fact, the two do have certain biographical similarities: Nasser, too, suffered a heart attack as a result of chain-smoking and stress.
19. *Bāb al-Ḥadīd* (*Cairo Station*, 1958), directed by Chahine, also features him in

the title role as Qinawi, a newspaper seller – a brilliant acting performance from Chahine.

20. The quote is taken from the following online review: http://www.chicagoreader.com/chicago/alexandria-again-and-forever/Film?oid=1071478.
21. The quote is taken from the following online review: http://www.allinoneboat.org/2011/02/19/alexandriaagain-and-forever-youssef-chahine-and-changing-egypt.
22. عمرو كان شبهك أيام ما كنّا في المدرسة. بس أنت كنت ممثل رائع! – لا هو أحسن. لما مثّل دوري اتلخبطت. ما بئتش عارف مين أنا ومين هوّ. يمكن هو كمان اتلخبط.
23. أنا باحبّه لحدّ دلوقتي! إسأليه هوّ!آه! بيحبّني زيّ ما أنا؟! ولاّ معلّق عالشبه اللي اخترعه في نافوخه؟!
24. In *Alexandria . . . Why?*, the young Yahya Mourad reenacts Hamlet's monologue to his mother in several episodes of the film, indicating his self-inclusion into the elite of the performative arts and, at the same time, offering a metaphor to Chahine's views on corruption in Egypt. *An Egyptian Story*, highlighting the autobiographical subject's identity crisis, is in itself a long meditation on "To be or not to be."
25. الناس بتفتكر إنك وحش مفترس. والحق إنك... شفّاف.
26. خُد عينيّ وشوفُه بيها. حتلاقيه جُوّاه جميل
27. سوستراتس، إسكاندر ... بيقولوا حتى المسيح درس هنا
28. جيجي تعرفني من وأحنا صغيّرين ... لما شافت الفيلم حسّت إنّك أنت أنا بالضبط. المليجي أبويا باللّي وأنت وأنا صغيّر باللّي. نظرة العين واحدة.
29. Mahmud al-Meligui (1910–1983) was a popular award-winning Egyptian actor, who reached stardom in the 1930s and acted in over 700 films throughout his long acting career. Because of his physical resemblance to the famous American actor, el-Meligui was nicknamed the "Marlon Brando of the East."
30. Here I use my own narrow definition of "performative autobiography," where the actual term allows for various other interpretations.

5

What Does My Avatar Say About Me? Autobiographical Cyber-writing and Postmodern Identity

> When we step through the screen into virtual communities, we reconstruct our identities on the other side of the looking glass. This reconstruction is our cultural work in progress.
>
> Sherry Turkle, *Life on the Screen*

1 New Sites of Autobiographical Production: *Autoblography*

In the first decades of the twenty-first century, cyberspace has integrated our lives in so many different ways. It is the source of instantaneous information: we read, hear, and watch the ever-changing news cycle, flipping through news channels, eyewitness reports, and individual opinions from every part of the world. It is where popular culture takes place: we read stories, watch films and TV videos, listen to music, and talk about our cultural experiences. It is where much of the social exchanges take place (for many people, it is where *all* of their social exchanges take place): Facebook, Twitter, YouTube, Internet gaming, Blogspot, and a myriad of similar sites provide unprecedented opportunities to construct communication lines between different cultures, generations, genders, and societal groups. In other words, for many, the ever-expanding cyber universe has become a place where a significant part of their living reality takes place.

From the identity studies point of view, cyberspace has truly revolutionized – and continues to do so – both our understanding of selfhood and the ways in which we perform our individual identities on a daily basis. The questions behind cyber identity are so many and so complex that one needs to navigate through all available theories on human subjectivity to even begin unwrapping the implications of cyber-living on general human experience. Avatars, gaming personalities, profiles on dating sites, blogs, twits, chat rooms, and personal webpages such as Facebook provide limitless prospects to create multiple – virtual – versions of our selves. Modern technology offers every one of us with a computer and Internet access a series of reincarnations in cyberspace, and ways to construct virtual bodies however we want and however we want *others* to see us. Sherry Turkle wrote about contemporary identity-making experiments that the Internet provided a medium for:

> Now, in postmodern times, multiple identities are no longer so much on the margins of things. Many more people experience identity as a set of roles that can be mixed and matched, whose diverse demands need to be negotiated . . . The Internet has become a significant social laboratory for experimenting with the constructions and reconstructions of self that characterize postmodern life. In its virtual reality, we self-fashion and self-create. (Turkle 1995: 180)

Moreover, cyber existences (there certainly could be more than one) challenge the traditional perceptions of selfhood and create numerous possibilities to better understand the dynamics of subjectivity and human agency, as argued in the words of Sidonie Smith and Julia Watson:

> As the platforms, templates, and modes of communicative exchanges increase and intersect hypertextually, they add to the forms of visual life narrative produced during the twentieth century virtual forms of social networking systems that link people around the world instantaneously and interactively. What subjectivity becomes in the fluidity of digital environments is the topic that will occupy scholars in coming decades. (Smith and Watson 2010: 167–8)

Whereas the medium of cyberspace provides diverse ways to articulate one's selfhood, for the purpose of this study I am particularly interested in the genre of autobiographical blogs. Personal and journalistic blogging has become increasingly popular in the last decade. Most news stations, newspapers, government institutions, universities and colleges, social clubs, and other numerous sociocultural and political organizations have blogs at the core of their discursive practices. Personal blogs on such websites as Worldpress, LiveJournal and Blogspot, too, have generated substantial interest from cyber readers, as they provided diverse accounts of both collective and individual experiences – from major historical events, such as the Iraq War and the Occupy Movement, to personalized private revelations that satisfy the everlasting human fascination with the "lives of others." Michael Keren wrote in 2010: "While it is hard to assess the exact magnitude of the [blogging] phenomenon, the number of people writing blogs, reading them, and commenting on that is estimated at tens of millions" (Keren 2010: 110). Although the expansion of the blogging universe is limited to areas where computers and the World Wide Web are readily available (books and films also have limited audiences, after all), these numbers prove the importance of cyberspace to communicative writing experiences – where writers and readers engage, often simultaneously, in identity-making practices online.

In the Arab world, blogging has become an even more important element in cultural life and a great platform for ideological movements – especially in the hands of younger generations. Providing a censorship-free medium (at least in those places where government does not have control over the Internet), the possibility of reaching wide audiences locally and internationally without having to earn a "name" in literary or filmmaking circles, and opportunities to overcome societal and cultural constraints by means of anonymity, blogs – *mudawwanāt* – offer artistic outlets for expressing one's selfhood with much innovative freedom. These new autobiographical forms challenged the established preconceptions and expectations of life-writing and self-referential writing. Thus, Gillian Whitlock wrote about Salam Pax's weblog, streamed from his apartment in Baghdad during the US invasion: "Pax and his blog 'fit badly' with what we know; they are elusive when translated into familiar ways of thinking about how autobiography touches the world" (Whitlock 2007: 25).

This chapter discusses what I term *autoblography*: a series of autobiographical blogs by the same author, often united by a common thematic thread. Autoblography can take various shapes: some focus on individual private autobiographical experiences, others tackle larger political and social issues, for example, providing eye-witness reports to a major event, but all of them essentially offer a chain of autobiographical experiences – or autobiographical utterances – in the form of separate blog entries. Autoblographies are very peculiar modes of self-expression since they provide a fresh outlook on the complex relationship between individual and collective: there is something very paradoxical about rendering highly individual, private narrative accounts in the highly public space of the World Wide Web. Moreover, bloggers are increasingly perceived as public figures, as "today the blogger is often seen as a public intellectual due to the expansion of 'public' to incorporate many private concerns discussed in blogs, and the opportunity given to a much larger number of people to comment on public affairs" (Keren 2010: 113–14).

Recently, autoblographies that have received substantial interest from their readers and the media have been published as books, translating the virtual cybertext into a more "solid" form and creating interesting connections between cyber and conventional discourses of life-writing. In Arabic, these included the concurrent publication in 2008 by Dar al-Shuruq[1] of the widely circulated blogs by three young Egyptian women: Ghada Abd al-Al's *ʿĀyizah ʾAtgawwiz* (*I Want to Get Married*), Ghada Muhammad Mahmud's *ʾAmmā Hadhihi . . . Fa Raqṣati ʾAnā* (*As for This, It is My Own Dance*), and Rihab Bassam's *ʾUrz bil-Laban li-Shakhṣayn* (*Rice Pudding for Two*). Arab autoblographies are also published in English, the most popular of which are Salaam Pax's *The Baghdad Blog* (2003), based on his widely read blog "Where is Raed?," and Riverbend's *Baghdad Burning: Girl Blog from Iraq* (2005) – both bloggers giving personalized on-the-ground coverage of the Iraq War.[2] In this chapter, I will focus on Ghada Abd al-Al's self-representational cyber-writing, where autobiographical blogging voices young Arab (Egyptian) generations and illustrates new ways in which individual identity is articulated through unconventional forms of cultural expression.

Before we proceed to discuss Abd al-Al's autoblography, I would like to outline some important aspects of the blogosphere with regard to articulating personal identity. First, blogging – with its accessibility and flexibility as a medium – completely changes the relationship between the author and the audience. Not only is there a direct communication line between blog writers and their readers – often in real time, but the instantaneous "back and forth" nature of online communication certainly has an impact on subsequent blog entries, therefore making the blog reader an active participant in the autobiographical act. Second, autoblography – just like the previously discussed autobiographical film – offers a medium that is particularly convenient for articulating fragmented subjectivities. But if in Chahine's trilogy we have experienced the subject's fragmentation primarily on the performative and visual levels emphasized by intertextuality, the very format of blogging – short and usually immediate narrative entries – illustrates the fragmented nature of human experience. I suggest looking at autoblographies as isolated autobiographical experiences – or single utterances of autobiographical transmission – strung together by a common thematic thread.

Unlike more conventional streamlined modes of life-writing, blogs offer very different experiences both for the autobiographical authors and their audiences. Cyber-writing as a medium – with possibilities for endless textual manipulation, alteration, and deletion – is as much related to oral folk tradition or storytelling as it is to written self-referential accounts. The storytelling aspect of autoblography is highlighted by the direct communication between the blogger and his or her readers – often in real time – through threaded comments and responses. Finally, weblogs render a different kind of text – a text that is multilayered and heterogeneous by definition. The hybrid of word and image, cyberspace is essentially nonlinear as it is penetrated with hyperlinks into other virtual dimensions – leading to other Internet sites, knowledge databases, videos, advertisements, and so on. Naturally, such complex textual fabric has an effect on the construction of narrative identity. In his analysis of digital biographies, Paul Longley Arthur wrote:

> A crucial difference between traditional biographies – including film and television – and people's lives represented in the online "space" is that online identities are easily manipulated at any time by the individual subject or by others. There is no doubt that even this single feature, the ability to "manage" online content at will, is changing the way we see ourselves and each other. (Arthur 2009: 76)

The quantity and quality of currently available personal blogs in Arabic suggest that this might be the new genre of self–representation. In her discussion of the young Egyptian women bloggers, Hoda Elsadda stressed that blogs resist strict classification and, in their fluidity and flexibility, offer new expressions of selfhood:

> They are forums for consciousness raising, social transformation and political mobilization. They are diaries, narratives of the self that are no longer locked up in drawers but made available to an audience. They probe the intimate secrets of the self, which is on display, even if under a false name. They are also messages or letters sent out to an imagined virtual audience. In actual fact, literary blogs defy generic classification: they are invariably a mélange of diaries, memoirs, autobiographical stories, to-do shopping lists, political manifestos, reflections, epistolary narratives, short stories and novels. (Elsadda 2010: 328)

And although some have claimed that blogging is globally losing its popularity due to the continuous "speeding up" and shortening of cyber discourses – Facebook posts, Twits, and instant messages,[3] autobiographical weblogs offer an insight into the making of identity politics of younger generations, especially in the second half of the 2000s – the time when blogging (both in Arabic and English) exploded on the Arab web. An important aspect of the blogosphere is that access is not restricted regionally or even linguistically (a large number of bloggers use English or at the very least are able to read blogs composed in English), and blog writers themselves acknowledge being influenced by other bloggers. Thus, Rihab Bassam talked about the online community of Middle Eastern bloggers and their mutual influences:

> When blogs started to pick up in 2003, 2004, this was right after the invasion of Iraq by the US. There were bloggers like Riverbend with Baghdad Burning . . . We used to follow more the Iraqi blogs, and the ones in Iran. Yes, this was some kind of connection . . . Mostly, I don't follow these now for people I liked to read stopped writing. They got busy, stopped writing. But I remember we had connections with many Arab bloggers because it was the same for them as for us: it was a place to express yourself. There was a famous blog from Saudi Arabia . . . there were these connections. (Rooney 2011: 470)

With this in mind, the future of autobiographical cyber-writing – whatever forms it may take – promises interesting developments in identity-making practices, especially with respect to configurations of national and regional identity, where the writers and their readers are no longer restricted by geographical and linguistic borders.

2 *I Want to Get Married . . .* Not!: Ghada Abd al-Al's Autobiographical Anti-Discourse

Ghada Abd al-Al's blog "wanna b a bride" (titled in English) received unprecedented popularity since its beginning on Blogspot in 2006. Full of satire and social commentary, Abd al-Al's blog challenged cultural prejudices and stereotypes on marriage. The blog was so successful that it appeared in a book form in 2008 as *ʿĀyizah ʾAtgawwiz* (*I Want to Get Married*) with over a dozen subsequent reprints, and was translated into English, Italian, German, and Dutch – all within only a few years of its initial publication. In addition to that, a TV series of the same title, starring Hind Sabri and co-written by Abd al-Al, was released in 2010 during the Ramadan season.[4]

With her autoblography, Abd al-Al – a pharmacist by training who began blogging when she was 27 – offered a glimpse into the lives and inspirations of Egyptian Gen Y-ers (the generation born in late 1970s–1980s), highlighting idiosyncrasies with regard to their cultural life, cross-generational relationships, and identity politics. Both in its cyber and book format, *I Want to Get Married* offers a series of stories about failed engagements (these are titled "The First," "The Second," and so on – up to "The Tenth") repeatedly interjected with short chapters-blogs containing more general meditations on issues of identity and, more specifically, the pitfalls of being a young urban woman in twenty-first-century Egypt, such as "Thirties Girl" and "In Defense of the Egyptian Women . . . the Bully." The text is composed almost entirely in colorful Egyptian colloquial, accentuated with idioms and expressions typical of Egyptian youth culture, English transliterations, and occasional segments in *fuṣḥā* (which often carry sarcastic connotations on the linguistic level). This, of course, veils certain nuances of the narrative from a non-native speaker and makes the narrative difficult to translate into another cultural paradigm – not only with regard to Western languages, but also in some ways limiting accessibility for speakers of other Arabic dialects. Nora Eltahawy, who produced an excellent tongue-in-cheek translation of *I Want to Get Married* into contemporary American English, wrote about numerous linguistic challenges faced by the text's translator:

Figure 9 Front page of Ghada Abd al-Al's blog *I Want to Be Married*
Screen shots courtesy of the author, Ghada Abd al-Al

In the course of her writing, Abdel al-Al offsets the Egyptian dialect she uses in the majority of the work, and which she manipulates alternately into lighthearted satire or angry speechifying, with religious citations, Arab cultural references, Modern Standard Arabic, transliterated English, and

> American celebrity culture. While this combination is far from unusual in a country exposed equally to the lived realities of the Middle East and the televised ones of the West, it is one that offers a particular challenge in translation. (Abd al-Al 2010: xiii)

Similarly, one of the comments on the article about the TV series *ʿĀyizah ʾAtgawwiz* stresses the blog's deep rooting in modern-day Egyptian culture: "I personally am a reader of her blog since its very beginning, post by post. Every post has many very Egyptian details, which makes it nearly impossible to be copied."[5] In addition to that, in order to fully appreciate Abd al-Al's humor and understand the nuances, one should be at least familiar with English since she very often uses transliterated and colloquialized English words in her writing. Thus, despite the fact that Abd al-Al's blog is circulating in the accessible medium of the Internet, its linguistic features limit its audience – or, at the very least, conceal some of the aspects of the narrative.[6]

Cyber-writing being a peculiar hybrid of private and public discourses, also offers a new perspective on the relationship between individual and collective identities. Abd al-Al asserts her individualism from the very first entries of her autoblography. She outlines her own reasons for wanting to get married, and explains in detail how these reasons set her apart from other women her age, placing particular emphasis on the uniqueness of her point of view: "Now *I* have a completely different set of reasons. Nothing Big and Important like the [other girls'] reasons I just listed" (Abd al-Al 2010: 6).[7] Soon after, she asserts her independence and the distinctiveness of her life choices:

> I'm saying it from the get-go: if it happens . . . if I don't get married and if I don't have children and if I can't follow society's grand plan, I will always have my independent nature and I will always have my own life and I will never be . . . a good-for-nothing. (*ibid.*: 15)

But while sharing some very personal stories with her readers – her encounters with potential grooms, private conversations with her female friends, insights into private matters of her family, and so on – Abd al-Al is at the same time very aware of the collective aspect of Egyptian womanhood and claims to be the voice of not only her generation, but of all Egyptian women:

> I represent 15 million of women between the ages of 25 and 35 who are on a daily basis pressured by society to get married, while it is not at all their fault that they have not been able to do so yet.[8]

Having stated this on her Internet profile, she further emphasizes the collective representational value of her blog in her very first entry:

> I, "Bride" (I'm using English here so people think I'm classy), have decided to write about this and explain the situation from all possible angles so that people who don't understand can get it, and so that people who don't know can find out – that girls are poor little things, that the pressure they're under gets worse every day, and that people judge them for something in which they have no hand. (Abd al-Al 2010: 5)

Therefore, although *I Want to Get Married* utilizes the Internet, an untraditional medium for autobiographical discourse, one can still notice some similarities with the earlier works of the genre where the collective was an active participant in the construction of personal identity and where the autobiographical narrator was seen as voicing a generation, a social class, or another form of community (see my discussion of autobiographies of Ahmad Amin, Salama Musa, and other earlier authors in the Introduction). This dichotomy of the highly personal versus the ever-present communal discourses is highlighted throughout the narrative even on a structural level: the individual "groom stories," detailing Abd al-Al's feelings and her interactions with family and friends, are intertwined with blogs dedicated to general reflections on marriage traditions and other challenges of Egyptian womanhood faced by young women of her generation. For example, between the "Groom No. 2" story, covering an encounter with a thief who pretended to be a potential groom in order to steal all her money, and the "Groom No. 3" episode, featuring the "Manly Man" suitor whose visit becomes a complete fiasco, Abd al-Al offers a blog titled "On Delicacy and Femininity," which rips into unrealistic expectations that Egyptian society imposes on women of all ages and generations. She ends it with a passionate proclamation in defense of Egyptian women:

> So, beloved husbands everywhere, don't be upset when your brides turn into somebody else after you marry them. They don't have any other option.

> Maybe if you put SOME effort and helped them, they'd have a little more time to look after themselves. And, beloved husbands, when you're looking for partners, pay attention to their upbringing and their manners and their faith instead of focusing on things like "delicacy" and "femininity." (*ibid.*: 23–4)

The writing style of direct communication with the reader, often addressing them in the second person throughout every blog entry, creates a sense of openness and sincerity, and establishes a semblance of trust between Abd al-Al and her audience. It is as if she is trying to say: look, I am just like you, I have my own personal story but I am also one of many, one of you. To compose her blog as a dialog with the reader, Abd al-Al often incorporates – or imitates – many elements of storytelling: her entries are short and direct; she tells stories while simultaneously talking about her feelings; she poses questions to readers throughout the narrative; and she even uses some features of spoken language in the typed text, such as multiplying the vowels to resemble speech (expressions of joy, sighing, and so on). The dialogical element of autoblography is further highlighted by means of readers' comments and remarks, which I will illustrate in the next section of this chapter.

On the content level, the most prominent feature of *I Want to Get Married* is the highly subversive and rebellious discourse that the blog offers to readers. Indeed, Abd al-Al's autoblography works hard to destabilize dominant sociocultural discourses in several different ways. She starts her very first entry with some blunt accusations of Egyptian society that, according to the author, continues to reinforce the patriarchal male–female binary and to objectify women:

> Honestly, the damn society we live in that rates girls according to marriages they land, and that values women who get married super quick and that thinks that there must be something wrong with the ones who don't, and that says, on the other hand, that it's a man's right to choose and be picky and that players are open-minded men of the world, and that sees nothing wrong with men getting married anytime after forty, even if it's to an eighteen-year-old . . . that society is just UNFAIR and cruel. (Abd al-Al 2010: 4–5)

While social commentary is in no way unusual in Arab cultural discourses, including autobiographical production, very rarely does it take such a forceful in-your-face approach. I should note though that the blog was initially anonymous – Abd al-Al wrote under the pseudonym "Bride" (using an English word transliterated into Arabic letters) – and one might account such boldness to the invisibility of the offline author and the lack of censorship restrictions in the blogosphere. However, when *I Want to Get Married* appeared in its book version with Ghada Abd al-Al's name on it, the text had not been modified and the sharp social critique remained as is.

Not only does the blog attack Egyptian society at large, but Abd al-Al goes after specific elements of this society, leaving no stone unturned. Expectedly, the author is very respectful of her parents, and even in the most humorous moments she writes about them with deep affection, yet she mercilessly mocks pretty much all other representatives of the older generation. The most frequent target of Abd al-Al's sarcasm in this category is Tant Shukreyyah, nicknamed Tant Hishariyyah – in Egyptian slang *hishariyyah* means "the one who intrudes in other people's business," translated as Auntie-Body in the English version of the book. Auntie-Body is featured in many blog entries as an embodiment of all that is superficial and hypocritical of her parents' generation. She is all urban kitsch ("they trailed in: Tante Shukreyya in an urban-trash couture dress" (Abd al-Al 2010: 40), her speech is full of fake mannerisms, and she forcefully inserts herself into everything that takes place in the Bride's household (which, among other things, included bringing her two grooms-disasters). The Bride even compares her – in a hilarious and highly sarcastic manner – to Al-Qaeda:

> What are the five things that Tante Shukreyya and Al-Qaeda have in common? . . . One: The two – regardless of whether we agree with them or disagree with them (you could, by the way, agree with Al-Qaeda, but it is impossible to agree with Tante Shukreyya) – will always be responsible for explosion and destruction and, more often than not, blood will be spilled. (*ibid.*: 36)

The young generation, however, is not left unscathed either. Abd al-Al emphasizes the superficiality of young people who live their lives through television shows and have lost their morals: "Baba gave her a look that meant:

it's obvious that he's a sleazeball and needs to have his eyes gouged out! . . . All men are like that now. This is the generation of satellite television, my friend!" (*ibid.*: 28). Abd al-Al criticizes their inability to gain control over their lives, their obsession with material things, their "loser mentality," and general uselessness. For example, she writes about her Groom No. 2, who posed as a suitor just to rob her, as a typical representative of the "youth generation" – while simultaneously mocking the rhetoric of the Mubarak era:

> He was carrying a briefcase and wearing a suit and tie and sunglasses. Looked like one of those guys from the Youth of the Future campaign ads Gamal Mubarak sponsored. "The youth of our generation . . . how quickly we'll rise . . . hear! Hear!" Remember them? (*ibid.*: 17)

A practicing Muslim, she goes after religious hypocrisy where faith is replaced with pretense and religiosity is manipulated for personal gain. Thus, she sarcastically criticizes young men who use religion to either control their fiancées and wives or to justify their own (often reckless and careless) behavior. Abd al-Al gives us an example of such hypocritical practices when she talks about engagements and the creation by men of rules convenient for themselves by dragging religion into it:

> you find him insisting that you don't go out together. He says, "It's forbidden in our religion! We aren't legally married yet and God wouldn't be happy with it." (Naturally, you realize that he's trying to save money he'd spend on the outings . . . because the boy doesn't even know what prayer looks like.) (*ibid.*: 139)

Even the "sacred of the sacred" subject of glorious ancient Egypt is ridiculed in *I Want to Get Married*, which further emphasizes the overall subversiveness of the blog. Whereas many other works of social commentary use ancient Egypt as a contrast to the current corrupt reality and as a calling to return to the past greatness, Abd al-Al makes fun of it. This may not be a central theme in her blog, but it serves to reinforce the general social anti-discourse in *I Want to Get Married*. For instance, she compares Groom No. 7 to the famous Ramses sculpture in downtown Cairo:

> Abeh Ashraf is my tante Rasha's son, and he's only seven years older than I am . . . I'm not entirely sure why we act like he's twenty or twenty-five

> years older than us. Maybe it's because he's levelheaded? . . . Or maybe because he and the statue of Ramses are two peas in a pod. The only difference between them is that Abeh Ashraf is respectable and would never stand in the middle of a public square wearing nothing but a miniskirt like that Ramses. (*ibid.*: 129)

While Abd al-Al offers ferocious commentary to various elements of contemporary Egyptian society, the prominent aspect of her blog that is particularly subversive to the dominant culture is cyber-feminism. As a term, cyber-feminism is a fluid construct that could acquire a number of definitions and could be applicable to various sociocultural and ideological settings, but its principal framework is based on the relationship between feminism and technology.[9] Traditionally, technology and science have been predominantly associated with the male/masculine culture due to various societal and ideological factors, such as access to adequate education, male dominance in the workforce, domestication of female labor, and so forth. As David Bell puts it, the gender–technology matrix highlights "the problematic equation of technology with men, the male and the masculine, and the concomitant exclusion of women from what we might call the 'circuit of technoculture'" (Bell 2001: 122). On the other hand, cyberspace can operate as a tool of empowerment and a space of liberation where one can overcome the restricting boundaries of one's sociocultural and domestic environment by crossing over into virtual reality:

> The internet promises women a network of lines on which to chatter, natter, work and play; virtuality brings a fluidity to identities which once had to be fixed; and multi-media provide a tactical environment in which women artists can find their space . . . Women are accessing the circuits on which they were once exchanged, hacking into security's controls, and discovering their own post-humanity. (Plant 2000: 265)

Ghada Abd al-Al writes about cyberspace as a means to share the inner life and articulate her opinions about her sociocultural milieu in a manner that allows frank confessions and unrestricted revelations. By going through the process of blog-writing she claims control over the discourse on marriage and thereby destabilizes the traditional social institution, while anonymity and lack of censorship provided by the cyber medium are perhaps the most favorable factors behind the author's self-liberation. In one of her blogs she elaborates on the progress of cyber-writing as an opportunity to express her true opinions and feelings that have previously been concealed from the public discourse:

> after I graduated, I, like many girls, entered a whirlwind of grooms and proposals and living-room meetings. Throughout it all, I was confronted with a number of situations and experiences that I kept to myself. When I looked for a way to communicate these experiences and my feelings, I found myself welcomed in cyberspace. (Abd al-Al 2010: 159)

The sense of empowerment is highlighted by the unusual boldness of her discourse: "men have become full of themselves and act like they're too good for all womankind (may their eyes and health be stricken, amen!)" (*ibid.*: 2), and Abd al-Al relentlessly goes after the "Egyptian male culture" and the social institutions supporting it. On the one hand, she is lamenting the fact that the romance is dead: "Marriages in general, and living-room marriages specifically, get treated by everyone like they're business transactions" (*ibid.*: 138). She rejects the discourse that trivializes love and reduces human relationships to a trade exchange. On the other hand, Abd al-Al's disenchanted cyber-self – "The Bride" – actively rebels against society's objectification of "the brides" to make them conveniently fit into the hegemonic system, and she channels her sentiment through her own version of cyber-feminism.

The highly subversive quality of Abd al-Al's autoblography unavoidably demands exaggerations, overgeneralizations, and stereotyping. All male characters featured in *I Want To Get Married*, with perhaps the only exception of The Bride's father, are overly negative. They scheme, cheat, and lie; they are unreasonable, lazy, entitled, and not very intelligent. Name any negative quality, and at least one of the men in Abd al-Al's blog possesses it. In her array of grooms (ten total), Abd al-Al offers a "typology" of men – or, rather, a typology of highly stereotyped masculinities. The first suitor is "The Freak Sportsguy," the second is "The Cheat," the third is "The Manly Man," the fourth is "The Impostor," the fifth is "Prince Charming," and so on. But the Egyptian men are not the only target of her scrutiny; Abd al-Al's goes after male hegemonic discourses elsewhere:

> But the good ol' Egyptian man is all talk. He isn't like the Indian man who'll fight with his wife and then pour kerosene all over her . . . and he isn't like the American who'll off his wife with a bullet to the head, throw her in the nearest river, and then pretend to look for her missing body with the police . . . and he isn't like the Frenchman who'll suggest that his wife find a boy toy to calm her nerves a little. (Abd al-Al 2010: 48–9)

Such awareness of sociocultural life in other parts of the world outside the author's immediate environment is typical of the blogosphere in general, where the infinite (and at times overwhelming) flow of information constructs a distinct global cultural zone which is situated in a virtual space, unrestricted by any type of boundaries. Yes, Abd al-Al's social commentary zooms in on Egyptian culture, but the latter is perceived as an integral part of the global discourse.

Abd al-Al's criticism is not limited to simply condemning men for their bad attitude and poor treatment of women: rather, she assesses the larger sociocultural framework that generates such unfortunate conditions for women and puts unbearable pressure upon them. Women, too, are often portrayed as catty and desperately vying for attention from men, indicating how they succumb to the pressures of society. Abd al-Al raises some important questions about societal conditions, as well as women's lack of psychological preparedness, which prevent an Egyptian female from living a fulfilled and self-sufficient single life. Moreover, Abd al-Al extends her argument onto the whole Middle East, not only Egypt. Thus, she emulates a condescending conversation that takes place between a married woman and the one that is single and childless at different levels of society, and then she engages the reader to think about the perils of female singledom in Egypt:

> It's the exact same conversation, taking place on all levels of society. And no amount of success in any field can replace getting married for a Middle Eastern girl. What about a woman who can't find anyone and who's missed the train and who's obsolete, as they say? Is she useless then? Should she go set herself on fire? Generally speaking, women aren't prepared emotionally or educationally or economically for a situation like that. (*ibid.*: 15)

What Abd al-Al does here is an active subversion and reconfiguring of the traditional Egyptian female narrative in cyberspace. Technology in this case serves as a tool of empowerment and gives the author control over construction of her own (female) identity, as well as a way to articulate her generation's womanhood – even if in quite blunt and uncompromising terms. Indeed, *I Want to Get Married* prompted very diverse reactions in all its three mediums: blog, book, and television series. It did have an evident impact on pop culture, as well as showcasing some previously unspoken contradictions in Egyptian society. It also inspired other young authors to voice their personal experiences and to talk about taboo subjects. One such example is Yasmin al-Mehayri's blog *ʾAnā Āsifah, Mish ʿĀyizah ʾAtnayyil* ("Sorry, I Don't Want to Mess Around"),[10] inspired by Abd al-Al's TV series *I Want to Get Married* where she shared some of her own experiences.[11]

3 Cybertext versus Conventional Text

A crucial feature of autoblography as a genre is that it relocates the autobiographical act into a new textual–visual dimension: cyberspace or cyberculture.[12] In *The Cybercultures Reader*, Michael Benedikt gives a number of poetic definitions of cyberspace, the following among them:

> Cyberspace: A new universe, a parallel universe created and sustained by the world's computers and communication lines . . . A common mental geography, built, in turn, by consensus and revolution, canon and experiment; a territory swarming with data and lies, with mind stuff and memories of nature, with a million voices and two million eyes in a silent, invisible concert to enquiry, deal-making, dream sharing, and simple beholding. (Benedikt 2000: 29)

Indeed, cyberspace's very essence – fluid, ever-changing, lacking solidity or any tangible markers – makes it very resistant to any concrete characterization.[13] For the purpose of this study specifically we will be looking into a number of aspects characteristic of cybertext that are fundamentally different from the conventional paper-based form, and the effect they have on the autobiographical process – both from the weblog writer's and reader's points of view.

While Ghada Abd al-Al's autoblography published in a book form delivers the main narrative elements and thematic structures of her online blog, the latter does offer various additional features and *textures* of the cybertext, most of which are impossible to transfer into a conventional book medium. These cybertextual features have an impact – in varying degrees – on the construction of autobiographical identity and on the autobiographical act itself. In what follows I will elaborate on some of these elements and will discuss their importance to the autobiographical process: the visual quality of the text, hyperlinks, and the communication between the writer and the reader.

Visual Textual Elements

One striking difference between the book *I Want to Get Married* and Abd al-Al's blog "wanna b a bride" is the visual quality of the online text. Let us look at the very first blog entry, dated August 22, 2006. The book is loyal to the online version with regard to reprinting the exact words and spellings, but it is still a traditional black-on-white print. Whereas the blog offers a dark maroon main text on a light yellow background, with several sentences typed in bright blue, dark green, and the final word *salām* (good-bye) is in purple. Such a multicolored environment commands a different experience for the reader-consumer of the text and, at the same time, illustrates the author's writing process. The segments colored differently from the main text stand out and create visual ruptures in the narrative. In many cases, these are utilized to indicate direct speech by other characters (rather than the conventional indenting of the lines) or intertextuality (such as excerpts from poems), but the coloring creates a *visual* effect of multiple voices – or layers of the text – that could be easily read as a separate narrative(s).[14]

In addition to multicoloring, the text is anything but linear when it comes to fonts and divisions between paragraphs, sentences, and words. If the book offers the usual right-to-left direction with indented dialogs, the weblog is chopped into spread-out paragraphs; varying spaces between lines; centered sentences, parts of sentences, and separate words; as well as varying font sizes, some of which create an effect of zooming in on particular segments of the narrative (see Figure 10). Moreover, it contains imbedded images and occasional smilicons[15] that add to the meaning of a written word – or sometimes reverse it. For example, the long blog entry of December 21, 2008[16] features a meditation on the life event of turning 30, and the text is punctuated by greeting-card images (in English) – most of them humorous – for the occasion of the thirtieth birthday, such as: "29 + 1 = Death" and "The longest 5 years in a woman's life are between twenty-nine and thirty." These pictures contribute to the satirical content of the blog that ends with "Today I am 30 years old. And next year, God willing, I am thinking about going back to 29."[17]

Hyperlinks

Perhaps the most prominent difference between a conventional text and a cybertext is that the latter contains hyperlinks and embedded interactive non-verbal content, such as video and audio segments and images. But what is the nature of hypertext? The term, coined by Theodor H. Nelson in the 1960s, nowadays refers to:

> a form of text made up of individual blocks of text and the links that join them together. Rather than being continuous and uninterrupted like most print texts, hypertext is comprised of independent text blocks (*lexias*) connected to other text blocks, documents, or hypermedia (photographs, graphics, videos). (Sloane 2001)

Or, in more simple terms, hypertext is "a computer-based text retrieval system that enables a user to access particular locations in webpages or other electronic documents by clicking on links within specific webpages or documents."[18] Hyperlinks deconstruct the narrative in some major ways: they disrupt the linearity of the text, create open-ended fluidity, and situate intertextuality as an essential quality of cybertext. As Rob Shields wrote in his study of hypertext links:

> The ontology of the World Wide Web is more than simply a question of space, sites, and pages; it is fundamentally concerned with links and motion . . . Rather than primarily cyberspacial, the Web must be understood as dynamic. It is not a timeless, ambient space in which "action takes place," but rather a vectoral space that does not exist apart from the action of calls out to remote servers and files and linkings from one page to another. (Shields 2000: 145–6)

When it comes to an autobiographical narrative, these features peculiar to cybertext unavoidably influence the nature of the autobiographical act. Cyber-writing is characterized by a polyphony of voices, where the web user/

reader is an active participant in the identity-making process through comments, messages, and other means of web communication, while intertextual segments connected to the main narrative by means of hyperlinks bring various accompanying content which, in turn, adds contextual layers to the identity-making process.[19]

Abd al-Al's blog in its current version[20] offers a mélange of hypertextual segments. The home page features the image of the *ʿĀyizah ʾAtgawwiz* book cover, as well as links to every international edition of the book – Italian, German, English, and Dutch – leading to Amazon.com pages that sell the editions. It also includes a link to a page featuring The Best Comedy Script Prize, awarded to Abd al-Al in 2010. As we scroll down, the page contains a drop-down menu of the Blog Archive organized by date, which allows movement between different entries; thumbnail pictures of Blogspot members following Abd al-Al's blog with links to their profiles (current number of followers: 1,579[21]); a link to Google News; links to Abd al-Al's other two blogs: "home of the bridez" (sic) ("beyt el-ʿarāīs wal-ʿorsān") and "men gowah";[22] and an interactive real-time clock showing local time in Egypt. Additional hypertext is present not only in the space surrounding the blog, but also occasionally in the actual entries: Abd al-Al includes links to online articles about herself and her blog, especially those in the English-language press such as the *Washington Post*, the BBC News, and the *LA Times*; an embedded video fragment of the TV series based on her autoblography; links to Facebook, such as her profile titled "Ghada Bride," or her book-signing event posted on Facebook; and other similar hypertexts. These various hyperlinks construct a multidimensional aspect to the autobiographical narrative. We are able to perceive Abd al-Al's autobiographical narrative *in context* by means of accessing diverse information provided in hypertext: by reading profile information of "wanna b a bride" subscribers we can learn a great deal about Abd al-Al's readership; by accessing links to her published books we see her as an accomplished writer who has been also acknowledged internationally; by reading Abd al-Al's other blogs we gain a more multidimensional perception of the autobiographical process of "wanna b a bride" and learn about the author and her style.

In other words, the cyber version of Abd al-Al's autoblography offers a much more polygonal and, at the same time, fluid narrative where different

انتي يا حبيبتي خلاص؟
خلاص إيه تاني يا طنط؟
خلاص بقوا العرسان يرفضوكي والا لسه بترفضي؟
لأ يا طنط من ده على ده ..بارفض و اترفض يعني عادي
آااه..ما اللى يعمل نفسه رده تنكشه الفراخ
حتى آخر مرة و انا رايحة الشغل و واحدة فيهم كانت مشغولة و بتدي
الزبالة ل "هيثم"الزبال بتاع المنطقة ..لقيتها بتمصمص شفايفها و هي
بتقول
ربنا يعدل المعووج
قام هيثم و إيمانا منه بضرورة تكاتف قوى الشعب العاملة و بالأصالة عن
نفسه و بالنيابة عن فئة الزبالين المتعلمين قرر إنه يشارك في الحملة الوطنية
لتعريف برايد بمقامها و راح قايل
بكرة اللي فى الحلة تطلعه المغرفة
(إيه العمارة البيئة اللي انا عايشة فيها دي؟)
بس انا مازعلتش من "هيثم" عشان عارفة انه مجروح من ساعة ما رفضته لما
اتقدملي بعد ماشاف فيلم "إنتبهوا أيها السادة مصر ترجع إلى الخلف" و
افتكر نفسه محمود يس و افتكرني ناهد شريف (فيه الخير برضه بس ربنا
يستر و مايتفرجش قريب على الرصاصة لا تزال في جيبي و يفتكرني محيي
إسماعيل)..و انا رغم إعجابي بشياكته (بييجي ياخد الزبالة و هو لابس
فيرساتشي و عامل شعرة سابايكي و دايما إيده في جيبه) و رغم إن الواد
كسيب (عنده عربية بيئة مصرية
اللي هي
B.M
بس موديل قديم)
زبااااااااالالااااااااااه
انا طبعا ماكنتش باخدها على نفسي خاالص مانتوا عارفين قلبي طيب أد
إيه و قعدت ادعيله أدعيله لغاية ربنا مارزقه بخطيبته الباشمهندسة نيرمين
نرجع بآة من ذكريات معركة السلم مارس 2008 لطنط حشرية و زوزن
حصلت؟...حصلت؟...حتى زوزن؟..يعني الأول نهى ..و دلوقتي..
زوزن؟...رجلي مابقتش شايلاني و اترميت على أول كرسي لقيته و ماما
2010, i hope it's not the last :)
Blog Archive
March (3)
Followers
Join this site
with Google Friend Connect
Members (1633) More »
Already a member? Sign in
Links
Google News
Edit-Me
Edit-Me
my other blogs
بيت العرايس و العرسان
من جوه

Figure 10 A typical screen image of one of the blogs in the series, featuring a very unlinear text with chopped up sentences and a variety of fonts and colors: this fragment alone contains text of six different colors (March 22, 2008 entry)

Screen shots courtesy of the author, Ghada Abd al-Al

additional pieces (readers' comments, other blogs, and other imbedded hypertext) bleed into the main story and add various meanings to it. Such multidimensional intertextuality – one of the key aspects of autoblography – has an important impact on the autobiographical act in that we experience the autobiographical self in various contexts simultaneously: through autobiographical voice in the blog; through other narrative articulations by the same voice; through reactions to this voice in comments; and so on. This, in turn, further emphasizes the complexity and fragmentality of cyber selfhood.

Communication with Blog Readers

In his *From Text to Hypertext*, Silvio Gaggi wrote about the crucial impact that hypertext has had on our subjectivities in general, and on the relationship between Internet writers and readers in particular:

> working with electronic textuality modifies our feeling of subjectivity. Traditional texts, both visual and verbal, address a localized spectator or reader – implied by logical vanishing points or by narrating voices that seem directed toward an individual reader . . . In electronic networks, no single author addresses any single reader . . . There is a polyphony of voices, and the authority of each of them is continually qualified by their mutually commenting on one another. An active . . . reader interrogates a conventional text and does not passively consume it, but interrogation is built into electronic conversations. (Gaggi 1997: 111)

Indeed, readers' comments constitute a crucially important part of the narrative environment in blogs: their comments and reactions, which are most of the time available for public viewing, not only help to outline the narrative's perception by different audiences, but they often shape the author's subsequent blogs. This is a crucial feature of an autoblography, since readers' active participation constructs what I call a *dialogic* autobiographical narrative and demonstrates some elements of a storytelling discourse where the invisible audience of the virtual space replaces traditional life audience.

In her post of August 17, 2008, Abd al-Al points out the participatory effect of her writing: the fifty-four blog entries generated 4,813 comments and attracted 263 visitors, in addition to hundreds of emails.[23] Every single blog entry of "wanna b a bride" has readers' commentary, varying in number from about fifty to over 200 per entry. Reading these comments and reactions is truly a fascinating experience that adds a completely new dimension to autobiographical writing: each subsequent reader has simultaneous access to the actual narrative, comments to the narrative from other readers, and comments to the comments. The self-referential process here has a circular nature where the articulation of the author's identity has a continuous impact on the readers' articulation of their personal identities and vice versa.

The commentary to "wanna b a bride" ranges from humorous reactions and thanking the author for her sharp critique of the contemporary Egyptian milieu, to marriage proposals, to preaching posts, such as those suggesting that the "Bride" spend more time praying and doing charity work, rather than wasting time on her blog. The impact of readers' comments is evident in Abd al-Al's writing: not only does she write her entries as if directly talking to her audience, but parts of the blog also sometimes address previous remarks from the readers. Thus, she dedicates a good half of her "O.L.D. M.A.I.D."[24] blog to respond to a harsh and judgmental comment on one of the previous entries:

> One time, for example, a girl left me a comment on my blog telling me that what I write about speaks to what she's going through and what a lot of girls are going through. Then some joker jumped in and said: "Well, why don't you gals start an organization and call it The Old Maids Club?!" Never mind me, I'll talk about me later. But I sat there and I tried to imagine how the girl who'd left me that comment and who'd read what the guy had written must have been feeling. (Abd al-Al 2010: 127)

The above quote is a snapshot of a complex relationship between the blog writer and the blog reader, where cyber interaction shapes self-perception on both sides. Some commentators are anonymous or write under a chosen "nickname," others do use full names – although it is unclear whether or not these are real. Anonymity behind blog writing and blog reading constitutes an important aspect of cyber communication by offering a convenient medium for practicing freedom of expression – especially in a society where societal and familial institutions are more restrictive and where different forms of censorship (from political to domestic) are practiced. Therefore, cyberspace in general and the blogosphere in particular are by default, an identity-making space where each user is free to choose – or create – an (online) identity for him- or herself. As Jacob Van Kokswijk wrote in his study on social and legal aspects of virtual identity, cyberspace is where one "can equip your own world, start your own society, build your own environment, and create your own identity. Irrestrictive of geography, culture, race, gender, class, education, well-being, et cetera, the phenomenon of virtual identity (VID) seems to have unrestricted possibilities" (Kokswijk 2007: 83). What I find extremely peculiar though, is that the concept of increased freedom, associated with cyberspace and at least partly informed by fluid and unobstructed online identities, still has not fully caught up with cyber-writers and readers. Thus, Abd al-Al herself sees the Internet as "restrictive" and looks at the book publication of her blog as something that would set it free: "I continued to dream that my writing would be freed from the restrictions of cyberspace and released into the expanse of the world" (Abd al-Al 2010: 159).

In any case, the direct, open, and unrestricted lines of cyber communication between the autobiographical author and the reader create a relationship between the two, completely redefined and unprecedented in its intimacy. Not only do readers of autoblography become active participants in the blogger's autobiographical act, but they also often end up creating their own mini articulations of personal identity via comments and remarks to the blog. In conclusion, Abd al-Al's articulations of personal identity in blogosphere illustrate a new cyber dimension of modern autobiographical discourse – a dimension that does not only offer novel narrative and visual tales of selfhood, but will also, I suspect, highlight the previously unknown mechanics of identity construction and shed a new light on human subjectivity as a whole.

Notes

1. Dār al-Shurūq is one of the major publishing houses in Egypt. Hoda Elsadda points at an interesting fact: Dār al-Shurūq is very much a mainstream publishing institution, which suggests that blogs (and writing in colloquial in general) are gradually entering Arab conventional publishing discourse: "Its [Dār al-Shurūq's] owner, Ibrahim al- Mu'allim, is president of the Union of Arab Publishers; it is hardly an avant-garde publisher, rather is very much a beacon of the status quo; its publishing history is predominantly liberal Islamic; and the

focus of its venture into the literary field has not been to discover new talent, but to republish the classics of Arabic literature" (Elsadda 2010: 315).

2. Following the success of their first autoblographies, Salaam Pax (real name Salam Abd al-Munʿim) republished his book in a US edition as *The Clandestine Diary of an Ordinary Iraqi* (2003), and Riverbend (real identity unknown, allegedly this is a pseudonym of a young Iraqi female of a mixed Sunni–Shia background) went on to publish the subsequent installment of her blog *Baghdad Burning II: More Girl Blog from Iraq* (2006).
3. Rihab Bassam, the author of *ʾUrz bil-Laban li-Shakhṣayn*, elaborated on the decreasing popularity of blogs in one of her interviews: "I get people asking me about the phenomenon of the blogs which I think is not so active now with Facebook and Twitter and lots of other media. I think the blogs are diminishing somehow and the amount of pressure we can mount is diminishing compared with a couple of years ago. There are an increasing number of blogs but a decreasing – let's not say quality – but these were different times, while now it is easier just to log on, on your mobile, to twitter and cover something you just saw right away. It's faster now" (Rooney 2011: 469).
4. Traditionally, Ramadan is the high season for television series in Egypt and the Arab world, the most anticipated series are always scheduled for release during that time.
5. The quote is taken from a reader's comment to the following online article: http://globalvoicesonline.org/2010/09/04/egypt-wanna-be-a-bride-from-blog-to-tv, accessed September 1, 2012.
6. To illustrate the linguistic texture of the text with some concrete examples, consider the following excerpt:

   وفجأة تخبطك الحقيقة على دماغك ... حالة "panic attack" على حبة ضربات قلب سريعة وضيق تنفس

   (Abd al-Al 2008: 88). The phrase "panic attack" is written in English in the middle of the Arabic script, which stands out in the text both visually and discursively. However, this nuance is, of course, unnoticeable in the English translation: ". . . and all of a sudden, the truth hits you upside the head . . . A panic attack, some accelerated heartbeats, a tight chest" (Abd al-Al 2010: 75).
7. For quotes from the book version of Abd al-Al's blog, I mostly use Nora Eltahawy's English translation, which superbly transplants the linguistic and cultural flavor of the original narrative into colloquial American English. For quotes from the weblog that are outside the purview of the book, I provide my own translations.

8. The quote is taken from Abd al-Al's profile on Blogger:

   أمثل 15 مليون بنت من سنّ 25 الى سنّ 35 واللي بيضغط عليهم المجتمع كل يوم عشان يتجوزوا مع إنه مش بايديهم إنهم لسه قاعدين.

   (accessed September 17, 2010). Interestingly, Abd al-Al's Blogger profile is not available to the public anymore and this page is no longer accessible.
9. In the article "Rethinking Cyberfeminism(s)," Jessie Daniels highlights the heterogeneous nature of this term: "Cyberfeminism is neither a single theory nor a feminist movement with a clearly articulated political agenda. Rather, 'cyberfeminism' refers to a range of theories, debates, and practices about the relationship between gender and the digital culture" (Daniels 2009: 102). In a special issue of *Rhizomes*, dedicated to the discussion of cyber-feminisms, Susanna Paasonen offers a similar definition of the term: "Since the early 1990s, 'cyber' has become something of a free-floating signifier for things to do with computers and information networks, and cyberfeminism has surfaced as a discursive arena for imagining and analyzing inter-connections of gender, new technology, and the Internet in particular" (Paasonen 2002).
10. Yasmin Al-Mehayri wrote these blog entries within her larger blog "A Piece of Mind," written primarily in English. The Arabic title of *ʾAnā Āsifah, Mish ʿĀyizah ʾAtnayyil* humorously imitates Abd al-Al's *ʿĀyizah Atgawwiz*, see at: http://zeww.blogspot.com/2010/08/0.html, accessed December 3, 2012.
11. Notably, Al-Mehayri's activities on the Internet are not limited to blogging: she went on to create *SuperMama* – the first of its kind Arabic website offering various expert tips and advice to mothers and expectant mothers, which has become a very successful business venture.
12. I use the terms "cyberspace" and "cyberculture" interchangeably, applying David Bell's argument that "setting up a distinction between cyberspace and cyberculture is a false dichotomy . . . cyberspace is always cyberculture, in that we cannot separate cyberspace from its cultural contexts" (Bell 2001: 8)
13. Benedikt, too, concludes his set of definitions with the declaration that "Cyberspace as just described does not exist" (Benedikt 2000: 30).
14. At times, Abd al-Al uses as many as six different colors in the same blog entry, as in the entry dated December 2, 2006: maroon, blue, green, purple, orange, and black. In other instances, the main text is split between maroon and black, as if dividing the narrative into two independent parts (for example, the November 18, 2006 entry).
15. A set of images, often conveyed by certain key combinations, featuring variations

on "smiley faces." Smilicons are widely used in instant messaging and various forms of online communication.

16. Abd al-Al's blog continues beyond the publication of her *I Want to Get Married*, with entries of varying lengths, the last one dated March 1, 2012, available at: http://wanna-b-a-bride.blogspot.com, accessed December 15, 2012.
17. My translation from Arabic:

النهاردة باه عندي 30 سنة ... والسنة الجاية إن شاء الله بأفكر أرجع وأبقى 29

(December 21, 2008, blog entry at: http://wanna-b-a-bride.blogspot.com, accessed November 30, 2012).

18. Definition taken from online Free Dictionary at: http://www.thefreedictionary.com/hypertext, accessed November 10, 2012.
19. Ananda Mitra and Elisia Cohen emphasized the intertextual nature of cybertext: "For the WWW text, intertextuality is not implicit or hidden. Rather, it is explicit and unambiguous, and the effectivity of hypertext often depends on its extent of intertextuality" (Mitra and Cohen 1999: 184).
20. Last accessed in December 2012 at: http://wanna-b-a-bride.blogspot.com.
21. *Ibid.*
22. The latter means "from within."
23. This information is taken from the August 17, 2008, entry at: http://wanna-b-a-bride.blogspot.com, accessed in December 2012. In fact, even though Abd al-Al has not added any new entries to the blog since March 1, 2012, the site's popularity does not seem to be diminishing: as of December 2012, the blog's statistics indicate over 790,000 visits, with an average off 130 views per day (statistics taken from http://www.sitemeter.com/?a=stats&s=s26wannababride).
24. In Arabic it is titled in a similar manner, as a letter–dot abbreviation:

ع. ا. ن. س.

Conclusion: Arab Autobiography in the Twenty-first Century

In this book, my goal has been to formulate a methodological approach to recent developments in the Arab autobiographical genre across different media and modes of identity. Rather than classifying works according to their geographical origin, the authors' gender, or linguistic composition (for instance, *fuṣḥā* versus colloquial, works written in Arabic versus English-language works by Arab authors), my typology categorizes the narratives by modes of autobiographical transmission; that is, thematic or form-based frameworks that dictate particular articulations of selfhood. Modes, or categories, chosen for this study are intentionally general and universal – nationalist, corporeal, multicultural, cinematic, and cyber – which suggests possibilities for comparison with autobiographical works produced in other cultures. I have pointed out in the Introduction that the list of categories is in no way complete and could certainly be extended in a number of ways. Moreover, this same method could be applied to a more historically and geographically specific categorization, such as autobiographical narratives of war or religious life-writing, among other possibilities.

Diverse autobiographical forms continue to mushroom and develop throughout the Arab world, and most of them are yet to be explored. Twitter, Facebook, graffiti and other forms of street art, performative art, painting, photography, artistic installations, graphic novels – these newly emerged and emerging genres of cultural expression offer modes of self-representation, remarkable in their newness, and ones that often challenge the conventional preconceptions of selfhood. As we have seen in the preceding chapters, the negotiations of personal identity in textual, cinematic, and cyber narratives give an insight into larger extratextual cultural and societal processes. Therefore, unveiling and studying the new and nontraditional developments of Arab autobiographical discourse would help us to better understand the internal workings of Arab society at large.

The range of autobiographical works discussed in the previous chapters illustrates the incredible internal diversity within Arab self-referential discourse. However, one may notice a number of elements that continue to recur in the works under study and that perhaps indicate some common tendencies within contemporary Arab autobiographical production. One such element is the continued emphasis on the collective. In earlier works of the genre, collective and communal identities have not only been actively participating in individual identity-making practices, but have often served as the justification for life-writing endeavors: the authors strived to depict their life stories as representational of their environment and, therefore, as contributing to the history of their milieu, rather than "narcissistic" self-portrayals that zoom in on their individual personas. In more recent works of the genre, the collective aspect is well suited to those modalities of autobiographical transmission where communal identities play a crucial role in the autobiographical process. As we have seen in Chapter 1, both Hanna Minah and Layla Abu Zayd rely heavily on their respective communal belonging when articulating an autobiographical selfhood whose primary markers are nationalism and postcolonialism. In Minah's *Baqāyā Ṣuwar*, the making of autobiographical identity is rooted in three characters who represent different aspects of Syrian nationalism; whereas Abu Zayd goes as far as reimagining her selfhood through the prism of a common Moroccan woman "Zahra" – a collective image of postcolonial Moroccan nationhood.

Muhammad Shukri, too – as radical and nontraditional with his graphic depictions of the autobiographical body as he may appear – keenly incorporates the notion of the collective in his narrative. His articulations of bodily identity rely on his communal affiliations, despite the fact that his community features Moroccan underground social groups, such as prostitutes, smugglers, and thieves, and, as a result, subverts conventional Arab autobiographical discourse. In other words, he sees himself as a product and a typical representative of his environment. When the autobiographical narrative engages in voicing the subaltern – be it a postcolonial and still-oppressed Muslim Moroccan, a colonized Christian Syrian, or a tabooed and socially silenced Moroccan – the collective appears to play a crucial role in the identity-making process. Even Ghada Abd al-Al's autoblography, which introduces a new and original medium of cyber-writing into Arab autobiographical discourse, integrates communal representation into her personal storytelling. While blogging about her highly personalized experiences with numerous grooms and engagement ceremonies, she also offers candid social commentary and aspires to speak on behalf of not only young "brides" of her generation, but all Egyptian women of various ages and social backgrounds.

Therefore, various notions of the collective continue to be recycled and reappropriated in the most recent Arab autobiographical production. At the same time, however, one can notice another interesting trend in our case studies that stands in sharp contrast to collective identity constructions: an increased emphasis on individualism. In Sumayyah Ramadan, Batul al-Khudayri, Nazik Saba Yarid, and much of Youssef Chahine's cinematic oeuvre, the autobiographical subject is essentially defined by the notion of difference. In *Leaves of Narcissus*, it is realized through linguistic and cultural dissimilarity which prevents the narrator from assimilating in either Egypt or Ireland, while al-Khudayri's autobiographical subject stands out in her environment by simultaneously possessing the contrasting "white" English tongue and brown skin and, therefore, demonstrates the conflicting essence of a biracial subjectivity. Nazik Saba Yarid's narrative, on the other hand, articulates a distorted perception of the autobiographical body where physical difference becomes the driving force behind identity construction. Finally, Youssef Chahine's autobiographical production highlights the intricate process of the subject's fragmentation rooted in the artist's deep sense of alienation. As distinct as these examples may appear, they all emphasize the *uniqueness* of autobiographical identities formulated in these texts.

Thus, even in the limited selection of autobiographical works discussed in this monograph, the dichotomy of collective versus individual continues to be a defining quality. Interestingly, this representational dualism is often expressed in drastic terms – the identity-making practices are either overwhelmingly collective or overly individualistic. This, I argue, is a reflection of the ongoing Arab identity crisis where traditional notions of the communal clash with ideas of individualism that are typical of modernity and postmodernity. Major historical events of the last fifty years both contributed to and highlighted identity tensions in the Arab world. The often violent process of decolonization, the Arab Defeat and continuing conflicts with Israel, the Lebanese Civil War, the Iran–Iraq War, the First Gulf War, the events of September 11, 2001, the highly intricate relationships with Western economic and military powers, and, finally, the still ongoing events of the Arab Spring – these historic moments escalated the tensions between various forms of Arab national(ist) identities (representing pan-Arab, local, and regional nationalism), religious and tribal affiliations, communal belonging (urban and rural communities, social classes, gender groups, generational groups), and increasing individualism.

In addition to collective versus individual tensions, autobiographical bodies – and physicality in general – become increasingly involved in the process of identity-making. In Chapter 2, I argued that Shukri's *Bare Bread* and Yarid's *Improvisations on a Missing String* express two different physical dimensions of subjectivity (sexual and aesthetic, respectively), but works discussed in other chapters, too, illustrate the growing importance of the bodily in Arab autobiographical narratives. Thus, in al-Khudayri's *A Sky So Close*, the Iraqi-English narrator is fixated on her skin's brownness – a very visual physical marker of her ethnic identity. Chahine's second part of his autobiographical trilogy, *An Egyptian Story*, largely takes place *inside* the autobiographical body during open-heart surgery on Chahine's cinematic alter ego, Yahya. Even the *absence* of a physical body can be a signifier. For example, in Abu Zayd the deliberately vague and ambiguous descriptions of the female body aid in formulating a highly abstract representation of a common post-colonial Moroccan, unified in its gender-less image.

As for narrative methods, several of these works show frequent and interesting instances of intertextuality. Of course, Abd al-Al's autoblography is intertextual by definition (its online version in particular), since hypertext is essentially hybrid and nonlinear. But other works, too, offer unorthodox constructions of intertextuality that play important roles in the autobiographical identity-making. If anything, intertextual autobiographical narrative highlights the subject's fragmented and multidimensional nature. For instance, Sumayyah Ramadan's subtle inclusions of English discourses into her Arabic text (references to James Joyce, Oscar Wilde, and Sylvia Plath) emphasize the narrator's struggle – and inability – to formulate a solid lingua-cultural identity. Whereas Youssef Chahine's intricate filmic intertextuality, which includes documentary chronicles and references to popular Hollywood genres, as well as fragments from his own films, establishes a set of complex relationships between the metatextual author and his numerous alter egos on screen.

These very diverse approaches to autobiographical narration only prove that negotiations of Arab identities – be it individual or collective, personal or communal identities – are far from over. At the same time, the overarching themes discussed here illustrate certain internal processes characteristic of Arab cultural zones in the last few decades. I argue that the most prominent of these processes, as articulated in the autobiographical texts under study, is the escalating tension between the individual and the collective. Every single work in this corpus – created by authors of both genders, of various religious affiliations, of several generations, and representing different cultural areas of the Arab world – offers its own take on the highly complex relationship between the individual and various forms of communal identity circulating in his or her environment. From Hanna Minah's *Baqāyā Ṣuwar*, written in 1978, to Youssef Chahine's experimentations with cinematic autobiography, to a very recent cybertext by Ghada Abd al-Al – autobiographical narratives produced in the last fifty years shed a light on how the rapidly changing sociocultural and ideological environment affects individual self-perception and self-expression. My case studies were written during and after crucial historical moments, such as anticolonial struggle, the Arab–Israeli War, the Iran–Iraq War, the First Gulf War, 9/11, and the 2003 Iraq War. Their authors observed and sometimes participated in the birth and further growth of important internal social and political developments – from feminism to the revival of Islamic movements. Finally, these texts have witnessed the astonishing technical revolution that placed a personal computer and a satellite dish in virtually every household; established lines of communication and the dissemination of information between the most distant corners of the world via the Internet (which together with satellite television continues to play a crucial role in the re-awakening of pan-Arabism, among other things); accelerated affordability of video-making technology; and offered a completely new medium of virtual reality. Therefore, an exploration of these works reveals more than just a narrative articulation of personal selfhood: it also illustrates the relationship between an individual and his or her society in a constantly changing world.

I look forward to seeing new, pioneering cultural narratives of selfhood that will come out of the current turmoil in the Middle East. A series of ongoing revolutions and civil wars accentuate the intricate structure of communal affiliations and the importance of belonging – or *not* belonging – even further. Sharpened tensions between religious and ethnic groups, such as Alawites and Sunni Muslims (Syria), and conservative and secular Muslims (Egypt), or, for example, the crisis of the complex tribal societal infrastructure (Libya and Yemen) will no doubt deepen and complicate the making of the autobiographical *I*. Moreover, the continuously evolving narrative media – social networking, cell phone video-making programs, Skype recordings, street art, music forms, and other progressive channels of self-expression and life-storytelling – promise to offer new ways to articulate individual selfhood. And to those claiming that autobiography is extinct and irrelevant, Candace Lang has already famously responded: "Autobiography is indeed everywhere one cares to find it." For in its myriad of modes, forms, and media, autobiographical narration is indeed our best guide into the wonder world of human subjectivity.

Bibliography

The date in brackets following the authors' names below is that of edition used. Where the date of first publication is different, it is given in square brackets.

Primary Sources

ʿAbbās, Ihsān (1996), *Ghurbat Al-Rāʿi: Sirah Dhātiyah*, Amman: Dār al-Shurūq.

ʿAbd al-ʿĀl, Ghādah (2008), *ʿĀyzah ʾAtjawwiz*, Madīnat Naṣr, Cairo: Dār al-Shurūq.

Abd al-Al, Ghadah (2010), *I Want to Get Married!: One Wannabe Bride's Misadventures with Handsome Houdinis, Technicolor Grooms, Morality Police, and Other Mr. Not-Quite-Rights*, trans. from Arabic by Nora Eltahawy, Center for Middle Eastern Studies, University of Texas at Austin.

Abū Zayd, Laylā (1987), *ʿĀm al-Fīl*, 2nd edn., Beirut: Dār al-Afāq al-Jadīdah.

Abū Zayd, Laylā (1993), *Rujūʿ ila al-Ṭufūlah*, Casablanca: Maṭbaʿāt al-Najāḥ al-Jadīdah.

Abū Zayd, Laylā (2005), *Al-Faṣl al-Akhīr*, Casablanca: al-Markaz al-Thaqāfī al-ʿArabī.

Abu Zayd, Layla (1989), *Year of the Elephant: A Moroccan Woman's Journey Toward Independence, and Other Stories*, trans. from Arabic by the author and Elizabeth Fernea, Center for Middle Eastern Studies, University of Texas at Austin.

Abu Zayd, Layla (1998), *Return to Childhood: The Memoir of a Modern Moroccan Woman*, trans. from Arabic by the author, Heather Logan Taylor, and Elizabeth Fernea, Center for Middle Eastern Studies, University of Texas at Austin.

Abu Zayd, Layla (2000), *The Last Chapter: A Novel*, trans. from Arabic by John Liechety, Cairo: American University in Cairo Press.

Amīn, Aḥmad (1961), *Ḥayātī*, Cairo: Maktabat al-Nahḍah al-Miṣriyah.

Amin, Ahmad (1978), *My Life: The Autobiography of an Egyptian Scholar, Writer and Cultural Leader*, trans. from Arabic by Issa J. Boullata, Leiden: Brill.

Bassām, Riḥāb (2008), *ʾUrz Bi-Al-Laban Li-Shakhṣayn*, Madīnat Naṣr, Cairo: Dār al-Shurūq.

Boudjedra, Rachid (1969), *La Répudiation*, Paris: Denoël.

Ḥulw, Laylā (1984), *Fa-lā Tansa Allāh*, al-Dār al-Bayḍā': Dār al-Rashād al-Ḥadīthah.

Hassan, Ihab (1986), *Out of Egypt: Scenes and Arguments of an Autobiography*, Carbondale, IL: Southern Illinois University Press.

Ḥusayn, Ṭāhā ([1929] 1958), *Al-'Ayyām*, Cairo: Dār al-Maʿaraf.

Husayn, Taha (1997), *The Days*, trans. from Arabic by E. H. Paxton, Hilary Wayment, and Kenneth Cragg, Cairo: American University in Cairo Press.

Idrīs, Yūsuf (1988), *Abū Rijāl/A Leader of Men*, bilingual edn., trans. Saad Elkhadem, Fredericton, NB: York Press.

Khuḍayrī, Batūl (1999), *Kam Badat al-Samā' Qarībah: Riwāyah*, Beirut: al-Mu'assasah al-ʿArabiyah lil-Dirāsāt wa al-Nashr.

Khudayri, Batul (2001), *A Sky So Close: A Novel*, trans. from Arabic by Muhayman Jamil, New York: Anchor Books.

Maḥfūẓ, Najīb ([1949] 1970), *Bidāyah wa Nihāyah*, Cairo: Maktabat Miṣr.

Maḥmūd, Ghādah Muḥammad (2008), *'Amma Hādhihi . . . Fa-Raqṣatī 'Anā*, Cairo: Dār al-Shurūq.

Mīnah, Ḥannā (1978), *Baqāyā Ṣuwar: Riwāyah*, Damascus.

Minah, Hanna (1993), *Fragments of Memory: A Story of A Syrian Family*, trans. from Arabic by Olive Kenny and Lorne Kenny, Center for Middle Eastern Studies, University of Texas at Austin.

Mūsa, Salāmah (1947), *Tarbiyat Salāmah Mūsa*, [Egypt]: Dār al-Kātib al-Miṣrī.

Mūsa, Salamah (1961), *The Education of Salama Musa = Tarbiyat Salamah Musa*, trans. from Arabic by L. O. Schuman, Leiden: Brill.

Nuʿaymah, Mikhā'īl ([1959] 1977), *Sabʿūn. Ḥikāyat ʿUmr: 1889–1959*, Beirut: Mu'assasat Nawfal.

Qabbānī, Nizār (1973), *Qiṣṣatī Maʿ Al-Shiʿr*, Beirut: Manshūrāt Nizār Qabbānī.

Qarah ʿAlī, Muḥammad (1988), *Suṭūr Min Ḥayātī*, Beirut: Mu'assasat Nūfil.

Quṭb, Sayyid ([1946] 1973), *Ṭifl Min Al-Qaryah*, Beirut, Cairo: Dār al-Shurūq.

Qutb, Sayyid (2004), *A Child From the Village*, trans. from Arabic by John Calvert and William Shepard, Syracuse, NY: Syracuse University Press.

Ramaḍān, Sumayyah (2001), *Awrāq Al-Narjis: Riwāyah*, Cairo: Dār Sharqiyāt.

Ramadan, Sumayyah (2002), *Leaves of Narcissus*, trans. from Arabic by Marilyn Booth, Cairo: American University in Cairo Press.

Saʿdawi, Nawāl (1999), *Mudhakkirāt Ṭabībah*, Beirut: Dār al-'Adab.

Saʿdawi, Nawal (1988), *Memoirs of A Woman Doctor*, trans. from Arabic by Catherine Cobham, London: Saqi Books.

Shidyāq, Aḥmad Fāris and Nasīb Wahībah Khāzin ([1855] 1966), *Al-Sāq ʿAla Al-Sāq*

Fī Mā Huwa Al-Fāryāq: Aw ʾAyyām Wa-Shuhūr Wa-Aʿwām Fī ʿAjam AlʿArab Wa Al-Aʿjām, Beirut: Dār Maktabat al-Ḥayāh.

Shukrī, Muḥammad (1982), *al-Khubz al-Ḥāfī: Sīrah Dhātiyah Riwāʾīyah, 1935–1956*, Beirut: Dār al-Sāqī.

Shukri, Muhammad ([1974] 2006), *For Bread Alone*, trans. from Arabic by Paul Bowles, San Francisco, CA: Telegram.

Ṭūqān, Fadwa (1985), *Riḥlah Jabalīyah, Riḥlah Ṣaʿbah*, Amman: Dār al-Shurūq.

Tuqan, Fadwa (1990), *A Mountainous Journey: An Autobiography*, trans. from Arabic by Olive Kenny and Naomi Shihab Nye, St. Paul, MN: Graywolf Press.

Yārid, Nāzik Sābā (1992), *Taqāsīm ʿAla Watar Ḍāʾiʿ: Riwāyah*, Beirut: Nawfal.

Yarid, Nazik Saba (1997), *Improvisations on a Missing String*, trans. from Arabic by Stuart Hancox, Fayetteville, AR: University of Arkansas Press.

Yārid, Nāzik Sābā (2008), *Dhikrayāt Lam Taktamil*, Beirut: Dār al-Sāqī.

Filmography

Aḥlām al-Madīnah (*Dreams of the City*), film, directed by Muḥammad Malaṣ, Syria: General Organization for Cinema, 1983.

Aḥlām Ṣaghīrah (*Little Dreams*), film, directed by Khālid Al-Ḥajar, Egypt: Misr International Films, 1993.

Bāb Al-Ḥadīd (*Cairo Station*), film, directed by Yūsuf Shāhīn, Egypt: Misr International Films, 1958.

Bayrūt al-Gharbīyyah (*West Beirut*), film, directed by Ziyād Duwayrī, Lebanon, France, Norway, Belgium: La Sept ARTE, 3B Productions, 1998.

Ḥaddūtah Maṣrīyah (*An Egyptian Story*), film, directed by Yūsuf Shāhīn, Egypt: Misr International Films, 1982.

Al-Ḥalfawiyīn (*Halfaouine: A Boy of the Terraces*), film, directed by Farīd Būghadīr, Tunisia, France: Ciné Télé Films, R.T.T., 1990.

Iskandarīyah Kamān Wa Kamān (*Alexandria Again and Forever*), film, directed by Yūsuf Shāhīn, Egypt: Misr International Films, 1990.

Iskandarīyah . . . Ley? (*Alexandria . . . Why?*), film, directed by Yūsuf Shāhīn, Egypt: Misr International Films, 1979.

Iskandarīyah . . . Nyū Yūrk (*Alexandria . . . New York*), film, directed by Yūsuf Shāhīn, Egypt: Misr International Films, 2004.

Al-Layl (*The Night*), film, directed by Muḥammad Malaṣ, Syria: General Organization for Cinema, 1992.

Secondary Sources

ʿAbbās, Ihsān (1967), *Fann al-Sīrah*, Beirut: Dār al-Thaqāfah.

ʿAbdel-Malek, Anouar (1983), *Contemporary Arab Political Thought*, London: Zed.

Abū Iyād and Fuʾād Abū Ḥajlah (1996), *Filasṭīni Bilā Huwīyah: "... Sayakūna La-Nā Dhāt Yawm Waṭan"*, Amman: Dār al-Jalīl lil-Nashr wa-al-Dirāsat wa-al-ʾAbḥāth al-Filasṭīnīyah.

Abu-Haidar, Farida (1989), "The Bipolarity of Rachid Boudjedra," *Journal of Arabic Literature*, 20(1): 40–56.

Aciman, Andre (1999), *Letters of Transit: Reflections on Exile, Identity, Language, and Loss*, New York: New Press.

Adham, ʿAlī (1978), *Limādhā Yashqʿa al-Insān: Fuṣūl Fī al-Ḥayāt wa-al-Mujtamaʿ wa-al-ʾAdab wa-al-Tārīkh, al-Fajjālah*, Cairo: Maktabat Nahḍat Miṣr.

Ahāmī, Muḥammad Aḥlūsh (2007), *Al-Tarjamah al-Dhātiyah Fī al-ʾAdab al-Andalusī Min Khilāl ʾAʿmal Ibn Hazm*, Rabat, Morocco.

Al-Issa, Ahmad and Laila S. Dahan (2011), *Global English and Arabic: Issues of Language, Culture and Identity*, New York: Peter Lang.

Allen, Roger (1991), "*Year of the Elephant*: A Moroccan Woman's Journey Toward Independence and Other Stories: Book Review," *International Journal of Middle Eastern Studies*, 23(4): 676–8.

Allen, Roger (1998), *The Arabic Literary Heritage: The Development of its Genres and Criticism*, New York: Cambridge University Press.

Althusser, Louis (1984), *Essays on Ideology*, London: Verso.

Anderson, Benedict R. O'G ([1983] 1991), *Imagined Communities: Reflections on the Origin and Spread of Nationalism*, London: Verso.

ʿArīs, Ibrahīm (2009), *Yūsuf Shahīn: Nazrat al-Ṭifl wa-Qabḍat al-Mutamarrid*, Cairo: Dār al-Shurūq.

Arthur, Paul Longley (2009), "Digital Biography: Capturing Lives Online," *Auto/Biography Studies*, 24(1): 74–92.

Ashcroft, Bill, Gareth Griffiths, and Helen Tiffin (1989), *The Empire Writes Back: Theory and Practice in Post-Colonial Literature*, New York: Routledge.

ʿAthāminah, Fāyiz Ṣalāḥ Qāsim (2007), *Al-Sīrah al-Dhātiyah Fī al-Urdun: al-Dhāt wa al-Iṭār al-Ijtimāʿī*, Damascus: al-Takwīn lil-Ṭibāʿah wa-lil-Nashr wa-al-Tawzīʿ.

ʿAṭṭār, Mahā Fāʾiq (1997), *Fann al-Sīrah al-Dhātiyah Fī al-ʾAdab al-ʿArabī: Ḥatta Awāʾil al-Thamānīniyāt*, Damascus.

Bakhtin, M. M. and Caryl Emerson (1984), *Problems of Dostoevsky's Poetics*, Minneapolis, MN: University of Minnesota Press.

Bakhtin, M. M. (1981), *The Dialogic Imagination: Four Essays*, ed. and trans. Michael Holquist, Austin, TX: University of Texas Press.

Banes, Ruth A. (1982), "The Exemplary Self: Autobiography in Eighteenth Century America," *Biography*, 5(3): 226–39.

Barakat, Halim Isber (1993), *The Arab World: Society, Culture, and State*, Berkeley, CA: University of California Press.

Baridī, Muḥammad (2005), *ʿIndamā Tatakallamu al-Dhāt: al-Sīrah al-Dhātīyah Fī al-Adab al-ʿArabī al-Ḥadīth*, Damascus: Ittihad al-Kuttāb al-ʿArab.

Barthes, Roland (1981), *Camera Lucida: Reflections on Photography*, New York: Hill & Wang.

Barthes, Roland ([1975] 2010), *Barthes by Roland Barthes*, trans. Richard Howard, New York: Hill & Wang.

Beard, Michael (1987), "Royal Gossip and the Meaning of Fencing," *New York Times Book Review*, February 1: 24.

Bechara, Miranda (2004), "Chahine's 'Alexandrie . . . New York,' a Personal Look at Arab-American Relations," *Al-Jadid*, 10(48), available at: http://www.aljadid.com/content/chahine%E2%80%99s-%E2%80%98alexandrie%E2%80%A6-new-york%E2%80%99-personal-look-arab-american-relations, accessed September 2, 2012.

Bell, David (2001), *An Introduction to Cybercultures*, New York: Routledge.

Benedikt, Michael (2000), "Cyberspace: First Steps," in David Bell and Barbara M. Kennedy (eds.), *The Cybercultures Reader*, New York: Routledge, pp. 20–44.

Ben Jelloun, Tahar (2011), "Literature After the Revolt: Arab Writers 'Should Not Be Invisible Anymore,'" Interview by Jess Smee, *Spiegel Online International*, September 15, available at: http://www.spiegel.de/international/world/literature-after-the-revolt-arab-writers-should-not-be-invisible-anymore-a-785689.html, accessed August 1, 2012.

Bhabha, Homi K. (1990), *Nation and Narration*, New York: Routledge.

Bhabha, Homi K. (1994), *The Location of Culture*, New York: Routledge.

Blaut, J. M. (1986), "A Theory of Nationalism," *Antipode*, 18(1): 5–10.

Boler, Megan (2007), "Hypes, Hopes and Actualities: New Digital Cartesianism and Bodies in Cyberspace," *New Media & Society*, 9(1): 139–68.

Booth, Marilyn (2003), "On Translation and Madness," *Translation Review*, 65(1): 47–53.

Brockelmann, Carl (1951), "Autobiography in Arabic literature," *Pakistan Quarterly*, 1: 21–5.

Brook, Clodagh (2005), "Screening the Autobiographical," in William Hope (ed.), *Italian Cinema: New Directions*, New York: Lang, pp. 27–52.

Brubaker, Rogers and Frederick Cooper (2000), "Beyond 'Identity,'" *Theory and Society*, 29(1): 1–47.

Bruss, Elizabeth (1980), "Eye for I: Making and Unmaking Autobiography in Film," in James Olney (ed.), *Autobiography: Essays Theoretical and Critical*, Princeton, NJ: Princeton University Press.

Brusted, Kristen (1997), "Imposing Order: Reading the Conventions of Representation in al-Suyuti's Autobiography," *Edebiyat: Journal of Middle Eastern Literatures*, 7: 327–44.

Butler, Judith (1990), *Gender Trouble: Feminism and the Subversion of Identity*, New York: Routledge.

Butler, Judith ([1987] 2004), "Variations on Sex and Gender: Beauvoir, Witting, Foucault," in Sara Salih (ed.), *The Judith Butler Reader*, Oxford: Blackwell, pp. 21–38.

Chejne, Anwar G. (1962), "Travel Books in Modern Arabic Literature," *Muslim World*, 52(3): 207–15.

Civantos, Christina (2006), "Literacy, Sexuality and the Literary in the Self-Inscription of Muhammad Shukr," *Middle Eastern Literatures*, 9(1): 23–45.

Coleman, Daniel (1993), "Masculinity's Severed Self: Gender and Orientalism in *Out of Egypt* and *Running in the Family*," *Studies in Canadian Literature/Etudes en Litterature Canadienne*, 18(2): 62–80.

Connell, R. W. (1995), *Masculinities*, Berkeley, CA: University of California Press.

Cook, Victoria (2005), "Exploring Transnational Identities in Ondaatje's *Anil's Ghost*," in Steven Tötösy de Zepetnek (ed.), *Comparative Cultural Studies and Michael Ondaatje's Writing*, West Lafayette, IN: Purdue University Press, pp. 6–15.

Cooke, Miriam (2000), *Hayati, My Life: A Novel*, Syracuse, NY: Syracuse University Press.

Cooke, Miriam (2001), *Women Claim Islam: Creating Islamic Feminism Through Literature*, New York: Routledge.

Couser, G. Thomas (1997), *Recovering Bodies: Illness, Disability, and Life-Writing*, Madison, WI: University of Wisconsin Press.

Dāhi, Muḥammad (2007), *Al-Ḥaqīqah al-Multabisah: Qirā'h Fī 'Ashkāl al-Kitābah 'An al-Dhāt*, Casablanca: Sharikat al-Nashr wa-al-Tawzī' al-Madāris.

Danet, Brenda and Susan C. Herring (2007), *The Multilingual Internet: Language, Culture, and Communication Online*, Oxford: Oxford University Press.

Daniels, Jessie (2009), "Rethinking Cyberfeminism(s): Race, Gender, and Embodiment," *Women's Studies Quarterly*, 37(1/2): 101–24.

Darwīsh, ʿAlī and Dīb Shāhīn (2005), *ʾAzmat al-Lughah wa-al-Tarjamah wa-al-Hawīyah: Fī ʿAṣr al-Intirnat wa-al-Faḍāʾīyāt wa-al-Iʿlām al-Muwajjah*, Melbourne: Sharikat Rāyatskūb al-Maḥdūdah.

Davies, Edward (2004), "Finding Ourselves: Postmodern Identities and the Transgender Movement," in Stacy Gillis, Gillian Howie, and Rebecca Munford (eds.), *Third Wave Feminism: A Critical Exploration*, Basingstoke: Palgrave Macmillan, pp. 110–21.

de Man, Paul (1979), "Autobiography as De-facement," *MLN*, 94(5): 919–30.

de Man, Paul (1984), *The Rhetoric of Romanticism*, New York: Columbia University Press.

Derrida, Jacques (1979), "Living On/Border Lines," in Harold Bloom (ed.), *Deconstructionism and Criticism*, New York: Seabury Press, pp. 75–176.

Derrida, Jacques (1985), *The Ear of the Other: Otobiography, Transference, Translation: Texts and Discussions with Jacques Derrida*, ed. Christie McDonald, New York: Schocken Books.

Descartes, René ([1637] 1968), *Discourse on Method, and Other Writings*, Harmondsworth: Penguin.

Durczak, Jerzy (1992), "*Out of Egypt*: Ihab Hassan's Confidential Criticism," *Studia Anglica Posnaniensia*, 24: 3–12.

During, Simon (1998), "Postcolonial and Globalization: A Dialectical Relation after All," *Postcolonial Studies*, 1(1): 31–47.

Eakin, Paul John (1985), *Fictions in Autobiography: Studies in the Art of Self Invention*, Princeton, NJ: Princeton University Press.

Eakin, Paul John (1999), *How Our Lives Become Stories: Making Selves*, Ithaca, NY: Cornell University Press.

Eakin, Paul John (2008), *Living Autobiographically: How We Create Identity in Narrative*, Ithaca, NY: Cornell University Press.

Egan, Eric (2003), "The City as Nation: Youssef Chahine's Alexandria," *Film & Film Culture*, 2: 33–41.

Elsadda, Hoda (2010), "Arab Women Bloggers: The Emergence of Literary Counterpublics," *Middle East Journal of Culture and Communication*, 3(3): 312–32.

Enderwitz, Susanne (1998), "Public Role and Private Self," in Robin Ostle, Ed de Moor, and Stefan Wild (eds.), *Writing the Self: Autobiographical Writing in Modern Arabic Literature*, London: Saqi Books.

Fahmi, Māhir Ḥasan (1970), *Al-Sīrah Tarīkh wa-Fann*, Cairo: Maktabat al-Nahḍah al-Maṣriyah.

Fahndrich, Hartmut (1995), "Fathers and Husbands: Tyrants and Victims in Some Autobiographical and Semi-Autobiographical Works from the Arab World," in Roger Allen, Hilary Kilpatrick, and Ed De Moor (eds.), *Love and Sexuality in Modern Arabic Literature*, London: Saqi Books, pp. 106–15.

Falcoff, Mark (1987), "Review of Out of Egypt by Ihab Hassan," *The American Spectator*, 22 (10): 48–9.

Fanon, Frantz (1968), *The Wretched of the Earth*, trans. Constance Farrington, New York: Grove Press.

Foucault, Michel ([1978] 1998), *The History of Sexuality*, London: Penguin.

Foucault, Michel (1980), *Power/Knowledge: Selected Interviews and Other Writings, 1972–1977*, ed. Colin Gordon, New York: Pantheon Books.

Freedman, Jonathan (1996), *Oscar Wilde: A Collection of Critical Essays*, Upper Saddle River, NJ: Prentice Hall.

Gabara, Rachel (2006), *From Split to Screened Selves: French and Francophone Autobiography in the Third Person*, Stanford, CA: Stanford University Press.

Gaggi, Silvio (1997), *From Text to Hypertext: Decentering the Subject in Fiction, Film, the Visual Arts, and Electronic Media*, Philadelphia, PA: University of Pennsylvania Press.

Ganim, John M. (2007), "Reversing the Crusades: Hegemony, Orientalism, and Film Language in Youssef Chahine's Saladin," in Lynn T. Ramey and Tison Pugh (eds.), *Race, Class, and Gender in "Medieval" Cinema*, New York: Palgrave Macmillan, pp. 45–58.

Gillett, James (2007), "Internet Web Logs as Cultural Resistance: A Study of the SARS Arts Project," *Journal of Communication Inquiry*, 31(1): 28–43.

Gillis, Stacy (2004), "Neither Cyborg Nor Goddess: The (Im)Possibilities of Cyberfeminism," in Stacy Gillis *et al.* (eds.), *Third Wave Feminism: A Critical Exploration*, Basingstoke: Palgrave Macmillan, pp. 185–96.

Gilmore, Leigh (2010), "American Neoconfessional: Memoir, Self-Help, and Redemption on Oprah's Couch," *Biography: An Interdisciplinary Quarterly*, 33(4): 657–79.

Gomaa, Sally (2003), "Alexandria as a Postmodern Space, as a Motive Force, and as an Articulated Moment in Youssef Chahine's Discourse: Again and Forever," in Yves Clavaron and Bernard Dieterle (eds.), *La Memoire des Villes/The Memory of Cities*, Saint-Etienne: Universite de Saint-Etienne, pp. 219–23.

Gusdorf, Georges (1980), "Conditions and Limits of Autobiography," in James

Olney (ed.), *Autobiography: Essays Theoretical and Critical*, Princeton, NJ: Princeton University Press, pp. 28–48.

Ḥāfiẓ, Ṣabrī (1993), *The Genesis of Arabic Narrative Discourse: A Study in the Sociology of Modern Arabic Literature*, London: Saqi Books.

Ḥāfiẓ, Ṣabrī (2002), "Raqsh al-Dhāt Lā Kitābatuhā: Taḥawwulāt al-Istrātījīyāt al-Naṣṣīyah Fī al-Sīrah al-Dhātīyah," *Alif: Journal of Comparative Poetics*, 22: 7–33.

Hall, M. (1995), "Leila Abouzeid's *Year of the Elephant*: A Post-colonial Reading," *Women: A Cultural Review*, 6(1): 67–79.

Halstead, John (1969), "A Comparative Historical Study of Colonial Nationalism in Egypt and Morocco," *African Historical Studies*, 2(1): 85–100.

Hammond, Andrew (2005), *Pop Culture Arab World!: Media, Arts, and Lifestyle*, Santa Barbara, CA: ABC Clio.

Haraway, Donna Jeanne (1991), *Simians, Cyborgs, and Women: The Reinvention of Nature*, New York: Routledge.

Ḥassan, Ihāb (1993), "Beyond Exile: A Postcolonial Intellectual Abroad," *Southern Review*, 29(3): 453–64.

Ḥassan, Ihāb (1995), *Rumors of Change: Essays of Five Decades*, Tuscaloosa, AL: University of Alabama Press.

Ḥassan, Ihāb (1997), "Counterpoints: Nationalism, Colonialism, Multiculturalism, etc., in Personal Perspective," *Third Text*, 11(41): 3–14.

Ḥassan, Ihāb (1998/9), "Postmodernism, etc.," interview with Frank L. Cioffi, available at: http://www.ihabhassan.com/cioffi_interview_ihab_hassan.htm, accessed September 29, 2012.

Ḥassan, Ihāb (2000), "Ihab Hassan in Focus," interview with Jerzy Durczak, available at: http://www.ihabhassan.com/durczak_interview_ihab_hassan.htm, accessed September 29, 2012.

Ḥassan, Ihāb (2002), "Identity and Imagination: David Malouf and Hossein Valamenesh in Process," *Religion and the Arts*, 6(4): 441–57.

Ḥassan, Ihāb (2005), "Maps and Stories: A Brief Meditation," *Georgia Review*, 59(4): 751–63.

Hassan, Omar (2010), "Real Queer Arabs: The Tension between Colonialism and Homosexuality in Egyptian Cinema," *Film International*, 8(1[43]): 18–24.

Hassan, Wail S. (2002), "Arab-American Autobiography and the Reinvention of Identity: Two Egyptian Negotiations," *Alif: Journal of Comparative Poetics*, (22): 7–35.

Ḥaydari, ʿAbd Allah Ibn ʿAbd al-Raḥmān (1998), *Al-Sīrah al-Dhātiyah Fi al-ʾAdab al-Saʿūdī*, Riyadh: Dār al-Miʿrāj al-Dawliyah lil-Nashr.

Ḥaydari, ʿAbd Allah Ibn ʿAbd al-Raḥmān (2006), *Iḍāʾāt Fī ʾAdab al-Sīrah wa al-Sīrah al-Dhātiyah: Buḥūth wa Maqālāt wa-Ḥiwārāt*, Riyadh: Dār al-Miʿrāj al-Dawliyah lil-Nashr.

Herman, Andrew and Thomas Swiss (2000), *The World Wide Web and Contemporary Cultural Theory*, New York: Routledge.

Hewitt, Kim (1997), *Mutilating the Body: Identity in Blood and Ink*, Bowling Green, OH: Bowling Green State University Popular Press.

Hirschmann, N. J. (1998), "Western Feminism, Eastern Veiling, and the Question of Free Agency," *Constellations–Oxford*, 5(3): 345–68.

Hollingsworth, Christopher (2001), *Poetics of the Hive: The Insect Metaphor in Literature*, Iowa City: University of Iowa Press.

Ibrāhīm, Zakariyā (1967), *Mushkilat al-Insān*, Cairo: Maktabat Miṣr.

Jenkins, Henry (1992), *Textual Poachers: Television Fans and Participatory Culture*, New York: Routledge.

Jenkins, Henry (2006), *Fans, Bloggers, and Gamers: Exploring Participatory Culture*, New York: New York University Press.

Johnson, Steven (1997), *Interface Culture: How New Technology Transforms the Way We Create and Communicate*, San Francisco, CA: HarperEdge.

Jones, Steve (1997), *Virtual Culture: Identity and Communication in Cybersociety*, Thousand Oaks, CA: Sage.

Jubūrī, Muḥammad Ṣābir ʿUbayd (1999), *Al-Sīrah al-Dhātiyah al-Shiʿriyah: Qirāʾah Fī al-Tajribah al-Sīriyah Li-Shuʿarāʾ al-Ḥadāthah al-ʿArabiyah*, al-Shāriqah: Dāʾirat al-Thaqāfah wa al-Iʿlām.

Kalantzis-Cope, Phillip and Karim Gherab Martin (2011), *Emerging Digital Spaces in Contemporary Society: Properties of Technology*, Basingstoke: Palgrave Macmillan.

Kennedy, Helen (2006), "Beyond Anonymity, or Future Directions for Internet Identity Research," *New Media & Society*, 8(6): 859–76.

Keren, Michael (2010), "Blogging and Mass Politics," *Biography*, 33(1): 110–26.

Khalīdī, Rashīd (1997), *Palestinian Identity: The Construction of Modern National Consciousness*, New York: Columbia University Press.

Khātib, Līnā (2007), "Bab El-Hadid/Cairo Station: Youssef Chahine, Egypt, 1958," in Gonul Donmez-Colin and Abbas Kiarostami (eds.), *The Cinema of North Africa and the Middle East*, London: Wallflower, pp. 23–9.

Khouri, Malek (2010), *The Arab National Project in Youssef Chahine's Cinema*, Cairo: American University in Cairo Press.

Khuḍayrī, Batūl (2005), Interview with Rana Safadi, available at: http://www.betoolkhedairi.com/press_en4.htm, accessed November 1, 2012.

Khuḍayrī, Batūl (2007), "Betool Khedairi on Mixed Parentage," audio interview with Steve Paulson, available at: http://ttbook.org/book/betool-khedairi-mixed-parentage, accessed November 11, 2012.

Kilpatrick, Hilary (1991), "Autobiography and Classical Arabic Literature," *Journal of Arabic Literature*, 22(1): 1–20.

Kilpatrick, Hilary (1995), "On Love and Sexuality in Modern Arabic Literature," in Roger Allen, Hilary Kilpatrick, and Ed De Moor (eds.), *Love and Sexuality in Modern Arabic Literature*, London: Saqi Books, pp. 9–15.

Kimmich, Allison (1998), "Writing the Body: From Abject to Subject," *Auto/Biography Studies*, 13(2): 223–34.

Kokswijk, Jacob Van (2007), *Digital Ego: Social and Legal Aspects of Virtual Identity*, Delft and Chicago: Eburon and University of Chicago Press.

Kramer, Martin (1993), "Arab Nationalism: Mistaken Identity," *Daedalus*, 122(3): 171–206.

Kroetsch, Robert (1989), *The Lovely Treachery of Words: Essays Selected and New*, Oxford: Oxford University Press.

Labbas, Jūzif Ṭāniyūs (2009), *Al-Ḥubb wa Al-Mawt min Manẓūr al-Sīrah al-Dhātīyah Bayna Miṣr wa-Lubnān Fī ʾAdab: Ṭāhā Ḥusayn, Tawfiq al-Ḥakīm, ʿĀʾishah ʿAbd al-Raḥmān, Mīkhāʾīl Nuʿaymah, Tawfiq Yūsuf ʿAwwād, Layla ʿUsayrān*, Beirut: Dār al-Mashriq.

Lang, Candace (1982), "Autobiography in the Aftermath of Romanticism," *Diacritics*, 12(4): 2–16.

Lazarus, Neil (2004), *The Cambridge Companion to Postcolonial Literary Studies*, Cambridge: Cambridge University Press.

Lejeune, Philippe (1971), *L'autobiographie en France*, Paris: Armand Colin.

Lejeune, Philippe (1975), *Le pacte autobiographique*, Paris: Seuil.

Lejeune, Philippe and Paul John Eakin (1989), *On Autobiography*, Minneapolis, MN: University of Minnesota Press.

Maalouf, Amin (2001), *In the Name of Identity: Violence and the Need to Belong*, New York: Arcade Publishing.

Mahrān, Rashīdah (1979), *Ṭāhā Ḥusayn Bayna al-Sīrah wa-al-Tarjamah al-Dhātiyah*, Alexandria: al-Hayʾah al-Miṣriyah al-ʿĀmmah lil-Kitāb.

Malti-Douglas, Fedwa (1988), *Blindness and Autobiography: Al-Ayyām of Taha Husayn*, Princeton, NJ: Princeton University Press.

Malti-Douglas, Fedwa (1991), *Woman's Body, Woman's Word: Gender and*

Discourse in Arabo-Islamic Writing, Princeton, NJ: Princeton University Press.

Malti-Douglas, Fedwa (2001), *Medicines of the Soul: Female Bodies and Sacred Geographies in a Transnational Islam*, Berkeley, CA: University of California Press.

Markus, Hazel, Patricia Mullally, and Shinobu Kitayama (1997), "Selfways: Diversity in Modes of Cultural Participation," in Ulrich Neisser and David Jopling (eds.), *The Conceptual Self in Context: Culture, Experience, Self-Understanding*, Cambridge: Cambridge University Press, pp. 13–61.

Marcus, Laura (1994), *Auto/Biographical Discourses: Theory, Criticism, Practice*, New York: Manchester University Press.

Marin, Louis (1981), "Montaigne's Tomb, or Autobiographical Discourse," *Oxford Literary Review*, 4(3): 43–58.

Mehrez, Samia (2001), "A Myriad of Leaves," *Spiegel Online International*, December 20–6, available at: http://weekly.ahram.org.eg/2001/565/cu4.htm, accessed July 15, 2012.

Mehrez, Samia (2010), *Egypt's Culture Wars: Politics and Practice*, Cairo: American University in Cairo Press.

Meijer, Roel (2000), *Alienation or Integration of Arab Youth: Between Family, State and Street*, Richmond: Curzon.

Minahan, Stella and Julie Wolfram Cox (2007), "Stitch'n'Bitch: Cyberfeminism, a Third Place and the New Materiality," *Journal of Material Culture*, 12(1): 5–21.

Minh-ha, Trinh (1989), *Woman, Native, Other: Writing Postcoloniality and Feminism*, Bloomington, IN: Indiana University Press.

Mitra, Ananda and Elisia Cohen (1999), "Analyzing the Web: Directions and Challenges." in Steve Jones (ed.), *Doing Internet Research: Critical Issues and Methods for Examining the Net*, London: Sage, pp. 179–202.

Moore-Gilbert, Bart (2011), "A Concern Peculiar to Western Man? Postcolonial Reconsiderations of Autobiography as Genre," in Patrick Crowley, Jane Hiddleston, and Dominique Combe (eds.), *Postcolonial Poetics: Genre and Form*, Francophone Postcolonial Studies (FPS): 2, Liverpool: Liverpool University Press, pp. 91–108.

Moukhlis, Salah (2003), "'A History of Hopes Postponed': Women's Identity and the Postcolonial State in *Year of the Elephant*" *Research in African Literatures*, 32(3): 66–83.

Muḥammad, Shaʿbān ʿAbd al-Ḥakīm (2009), *Al-Sīrah al-Dhātiyah Fī al-ʾAdab al-ʿArabi al-Ḥadīth: Ruʾyah Naqdiyah*, Dasuq: Dār al-ʿIlm wa al-Īmān.

Munro, Ian (2003), "Interview with Leila Abouzeid, Moroccan Writer," *Journal of Commonwealth and Postcolonial Studies*, 10(2): 1–12.

Murray, Donald M. (1991), "All Writing is Autobiography," *College Composition and Communication*, 42(1): 66–74.

Mūsawī, Muḥsin (2003), *The Postcolonial Arabic Novel: Debating Ambivalence*, Leiden: Brill.

Muṣṭafa, Dāliyā Saʿīd (2010), "Taʿammulāt Ḥawla al-Dhākirah wa al-Ṣadmah ʿInda Yūsuf Shāhīn," *Alif: Journal of Comparative Poetics*, 30: 176–205.

Nabokov, Vladimir Vladimirovich (1954), *Drugie Berega*, New York: Izdatelstvo imeni Chekhova.

Neuman, Shirley (1981), "The Observer Observed: Distancing the Self in Autobiography," *Prose Studies*, 4: 317–36.

Neuman, Shirley (1989), "'An Appearance Walking in a Forest the Sexes Burn': Autobiography and the Construction of the Feminine Body," *Signature: Journal of Theory and Canadian Literature*, 2(Winter): 1–26.

Neuman, Shirley ([1991] 1998), "Autobiography, Bodies, Manhood," in Sidonie and Julia Watson Smith (eds.), *Women, Autobiography, Theory*, Madison, WI: University of Wisconsin Press, pp. 415–28.

Nice, Pamela (2000), "Chahine on Chahine: The Alexandria Trilogy," *Al-Jadid*, 6(32), available at: http://www.aljadid.com/content/chahine-chahine-alexandria-trilogy, accessed September 2, 2012.

Nichols, Bill (2010), *Introduction to Documentary*, Bloomington, IN: Indiana University Press.

Nijland, C. (1975), *Mikhail Nuʿaymah, Promotor of the Arabic Literary Revival*, Leiden: Nederlands Historisch-Archaeologisch Instituutte Istanbul.

Okonkwo, Chidi (1999), *Decolonization Agonistics in Postcolonial Fiction*, New York: St. Martin's Press.

Ostle, Robin, Ed de Moor, and Stefan Wild (eds.), *Writing the Self: Autobiographical Writing in Modern Arabic Literature*, London: Saqi Books.

Paasonen, Susanna (2002), "Thinking Through the Cybernetic Body: Popular Cybernetics and Feminism," *Rhizomes: Cultural Studies Emerging*, 4, available at: http://www.rhizomes.net/issue4/paasonen.html, accessed August 13, 2012.

Paasonen, Susanna (2005), *Figures of Fantasy: Internet, Women, and Cyberdiscourse*, New York: Peter Lang.

Parry, Benita (2004), *Postcolonial Studies: A Materialist Critique*, New York: Routledge.

Peled, Mattityahu (1985), "Al-Sāq Ala al-Sāq: A Generic Definition," *Arabica*, 32(1): 31–46.

Peterson, Mark Allen (2011), *Connected in Cairo: Growing up Cosmopolitan in the Modern Middle East*, Bloomington, IN: Indiana University Press.

Philipp, Thomas (1993), "The Autobiography in Modern Arab Literature and Culture," *Poetics Today*, 14(3): 573–604.

Plant, Sadie (1997), *Zeroes + Ones: Digital Women + The New Technoculture*, New York: Doubleday.

Plant, Sadie (2000), "On the Matrix: Cyberfeminist Simulations," in Fiona Hovenden *et al.* (eds.), *The Gendered Cyborg: A Reader*, London: Routledge, pp. 265–75.

Provence, Michael (2005), *The Great Syrian Revolt and the Rise of Arab Nationalism*, Austin, TX: University of Texas Press.

Qāsim, Maḥmūd (1995), "Sīrat Fannān al-Dhātiyah fi al-Sīnemā al-ʿArabiyyah," *Alif: Journal of Comparative Poetics*, (15): 22–37.

Quinby, Lee (1992), "The Subject of Memoirs: The Woman Warrior's Technology of Ideographic Selfhood," in Sidonie Smith and Julia Watson (eds.), *De-Colonizing the Subject: The Politics of Gender in Women's Autobiography*, Minneapolis, MN: University of Minnesota Press, pp. 297–320.

Reynolds, Dwight F. (1997), "Arabic Autobiography," *Edebiyat: Journal of Middle Eastern Literatures*, 7(2): 207–14.

Reynolds, Dwight F. (1997), "Childhood in One Thousand Years of Arabic Autobiography," *Edebiyat: Journal of Middle Eastern Literatures*, 7(2): 379–92.

Reynolds, Dwight F. (ed.) (2001), *Interpreting the Self: Autobiography in the Arabic Literary Tradition*, Berkeley, CA: University of California Press.

Robinson, Laura (2007), "The Cyberself: The Self-Ing Project Goes Online, Symbolic Interaction in the Digital Age," *New Media & Society*, 9(1): 93–110.

Roden, Frederick (2004), *Palgrave Advances in Oscar Wilde Studies*, Basingstoke: Palgrave Macmillan.

Rooke, Tetz (1997), *In My Childhood: A Study of Arabic Autobiography*, Stockholm: Stockholm University Press.

Rooney, Caroline (2011), "In Less than Five Years: Rehab Bassam Interviewed by Caroline Rooney, Dar al-Shorouk, Nasr City, Cairo, April 2010," *Journal of Postcolonial Writing*, 47(4): 467–76.

Rosenfield, Israel (1992), *The Strange, Familiar, and Forgotten: An Anatomy of Consciousness*, New York: Knopf.

Rugg, Linda Haverty (2006), "Keaton's Leap: Self-Projection and Autobiography in Film," *Biography*, 29(1): v–xiii.

Russell, Adrienne and Nabil Echchaibi (2009), *International Blogging: Identity, Politics, and Networked Publics*, New York: Peter Lang.

Rustin, Michael (1989), "The Politics of Post-Fordism: Or, the Trouble with 'New Times,'" *New Left Review*, 175: 54–77.

Saadallah, Sherin (2004), "Muslim Feminism in the Third Wave: A Reflective Inquiry," in Stacy Gillis, Gillian Howie, and Rebecca Munford (eds.), *Third Wave Feminism: A Critical Exploration*, Basingstoke: Palgrave Macmillan, pp. 216–26.

Sacks, Oliver (1990), "Neurology and the Soul,", *New York Review of Books*, 22 (November), pp. 44–50.

Said, Edward (1978), *Orientalism*. New York: Pantheon Books

Said, Edward (1999), "No Reconciliation Allowed," in Andre Aciman (ed.), *Letters of Transit: Reflections on Exile, Identity, Language, and Loss*, New York: New Press, pp. 87–114.

Salti, Ramzi (2001), "A Different Leader of Men: Yusuf Idris Against Arab Concepts of Male Homosexuality," *World Literature Today*, 75: 246–56.

Ṣāwī, Muḥammad (1990), *Sīnimā Yūsuf Shāhīn: Riḥlah Aydiyūlūjīyah*, Alexandria and Beirut: Dār al-Maṭbūʿāt al-Jadīdah and Dār Āzāl.

Schehr, Lawrence R. (1997), *Parts of an Andrology: On Representations of Men's Bodies*, Stanford, CA: Stanford University Press.

Shaykh, Khalīl (2005), *Al-Sīrah wa al-Mutakhayyal: Qirāʾāt Fī Namādhij ʿArabīyah Muʿāṣirah*, Amman: Azminah.

Shail, Andrew (2004), "'You're Not One of Those Boring Masculinities, Are You?' The Question of Male-Embodied Feminism," in Stacy Gillis, Gillian Howie, and Rebecca Munford (eds.), *Third Wave Feminism: A Critical Exploration*, Basingstoke: Palgrave Macmillan, pp. 97–109.

Shākir, Tahānī ʿAbd al-Fattāh (2002), *Al-Sīrah al-Dhātīyah Fī al-Adab al-ʿArabī: Fadwa Ṭūqān wa Jabrā Ibrāhīm Jabrā wa Iḥsān ʿAbbās, Namūdhajan*, Beirut: al-Muʾassasah al-ʿArabiyah lil-Dirāsāt wa al-Nashr.

Shamīṭ, Walīd (2001), *Yūsuf Shāhīn: Ḥayāh lil-Sīnimā*, Beirut: Riyāḍ al-Rayyis lil-Kutub wa al-Nashr.

Sharaf, ʿAbd al-ʿAzīz (1992), *ʿAdab al-Sīrah al-Dhātiyah*, Beirut and al-Duqqī, al-Jīzah: Maktabat Lubnān and al-Sharikah al-Miṣriyah al-ʿĀlamiyah lil-Nashr, Lūnjmān.

Shāwī, ʿAbd al-Qādir (1998), *Al-Kitābah wa-al-Wujūd: Al-Sīrah al-Dhātīyah Fī al-Maghrib*, Casablanca: Afrīqīyā al-Sharq.

Shāwī, ʿAbd al-Qādir (2003), *Al-Mutakallim Fī al-Naṣṣ: Maqālāt Fī al-Sīrah al-Dhātīyah*, [Casablanca?]: Manshūrāt al-Mawjah.

Sheehi, Stephen (1999), "Desire for the West, Desire for the Self: National Love and the Colonial Encounter in an Early Arabic Novel," *Jouvert: Journal of Postcolonial Studies*, 3(3), available at: http://search.ebscohost.com/login.aspx?direct=true&db=mzh&AN=1999068317&site=ehost-live, accessed May 20, 2012.

Sheehi, Stephen (2004), *Foundations of Modern Arab Identity*, Gainesville, FL: University Press of Florida.

Shields, Rob (2000), "The Ethic of the Index and Its Space-Time Effects," in Andrew Herman Thomas Swiss (eds.), *The World Wide Web and Contemporary Cultural Theory: Magic, Metaphor, Power*, Routledge, pp. 145–60.

Shotter, John (1993), *Conversational Realities: Constructing Life Through Language*, Thousand Oaks, CA: Sage.

Shotter, John and Kenneth J. Gergen (1989), *Texts of Identity*, Newbury Park, CA: Sage.

Shukrī, Muḥammad (1986), "Al-Kayān wa al-Makān," *Alif: Journal of Comparative Poetics*, (6): 67–78.

Sloane, Thomas O. (2001), *Encyclopedia of Rhetoric*, Oxford: Oxford University Press.

Smith, Sidonie (1987), *A Poetics of Women's Autobiography: Marginality and the Fictions of Self-Representation*, Bloomington, IN: Indiana University Press.

Smith, Sidonie (1993), *Subjectivity, Identity, and the Body: Women's Autobiographical Practices in the Twentieth Century*, Bloomington, IN: Indiana University Press.

Smith, Sidonie and Julia Watson (1992), *De-colonizing the Subject: The Politics of Gender in Women's Autobiography*, Minneapolis, MN: University of Minnesota Press.

Smith, Sidonie and Julia Watson (1996), *Getting a Life: Everyday Uses of Autobiography*, Minneapolis, MN: University of Minnesota.

Smith, Sidonie and Julia Watson (1998), *Women, Autobiography, Theory: A Reader*, Madison, WI: University of Wisconsin Press.

Smith, Sidonie and Julia Watson (2001), *Reading Autobiography: A Guide for Interpreting Life Narratives*, Minneapolis, MN: University of Minnesota Press.

Smith, Sidonie and Julia Watson (2005), *Interfaces: Women, Autobiography, Image, Performance*, Ann Arbor, MI: University of Michigan Press.

Smith, Sidonie and Julia Watson (2010), *Reading Autobiography: Interpreting Life Narratives*, Minneapolis, MN: University of Minnesota Press.

Somekh, Sasson (1991), *Genre and Language in Modern Arabic Literature*, Wiesbaden: Harrassowitz.

Somekh, Sasson (1995), "Biblical Echoes in Modern Arabic Literature," *Journal of Arabic Literature*, 26(1): 186–200.

Spivak, Gayatri Chakravorty (1988), "Can the Subaltern Speak?" in Cary Nelson and Lawrence Grossberg (eds.), *Marxism and the Interpretation of Culture*, Basingstoke: Macmillan, pp. 271–313.

Starkey, Paul (1998), "Fact and Fiction in Al-Sāq ala al-Sāq," in Robin Ostle, Ed de Moor, and Stefan Wild (eds.), *Writing the Self: Autobiographical Writing in Modern Arabic Literature*, London: Saqi Books, pp. 30–8.

Stauffer, Zahr Said (2004), "The Politicisation of Shakespeare in Arabic in Youssef Chahine's Film Trilogy," *English Studies in Africa: Journal of the Humanities*, 47(2): 41–56.

Stroinska, Magda and Vittorina Cecchetto (eds.) (2003), *Exile, Language and Identity*, Frankfurt am Main: Peter Lang.

Suleiman, Yasir (2003), *The Arabic Language and National Identity: A Study in Ideology*, Washington, DC: Georgetown University Press.

Suleiman, Yasir (2011), *Arabic, Self and Identity: A Study in Conflict and Displacement*, New York: Oxford University Press.

Suyūṭī, Jalāl al-Dīn (1975), *Jalāl al-Dīn al-Suyūṭī: Al-Taḥadduth Bi-Niʿmat Allah*, Cambridge: Cambridge University Press for the Faculty of Oriental Studies.

Tamīmi, Amal (2005), *Al-Sīrah al-Dhātīyah al-Nisāʾīyah Fī al-ʾAdab al-ʿArabī al-Muʿāṣir: Dirāsah Fī Namādhij Mukhtārah*, Casablanca: al-Markaz al-Thaqāfī al-ʿArabī.

Tanoukhi, Nirvana (2003), "Rewriting Political Commitment for an International Canon: Paul Bowles's *For Bread Alone* as Translation of Mohamed Choukri's *Al-Khubz Al-Hafi*," *Research in African Literatures*, 34(2): 127–44.

Truffaut, François (2008), *François Truffaut: Interviews*, ed. Ronald Bergan, Jackson, MS: University Press of Mississippi.

Ṭurayṭir, Jalīlah (2004), *Muqawwimāt al-Sīrah al-Dhātīyah Fī al-ʾAdab al-ʿArabī al-Ḥadīth: Baḥth Fī al-Marjaʿīyāt*, Tūnis: Markaz al-Nashr al-Jāmiʿī.

Turkle, Sherry (1984), *The Second Self: Computers and the Human Spirit*, New York: Simon & Schuster.

Turkle, Sherry (1995), *Life on the Screen: Identity in the Age of the Internet*, New York: Simon & Schuster.

Turkle, Sherry (2011), *Alone Together: Why We Expect More from Technology and Less From Each Other*, New York: Basic Books.

Wajcman, Judy (2004), *TechnoFeminism*, Cambridge: Polity Press.

Weedon, Chris (2004), *Identity and Culture: Narratives of Difference and Belonging*, Maidenhead: Open University Press.

Whitlock, Gillian (2007), *Soft Weapons: Autobiography in Transit*, Chicago, IL: University of Chicago Press.

Wild, Stefan (1995), "Nizar Qabbani's Autobiography: Images of Sexuality, Death and Poetry," in Roger Allen, Hilary Kilpatrick, and Ed De Moor (eds.), *Love and Sexuality in Modern Arabic Literature*, London: Saqi Books, pp. 200–9.

Wild, Stefan (1998), "Searching for Beginnings in Modern Arabic Autobiography," in Robin Ostle *et al.* (eds.), *Writing the Self: Autobiographical Writing in Modern Arabic Literature*, London: Saqi Books, pp. 82–99.

Selection of Arab Autobiographical and Semi-Autobiographical Works Written in and Translated to English

English translations of primary sources are listed in the corresponding section.

Abdel-Fattah, Randa (2007), *Does My Head Look Big in This?* New York: Orchard Books.

Abinader, Elmaz (1991), *Children of the Roojme: A Family's Journey*, New York: Norton.

Abu-Jaber, Diana (2005), *The Language of Baklava: A Memoir*, New York: Anchor Books.

Ahmad, Layla Abd al-Latif (1999), *A Border Passage: From Cairo to America – A Woman's Journey*, New York: Farrar, Straus & Giroux.

Amiry, Suad (2006), *Sharon and My Mother-in-Law: Ramallah Diaries*, New York: Anchor Books.

Ashur, Radwa ([1999] 2011), *Specters*, trans. from Arabic by Barbara Romaine, Northamton, MA: Interlink Books.

Attar, Samar (1994), *Lina: A Portrait of a Damascene Girl*, trans. from Arabic by the author, Washington, DC: Three Continents Press.

Baradah, Muhammad (1996), *The Game of Forgetting*, trans. from Arabic by Issa J. Boullata, Center for Middle Eastern Studies, University of Texas at Austin.

Barghuti, Murid (2000), *I Saw Ramallah*, trans. from Arabic by Ahdaf Soueif, Cairo: American University in Cairo Press.

Basrawi, Fadia (2009), *Brownies and Kalashnikovs: A Saudi Woman's Memoir of American Arabia And Wartime Beirut*, Reading: South Street Press.

Bih, Fatinah (2008), *Talk of Darkness*, trans. from Arabic by Mustapha Kamal and Susan Slyomovics, Center for Middle Eastern Studies, University of Texas at Austin.

Bilal, Wafaa and Kari Lydersen (2008), *Shoot an Iraqi: Art, Life and Resistance Under the Gun*, San Francisco, CA: City Lights.

Buqari, Muhammad Hammazah (1991), *The Sheltered Quarter: A Tale of a Boyhood in Mecca*, trans. from Arabic by Olive Kenny and Jeremy Reed, Center for Middle Eastern Studies, University of Texas at Austin.

Chraibi, Driss (1972), *Heirs to the Past*, trans. from French by Len Ortzen, London: Heinemann Educational.

Chraibi, Driss ([1954] 1990), *The Simple Past*, trans. from French by Hugh A. Harter, Washington, DC: Three Continents Press.

Daoud, Hassan (1999), *The House of Mathilde*, trans. from Arabic by Peter Theroux, London: Granta Books.

Darwish, Mahmud ([1995] 2013), *Memory for Forgetfulness: August, Beirut, 1982*, trans. from Arabic by Ibrahim Mulawi, Berkeley, CA: University of California Press.

Dib, Muhammad (2012), *Tlemcen or Places of Writing*, trans. from French by Guy Bennett, Los Angeles, CA: Otis Books/Seismicity Editions.

Djebar, Assia ([1985] 1993), *Fantasia, An Algerian Cavalcade*, trans. from French by Dorothy S. Blair, Portsmouth, NH: Heinemann.

Faqir, Fadia and Shirley Eber (eds.), (1998), *In the House of Silence: Autobiographical Essays by Arab Women Writers*, Reading: Garnet.

Feraoun, Mouloud (2005), *The Poor Man's Son: Menrad, Kabyle Schoolteacher*, trans. from French by Lucy McNair, Charlottesville, VA: University of Virginia Press.

Fernea, Elizabeth Warnock (ed.), (2002), *Remembering Childhood in the Middle East: Memoirs From a Century of Change*, Austin, TX: University of Texas Press.

Geha, Joseph (2009), *Through and Through: Toledo Stories*, Syracuse, NY: Syracuse University Press.

Ghali, Waguih (1964), *Beer in the Snooker Club*, New York: Knopf.

Hakim, Tawfiq (1992), *The Prison of Life: An Autobiographical Essay*, trans. from Arabic by Pierre Cachia, Cairo: American University in Cairo Press.

Halaby, Laila (2003), *West of the Jordan: A Novel*, Boston, MA: Beacon Press.

Ibrahim, Sun' Allah (2013), *That Smell and Notes from Prison*, trans. from Arabic by Robyn Cresswell, New York: New Directions.

Idlibi, Ulfat (1995), *Sabriya: Damascus Bitter Sweet*, trans. from Arabic by Peter Clark, New York: Interlink Books.

Jabra, Jabra Ibrahim (1995), *The First Well: A Bethlehem Boyhood*, trans. from Arabic by Issa J. Boullata, Fayetteville, AS: University of Arkansas Press.

Jarrar, Randa (2008), *A Map of Home: A Novel*, New York: Other Press.

Kahf, Mohja (2006), *The Girl in the Tangerine Scarf: A Novel*, New York: Carroll & Graf.

Kanafani, Fay Afaf (1998), *Nadia, Captive of Hope: Memoir of an Arab Woman*, Armonk, NY: M. E. Sharpe.

Kharrat, Idwar (1989), *City of Saffron*, trans. from Arabic by Frances Liardet, London: Quartet.

Kharrat, Idwar (1993), *Girls of Alexandria*, trans. from Arabic by Frances Liardet, London: Quartet Books.

Mahfuz, Najib (1997), *Echoes of an Autobiography*, trans. from Arabic by Denys Johnson-Davies, New York: Doubleday.

Mahjoub, Jamal (2004), *Travelling with Djinns*, London: Vintage.

Makdisi, Jean Said (1990), *Beirut Fragments: A War Memoir*, New York: Persea Books.

Makdisi, Jean Said (2005), *Teta, Mother and Me: An Arab Woman's Memoir*, London: Saqi Books.

Mamduh, Aliyah (2005), *Naphtalene: A Novel of Baghdad*, trans. from Arabic by Peter Theroux, New York: Feminist Press at the City University of New York.

Mazini, Ibrahim Abd al-Qadir (1976), *Ibrahim the Writer*, trans. from Arabic by Magdi Wahba, Cairo: General Egyptian Book Organization.

Memmi, Albert (1992), *The Pillar of Salt*, trans. from French by Edouard Roditi, Boston, MA: Beacon Press.

Mernissi, Fatima (1994), *Dreams of Trespass: Tales of a Harem Girlhood*, Reading, MA: Addison-Wesley.

Mrabet, Mohammed (1975), *Look and Move On*, trans. and ed. Paul Bowles, Los Angeles, CA: Black Sparrow Press.

Munif, Abd al-Rahman (1996), *Story of a City: A Childhood in Amman*, trans. from Arabic by Samira Kawar, London: Quartet.

Nasr, Hasan (2006), *Return to Dar al-Basha: A Novel*, trans. from Arabic by William Hutchins, Syracuse, NY: Syracuse University Press.

Nusseibeh, Sari (2007), *Once Upon a Country: A Palestinian Life*, trans. from Arabic by Anthony David, New York: Farrar, Straus & Giroux.

Qashu, Sayed (2004), *Dancing Arabs*, trans. from Hebrew by Miriam Shlesinger, New York: Grove Press.

Qazwini, Iqbal (2008), *Zubaida's Window: A Novel of Iraqi Exile*, trans. from Arabic by Azza El Kholy and Amira Nowaira, New York: Feminist Press at the City University of New York.

Radi, Nuha (2003), *Baghdad Diaries: A Woman's Chronicle of War and Exile*, New York: Vintage.

Ramli, Muhsin (2003), *Scattered Crumbs*, trans. from Arabic by Yasmeen Hanoush, Fayetteville, AS: University of Arkansas Press.

Riverbend (2005), *Baghdad Burning: Girl Blog from Iraq*, New York: Feminist Press at the City University of New York.

Riverbend (2006), *Baghdad Burning II: More Girl Blog From Iraq*, New York: Feminist Press at the City University of New York.

Sa'dawi, Nawal (1999), *A Daughter of Isis: The Autobiography of Nawal El Saadawi*, trans. from Arabic by Sherif Hetata, London: Zed Books.

Sa'dawi, Nawal (1986), *Memoirs from the Women's Prison*, trans. from Arabic by Marilyn Booth, Berkeley, CA: University of California Press.

Said, Edward W. (1999), *Out of Place: A Memoir*, New York: Knopf.

Salam, Pax (2003), *Salam Pax: The Clandestine Diary of an Ordinary Iraqi*, New York: Grove Press.

Salem, Salwa (2007), *The Wind in my Hair*, trans. from Italian by Yvonne Freccero, Northampton, MA: Interlink Books.

Sebbar, Layla (ed.) (2001), *An Algerian Childhood: A Collection of Autobiographical Narratives*, trans. from French by Marjolijn de Jager, Minneapolis, MN: Ruminator Books.

Sha'rawi, Huda (1986), *Harem Years: The Memoirs of an Egyptian Feminist (1879–1924)*, trans. from Arabic by Margot Badran, London: Virago.

Shihab, Aziz (2007), *Does the Land Remember Me?: A Memoir af Palestine*, Syracuse, NY: Syracuse University Press.

Shukri, Muhammad (1996), *Streetwise*, trans. from Arabic by Ed Emery, London: Saqi Books.

Siba'i, Ahmad (2009), *My Days in Mecca*, ed. and trans. from Arabic by Deborah Akers and Abu Bakr Ahmad Baqadir, Boulder, CO: First Forum Press.

Soueif, Ahdaf (1992), *In the Eye of the Sun*, New York: Vintage.

Tahawi, Miral (2002), *Blue Aubergine*, trans. from Arabic by Anthony Calderbank, Cairo: American University in Cairo Press.

Turki, Fawaz (1972), *The Disinherited: Journal of a Palestinian Exile*, New York: Monthly Review Press.

Turki, Fawaz (1988), *Soul in Exile: Lives of a Palestinian Revolutionary*, New York: Monthly Review Press.

Turki, Fawaz (1993), *Exile's Return: The Making of a Palestinian American*, New York: Free Press.

Yazbik, Samar Weiss Max (2012), *A Woman in the Crossfire: Diaries of the Syrian Revolution*, trans. from Arabic by Max Weiss, London: Haus.

Zangana, Haifa ([1995] 2009), *Dreaming of Baghdad*, trans. from Arabic by the author and Paul Hammond, New York: Feminist Press at the City University of New York.

Zaydan, Aminah (2010), *Red Wine*, trans. from Arabic by Sally Gomaa, Cairo: American University in Cairo Press.

Zaydan, Jurji (1979), "The Autobiography of Gurgi Zaidan," in *Ǧurǧī Zaidān, His Life and Thought*, trans. from Arabic by Thomas Philipp, Beirut: Orient-Institut der Deutschen Morgenländischen Gesellschaft.

Zayyat, Latifah (1996), *The Search: Personal Papers*, trans. from Arabic by Sophie Bennett, London: Quartet.

Zayyat, Latifah (2000), *The Open Door*, trans. from Arabic by Marilyn Booth, Cairo: American University in Cairo Press.

Index